Spring Training Handbook

Second Edition

Spring Training Handbook

A Comprehensive Guide to the Grapefruit and Cactus League Ballparks

Second Edition

JOSH PAHIGIAN

McFarland & Company, Inc., Publishers

Jefferson, North Carolina, and London

All photographs are by the author unless otherwise noted.

LIBRARY OF CONGRESS CATALOGUING-IN-PUBLICATION DATA

Pahigian, Josh.
Spring training handbook : a comprehensive guide to the
Grapefruit and Cactus league ballparks / Josh Pahigian. — Second edition.
p.   cm.
Includes bibliographical references and index.

ISBN 978-0-7864-7195-9
softcover : acid free paper ∞

1. Spring training (Baseball)— Florida. 2. Spring training
(Baseball)— Arizona.   3. Baseball fields— Florida — Guidebooks.
4. Baseball fields— Arizona — Guidebooks. 5. Florida — Guidebooks.
6. Arizona — Guidebooks. I. Title.
GV875.6.P35 2013   796.357'64—dc23   2013014981

BRITISH LIBRARY CATALOGUING DATA ARE AVAILABLE

On the cover: View of Champion Stadium in
Lake Buena Vista, Florida (photograph by the author)

Manufactured in the United States of America

*McFarland & Company, Inc., Publishers
Box 611, Jefferson, North Carolina 28640
www.mcfarlandpub.com*

Contents

II. Arizona's Cactus League

Acknowledgments

I thank my wife, Heather, for her patience and encouragement and my son Spencer for being an amazingly loving and good humored little guy. I also thank all of my family members and friends who support my writing. Special thanks too, go to my literary agent, Colleen Mohyde, at the Doe Coover agency. Finally, I thank George Gratto and Jim Tootle, who shared generously from their respective photo collections so that I could include some of their work in these pages.

Introduction

Like baseball itself, the game's annual season of renewal never stops evolving. With each passing spring, new players arrive at baseball's spring training practice fields, new traditions are born, and larger and larger crowds gather to watch the Boys of Summer prepare for the regular season. And yet, some things remain constant: the spring game continues to offer fans access to idyllic little diamonds that provide more intimate settings for the game and greater access to its players than the regular season stadiums do. Back home the temperature may be struggling to reach the freezing mark, but it's little matter to the snowbirds who descend on Florida and Arizona. The ballparks of the Grapefruit and Cactus Leagues sparkle under the March sun, while the players happily sign autographs, and the fans and players alike look hopefully forward to the season ahead. Remarkably, these delightful aspects of the spring version of America's Game have endured for a century, even while the physical landscapes of the Grapefruit and Cactus Leagues have undergone great change. In the years since St. Petersburg Mayor Al Lang first lured the St. Louis Browns to Florida in 1914, and New York Giants owner Horace Stoneman and Cleveland Indians owner Bill Veeck first brought their clubs to Phoenix and Tucson in 1947, the two spring leagues have seen many ballparks and cities come and go.

A period of particularly great change occurred in the decade spanning the publication of the first edition of this book in 2004 and the publication of the second edition, which you hold in your hands. With the addition and subtraction of ballparks, and the relocation of several teams during this time, the Cactus League grew to at long last equal the Grapefruit League in teams. Today's Cactus League includes fully half of the game's 30 major league teams. To put this shift of power in perspective: when *Spring Training Handbook*'s first edition was published, 18 teams trained in Florida and 12 trained in Arizona. Then there were 17 ballparks in Florida, nine parks in Phoenix Valley, and two parks in Tucson. Today, there are 14 parks in Florida and ten in Phoenix Valley. Like the four Florida cities that lost their spring affiliations with major league teams in the first decade of the 2000s (Vero Beach, St. Petersburg, Fort Lauderdale, and Winter Haven), Tucson, also became estranged from the spring game.

Since the first edition, five new spring ballparks have opened, including three in the Cactus League. All three of the new Arizona parks are in Phoenix Valley and all three house two home teams rather than just one. Thus, these new parks have cemented a traveler-friendly Cactus League footprint that places all of the league's parks within an hour's drive of one another. With the opening of Camelback Ranch-Glendale in 2009, Phoenix Valley convinced the Dodgers to leave their legendary Dodgertown campus in Vero Beach and the White Sox to leave Tucson Electric Park. With the opening of Goodyear Ballpark also in 2009, Phoenix Valley lured the Indians and Reds from their Grapefruit League parks in Winter Haven and Sarasota. And with the opening of Salt River Fields at Talking Stick in 2011, Phoenix Valley signaled the end of Tucson's long run as a Cactus League bastion by luring the Diamondbacks from Tucson Electric Park and the Rockies from iconic Hi Corbett Field.

As the Cactus League has consolidated its teams in Greater Phoenix, the Grapefruit League has also undergone a shift in recent years. As it has lost teams to Arizona and watched other teams move within the state, the Florida circuit's map has tilted west, so that eight of its fifteen teams now train on Florida's western Gulf Coast. Meanwhile, three Florida teams train in the center of the state, and four teams (represented by three ballparks) remain on the eastern Atlantic Coast. Besides losing the Dodgers, Reds, and Indians to the Cactus League in the interval between this book's two editions, the Grapefruit League has seen the Orioles relocate from Fort Lauderdale to Sarasota, the Rays relocate from St. Petersburg to a significantly remodeled version of a former Rangers ballpark in Port Charlotte, and the Red Sox move into a Fenway Park replica in Fort Myers, where they had outgrown their previous home.

For the most part, all of this change has been a positive development from the perspective of the traveling fan. With their sunken seating bowls, open concourses that encircle the entire field, and spacious outfield seating berms, today's stadiums are even more luxurious and intimate than their predecessors. Today's camps are also designed to allow fans greater walking access to the fields where the players of each organization work out in February, before the official start of spring games, and in March, when games are not in progress. And yet, with the closure of the historic ballparks that once stood in St. Petersburg, Vero Beach, and Tucson, something has been lost. In those towns, Al Lang Field, Holman Stadium, and Hi Corbett Field were as rich in lore and history as many of the game's legendary regular season stadiums came to be. This edition of the book endeavors to do justice to these hallowed grounds by telling the history of the Grapefruit and Cactus Leagues within the framework of its stated purpose to serve as a travel guide to the spring training parks.

The book is divided into 24 chapters, one for each of today's spring baseball grounds. Each chapter describes the focal ballpark as it exists and provides photographs to illustrate its intricacies. Each chapter also includes historical information about the stadium, as well as historical information about previous stadiums that stood or still stand in the city. The chapter introductions also recall the full spring training history of the ballpark's resident team (or teams, in the case of the six shared parks). The book also describes the various fan traditions and foods that characterize a day spent at each of the parks. Finally, each chapter describes the landscape surrounding the focal ballpark, providing information about other baseball and sports-related attractions in the area. Many of the game's older teams have trained at more than a dozen sites in their history. In such cases, the book highlights the most unique or historically significant locations, while alluding to the others. A full listing of every team's spring training sites since 1914, the year that most historians recognize as the birth date of the Grapefruit League, is at the back of the book.

My hope is that after reading this book, every fan will agree that he or she deserves to spend at least one March in Florida, Arizona, or both. For some, this may be a goal attained with buddies during or following their high school or college years. For others, spring training will be a family vacation destination. For others, it will offer a pleasant diversion during business travel. Still others will wait until their retirement to pack up a camper and head south. At any point in one's life, the experience of watching baseball's brightest stars, intriguing newcomers and beleaguered veterans in the relaxed and up-close environment of spring training is enjoyable and rewarding.

My hope is that those unable to readily travel will also find the book enjoyable and informative to read. More than just serving as a travel guide, *Spring Training Handbook* aspires to serve as a comprehensive historical guide to the cities and ballparks of the spring game. The book tells the stories of how baseball first arrived in Florida and Arizona; how the Grapefruit League got its unusual name; how Florida's Yankees and Arizona's Giants traded spring camps one year; how Dizzy Dean opened a gas station in Bradenton, Florida, when he was a player, and then became the hunting-buddy of a Scottsdale, Arizona, bar owner when he was a broadcaster. It also recalls Mickey Mantle's debut camp in Phoenix, Ichiro Suzuki's first camp in Peoria, and the years when basketball legend Michael Jordan and country music star Garth Brooks donned big league uniforms at big league camps in Sarasota and Peoria. The book shares countless other historical tidbits, too.

As the game's players and fans create more special moments at baseball's spring training ballparks in the years ahead, no doubt the rich reservoir of anecdotes and lore devoted to the March version of the game will deepen still. The ballparks of the Grapefruit and Cactus Leagues will no doubt continue to evolve as well, as cities in Florida and Arizona strive to perfect their spring baseball oases. Whether some future edition of this book will characterize a Cactus League that has surpassed the Grapefruit League in terms of its number of teams remains to be seen. Likewise, it is impossible to predict whether the Florida league's migration to the Gulf Coast will continue. But one thing seems certain: the Grapefruit and Cactus Leagues will continue to present a unique baseball atmosphere that the game's players and fans treasure.

I.

FLORIDA'S GRAPEFRUIT LEAGUE

George M. Steinbrenner Field

(TAMPA) New York Yankees

George M. Steinbrenner Field
1 Steinbrenner Drive, Tampa
813-879-2244
http://www.steinbrennerfield.com/
http://newyork.yankees.mlb.com
Opened: 1996. Seating Capacity: 11,076
• 17 miles west to Clearwater (Phillies)
• 23 miles west to Dunedin (Blue Jays)
• 40 miles east to Lakeland (Tigers)
• 46 miles south to Bradenton (Pirates)

As THE MOST SUCCESSFUL franchise in the history of the Grand Old Game, the New York Yankees have always made mystique and extravagance their hallmarks. And through the years, the three different incarnations of Yankee Stadium have consistently reflected the legendary pinstripe bravado. But despite the Yankees' tremendous regular season success and rich tradition in the Bronx, the team's spring training history was a transitory one, spent largely in unremarkable ballparks until 1996, when the Yankees opened a miniature version of Yankee Stadium in Tampa. It seems appropriate, given all else that former Yankee owner George M. Steinbrenner did to usher in a new era of Yankee dominance, that today a life-sized bronze of Mr. Steinbrenner stands outside the Yankees' Grapefruit League home. And it seems fitting that the facility, originally known as Legends Field, has since been rechristened in the late Boss's honor.

Steinbrenner Field reflects many of the design elements that make Yankee Stadium beloved, appealing at once to the region's many transplanted New Yorkers and to native Floridians who may never have opportunity to step foot in the Bronx. The seats are Yankee Stadium Blue and the field dimensions replicate those of Yankee Stadium. The home run porch in right field is just 314 feet from home plate, the fence in straight-away center measures 408 feet, "Death Valley" in left-center measures 399 feet, and the left field foul pole is planted 318 feet from home plate.

Decorative white arches and filigree extend high above the seats on the facing of the roof, mimicking the trademark Yankee filigree that adorns the roof at new Yankee Stadium and which also appeared at the two previous versions of the Yankees' regular season home. Above the last row of seats, meanwhile, fans find giant blue windscreens that together spell out YANKEES.

Outside, the statue of Mr. Steinbrenner is joined by a miniature version of Yankee Stadium's famous Monument Park. The Tampa edition consists of pinstriped plaques honoring Yankee heroes whose uniform numbers have been retired. Many of the plaques include quotations from the players themselves, while others summarize their accomplishments, or offer general words of praise. Joe DiMaggio's plaque reads: "I want to thank the good Lord for making me a Yankee." Babe Ruth's reads: "Single-handedly lifted baseball to new heights. The most celebrated athlete who ever lived."

The surrounding landscape welcomes fans to grounds as immaculately clean as they are inviting. Fountains shoot streams of water high into the air, while ducks paddle and quack in a man-made lake. Ferns unfurl and tropical flowers blossom in lush gardens. Palm trees sway in the breeze. A small ballpark adjacent to the main stadium, named "NY Yankees Community Field" serves as the home diamond of the Hillsboro Community College Hawks.

Once the game begins, Steinbrenner Field offers fans the chance to feel like they're watching a game in a scaled down version of Yankee Stadium. With its high roof, steep seating bowl, and stricter-than-usual ushers, the park gives the impression that it is too big and too serious to be "just" a spring training venue. The fans play their part in perpetuating this notion too. In some towns, spectators view spring training as a chance to familiarize themselves with the home team's new players, reconnect with the veterans, and enjoy a few relaxing days in the sun. In Tampa, the dynamic is quite different. As a general rule, the fans that attend games at Steinbrenner Field are younger and hipper than the retirees who populate the

The grounds of Steinbrenner Field are adorned by royal palms.

stands in other spring cities. And these Yankee rooters aren't interested in watching players build arm strength or get a few at bats and then head to the showers. They want to see their team get a win. Just like in New York, they scream with indignation when a member of the home team hits into a double play or makes an error in the field. And they cheer with delight when the home team wins. As in New York, every game concludes with fans singing along to Frank Sinatra's "New York, New York," which blares through the public address system as fans file to the exits. Further contributing to the regular season flavor, the Yankees utilize professional security officers, ushers, and food service personnel, rather than the friendly senior citizens often found filling these roles at other spring parks.

Although Steinbrenner Field is visually pleasing, it must be an intimidating place to play as a visiting player, especially for the minor leaguers who typically fill out spring rosters. With an official capacity of just over 11,000 and two levels of luxury boxes built into the concrete façade behind home plate, Steinbrenner Field is the largest Grapefruit League stadium, narrowly edging the Red Sox's Jet Blue Park for the distinction. What's more, the Yankees perennially average more than 10,500 fans per game and lead the Grapefruit League in attendance. With the opening of Jet Blue Park in 2012, the Red Sox were expected to vie with the Yankees for

The façade features windscreens that spell out "YANKEES."

attendance bragging rights, but when the ticket stubs were tallied at the end of that spring they showed the Yankees had drawn an average of 10,855 per game, while the Red Sox had attracted an average of 9,464.

Steinbrenner Field sits on a 31-acre parcel across the street from the NFL Tampa Bay Buccaneers' Raymond James Stadium. The football field is laid on the same land where Al Lopez Field once stood. The Grapefruit League field served as the home of the White Sox from 1955 to 1959 and of the Reds from 1960 to 1987. From a design perspective Al Lopez Field was rather straight forward and unremarkable, but the park was notable for contributing one nice tradition to the spring version of the game. On March 17, 1978, Reds general manager Dick Wagner sent his team onto the field in Tampa wearing green uniforms. Thus, the successor of the Reds GM who had created "The Big Red Machine" had created his own legacy; in the years ahead the St. Patrick's Day tradition of outfitting players in special green jerseys and/or green caps has continued.

After Lopez Field was demolished in 1989, Steinbrenner Field was built at a cost of $30 million in 1994 and 1995. The Tampa Sports Authority funded the project, intended from the start to house the Yankees. Mr. Steinbrenner was a long-time Tampa resident and his connection to the city was the impetus for the deal. Plans to bring the Yankees to Tampa were unveiled in September of 1993 when the Tampa Sports Authority announced it intended to construct the ballpark along with Raymond James Stadium and the Tampa Bay Times Forum, home of the National Hockey League's Tampa Bay Lightning. Steinbrenner Field was the first of the three projects to be completed. On March 1, 1996, the Yankees beat the Indians

Babe Ruth's plaque in Tampa's version of Monument Park. 5–2 in the park's inaugural

The field dimensions of Steinbrenner Field mimic those of Yankee Stadium.

game. A number of legendary Yankee pitchers were on hand to mark the occasion, including Whitey Ford, Catfish Hunter, and Ron Guidry. But when it came time to toss out the ceremonial first pitch, former shortstop Phil Rizzuto did the honors.

In 2006, Hillsborough County approved a $7.5 million addition to add an expanded seating area in right field home run territory. The new pavilion-style seating section, known as the Tampa Tribune Deck, opened in 2008. That same spring, the ballpark was renamed "Steinbrenner Field." As for the bronze of Mr. Steinbrenner, it was added to the complex shortly after the Boss's death, in time for the start of the 2011 spring season.

Between 1900 and 1962, the Yankees made camp in 16 different spring cities. Five of these towns eventually fielded regular season big league teams: Baltimore (1901), Atlanta (1907, 1908, 1912), Houston (1914), St. Petersburg (1925–1942, 1946–1950, 1952–1961), and Phoenix (1951). In 1913 the Yankees trained in Hamilton, Bermuda, only to see star first baseman Hal Chase fall off a bicycle and break his leg. Although he eventually recovered, Chase was never again the player he'd been before the injury.

When the Yankees inked Ruth to a new $80,000 contract in St. Petersburg during the spring of 1930, a reporter informed the slugger that he would be earning more money than President Hoover. Ruth responded, "I had a better year." In 1936 DiMaggio's Yankee debut was delayed when a trainer accidentally over-heated his left ankle during treatment in St. Petersburg. The ailment sidelined the future "Yankee Clipper" until May.

In 1951 the Yankees swapped spring sites with the New York Giants for one season. The Giants traveled to the Yankees' usual home in St. Petersburg and the Bronx Bombers traveled to the Giants' spring home in Phoenix. This marked the only year since 1919 (excepting the World War II years) that the Yankees did not train in Florida. The move allowed Yankees co-owner Del Web, a resident of Phoenix, to showcase his championship team to his friends back home. Later in the 1951 season, the two teams met in the World Series, with the Yankees prevailing in six games.

From 1962 to 1995 the Yankees played their Grapefruit League games at unspectacular Fort Lauderdale Stadium. Although a generation of Yankee fans traveled to Florida's east coast to follow the team's vernal exploits, the Yankees always maintained a loyal fan base in the Tampa Bay area thanks to their three spring stints in St. Petersburg.

As for the history of spring baseball in Tampa, several teams fielded Grapefruit League squads in the city before the Yankees. The Chicago Cubs trained in Tampa from 1913 to 1916, the Boston Red Sox in 1919, the Washington Senators from 1920 to 1929, the Detroit Tigers in 1930, the Chicago White Sox from 1954 to 1959, and the Cincinnati Reds from 1931 to 1987. The Reds ultimately left the aforementioned Al Lopez Field to move east to Plant City, thus beginning a decade-long spring training drought for Tampa fans.

Today, with Steinbrenner Field in place, it would appear that the marriage between Tampa and the Yankees will endure. The whole region is Yankee-crazy, to the extent that the owners of the Tampa Bay Rays have cited the local affinity for pinstripes as one reason why the Rays have struggled to establish a fan base. It is telling that the Rays average about 20,000 fans per game overall at Tropicana Field, but when the Yankees are the visitors they draw 35,000 or so. South though it may be, there's no disputing that Tampa is Yankee Country and Steinbrenner Field is the regional capital.

GETTING TO THE PARK. Take Route I-275 to Exit 41B and follow Dale Mabry Highway north for three miles. Steinbrenner Field is on the left. A spacious parking lot sits across the street from the ballpark, adjacent to Raymond James Stadium. A pedestrian bridge allows fans to access the stadium.

SEATING. Steinbrenner Field does not offer any general admission, standing room, bleacher, or lawn tickets, which makes it something of an anomaly in the spring game. The seating bowl consists of 16 rows of Field Box seats below a midlevel walkway, and 16 rows of Upper Reserved seats above the walkway.

TicketMaster manages all Steinbrenner Field advance sales through the Internet and telephone, which means that fans who don't buy tickets in person at the box office are subjected to surcharges and handling fees. But it is not advisable to wait to procure ticket until game-day. Games often sell out.

The Field Box seats are the ones below the midlevel walkway. Section 102 is located in shallow right field, while Sections 110 and 111 are behind the plate, and Section 120 is just beyond the third base bag in shallow left. On both sides of the diamond, the bullpens fill the remaining space between the end of the seating and the nearest foul pole. The first row is marked AA, while the last is PP. The majority of the seats in these sections are reserved for season ticket holders or for those with corporate connections. Only the outfield-most sections are available to the general public. Sections 102 and 103 are in right field, while Sections 119 and 120 are in left.

Above the walkway, the Upper Reserved seats appear in Sections 201 to 221. Section 201 is in right field, Sections 210 and 211 are behind the plate, and Section 221 is in left field. Seats in Sections 201, 202, 220, and 221 sell for considerably less than the rest of the seats because they are farthest from the infield. The seats in this part of the park are in Rows A–P, with Rows K–P covered by the sunroof.

THE BALLPARK EXPERIENCE. A large sign immediately reminds fans arriving at Steinbrenner Field of just how many World Championships the Yankees have won. The *New York Post* and *New York Daily News* are available in news boxes out front too, to keep road-trippers in touch with the happenings back home. The gift shop — by far the most elaborate souvenir outlet in the Grapefruit League — predictably offers exclusively Yankees garb and memorabilia. This so-called "Legends Room" has a more expansive collection of keepsakes than the three souvenir stands inside the stadium.

Upon passing through the turnstiles — which are located atop a set of concrete steps that empty onto the concourse beneath the grandstand — fans encounter banners celebrating great players and teams in Yankee history. Among the individuals honored by this assortment of classy black and white photographs are: Ruth, DiMaggio, Rizzuto, Ford, Maris, Martin, Mantle and Gehrig. The team photos include the championship squads of 1927, 1951, 1956 and 1977.

Several runways lead from the wide concourse beneath the stands to the interior walkway that bisects the seating bowl. The unsympathetic ushers don't allow anyone — not even the kids and not even during batting practice — to access the Field Box seats without a ticket. These seats are guarded more tightly than the good seats at most regular season parks! As a result, the lower seats are sparsely populated during warm-ups and those autograph seekers who do possess legitimate tickets down low face limited competition near the Yankees' first base dugout.

Another strategy that autograph seekers sometimes employ is to wait outside the park for retired players and celebrities to arrive. More famous people are sighted at Steinbrenner Field than at any other spring park. Regular visitors include Warren Sapp, Wayne Gretzky, Dick Vitale, Rudy Giuliani, Jeb Bush, and retired Yankees like Daryl Strawberry, Dwight Gooden and Reggie Jackson. Inside the park these folks are inaccessible to regular fans because they sit in the luxury boxes, but outside the park they are fair game.

Probably the best bet for those intent on getting autographs, is to arrive on a day when the Yankees don't have a game, or several hours before game-time, and to head to the practice field behind the main stadium. Sometimes Yankee rookies and minor leaguers take batting practice there.

As for the ballpark concessions, let's just say that big eaters will be pleased with Steinbrenner Field. The stadium ranks near the top of the pack compared to other Grapefruit League venues in terms of the quality and diversity of its offerings. Vendors line both sides of the concourse, offering a veritable smorgasbord. In addition to different types of hot dogs, fans find Smoked Turkey Legs, Funnel Cakes, Deviled Crabs, Cuban Sandwiches, Meatball Parmesan Sandwiches, and a Pizza big enough to feed a family of four.

ON THE TOWN. Tampa is the largest city that fans visit while touring the Grapefruit League, and it's a city with a lot to offer in the way of sports and entertainment. Unfortunately the streets immediately surrounding the ballpark do not put the town's best foot forward. The ballpark neighborhood offers strip malls, strip clubs and the occasional restaurant. Many fans choose to bunk across the bay in St. Petersburg, where the streets are less congested, the air is more pristine and the pace of life more relaxed.

Early arrivals at Steinbrenner Field sometimes walk next door to check out **Raymond James Stadium**, which opened in 1998. Its trademark 103-foot-long, 19th century pirate ship replica cost $3 million to build. The ship sits in the north end zone where it flies a 32-by-50-foot sail atop a 78-foot mast. This was a publicly financed project, pirate ship and all.

Fans wishing to watch New York's minor league workouts visit the **Yankees' Minor League Complex** (3102 North Himes Avenue). A stop at the camp offers the chance to see not just rookies but also many retired Yankee stars. The Yankees are famous for utilizing their alumni to instruct young players in their organization.

A bronze plaque outside Al Lang Field in St. Petersburg honors the man who brought spring baseball to Florida in 1914.

That way, by the time rookies reach the big leagues they already have an appreciation of what it means to wear pinstripes.

For those who can't get enough baseball, the University of South Florida plays Division I hardball at **USF Baseball Stadium** (4202 East Fowler Avenue). The field is laid out on the very footprint of old Red McEwen Field, which was home to the Bulls from 1967 through 2010. That field saw its first night game in 1977, after Mr. Steinbrenner donated a set of stadium lights to the University. The Bulls, who joined the Big East Conference in 2005, play a competitive schedule throughout the spring, including an annual series against Division I powerhouse Miami. Most weekday games start at 7:00 P.M., while weekend tilts begin at 1:00 P.M. In 2012, the Bulls played an exhibition game against the Yankees at Steinbrenner Field, losing 11–0.

Another nearby baseball landmark is old **Al Lang Field** (180 Second Avenue Southeast, St. Petersburg). This venerable waterfront park was the spring home of the Rays until they moved to Port Charlotte in 2009. And it was home of the spring Yankees from 1947 through 1961 (excepting the aforementioned 1951 season when they traded sites with the Giants). It also hosted the Orioles, Mets and Cardinals at various points. Today it is used as a North American Soccer League stadium, hosting the Tampa Bay Rowdies. Fans visit the park during spring training to check out the plaque honoring Mr. Al Lang, the man widely regarded as the grandfather of the Grapefruit League. As mayor of St. Petersburg, Lang brokered a deal to bring the St. Louis Browns to the small fishing village in February and March of 1914. That year, a number of other teams traveled south to play exhibition games against the Browns and, finding the Florida air to their liking, a new spring tradition was born.

St. Petersburg's **Baseball Boulevard**, which begins at Al Lang Field and ends at **Tropicana Field** (1 Tropicana Drive) a mile away, provides a nice overview of the region's baseball history. The bronze markers laid in the sidewalk contain a wealth of spring lore that fans enjoy reading as they stroll along the streets of this scenic city.

Another sports destination worth visiting back in Tampa is **The Tampa Bay Times Forum** (401 Channelside Drive). Located in the city's Garrison Seaport District, the home of the Lightning usually hosts seven or eight NHL games in the month of March. The Tampa Bay Storm of the Arena Football League also calls the Forum home. The gridders typically play one or two home games in March.

Fans looking for a sports bar in Tampa will find plenty of chain-type places. Those looking for a joint with more reasonable prices, good food and a whole lot more character than the chains will find **Walter's Press Box, Sports Emporium and Eatery** (222 S. Dale Mabry Highway) fits the bill.

Bright House Field

(CLEARWATER) Philadelphia Phillies

Bright House Field
601 Old Coachman Road, Clearwater
727–442–8496
http://www.milb.com/team1/page.jsp?content_id=526706&fext=.jsp&sid
    =t566&vkey=team1_t566&ymd=20090319
http://philadelphia.phillies.mlb.com
Opened: 2004. Seating Capacity: 9,200
• 7 miles north to Dunedin (Blue Jays)
• 16 miles west to Tampa (Yankees)
• 42 miles south to Bradenton (Pirates)
• 52 miles east to Lakeland (Tigers)

IN 2004 THE PHILADELPHIA PHILLIES unveiled not one, but two spectacular new ballparks. In March, the team opened Bright House Field in Clearwater, then just a month later it opened Citizens Bank Park in Philadelphia. Although the team's new regular season park was universally applauded, it did not reinvent its genre in the way Bright House Field did, raising the bar for the next generation of Grapefruit League facilities. The Clearwater stadium was the first new addition to the Grapefruit League landscape since Cracker Jack Stadium and Roger Dean Stadium opened six years earlier in 1998. From its very start Bright House presented hardball aficionados with a temple to the spring game unlike any other park in the Sunshine State. The sight lines are exceptionally pure and completely unobstructed, the amenities are many, and the stadium is architecturally stunning.

Bright House projects a decidedly Floridian facade. The stadium also bears noticeable similarities to the ballpark in Philadelphia. Bright House was designed, in fact, by the same architectural tandem that drew up Citizens Bank Park: the well-known ballpark architects of HOK Sport (now Populous) working in tandem with Ewing-Cole-Cherry-Brott of Philadelphia. In addition to borrowing from the Citizens Bank Park prints in crafting Bright House, these designers also clearly drew inspiration from the local football gridiron — Raymond James Stadium, home of the Tampa Bay Buccaneers.

A statue of Phillies legend Steve Carlton rises outside the main entrance.

Bright House is one of the most fan-friendly facilities in the Grapefruit League. As such, many fans arrive two hours before the game and stay for an hour or two afterward, eating and drinking at the festive tiki bar in left field home run territory while listening to live music. This unique ballpark sitting area was designed specifically to capture the atmosphere of the Pirate Ship at Raymond James Stadium.

In a nod to a design element common to many of the Cactus League stadiums, the Bright House playing surface is sunken below street level and the first level seats appear below a wide concourse that encircles the entire field. Not only does sinking the field and seats reduce the wind's effect on the game, but it allows fans to walk laps around the field. Fans can pursue concessions, souvenirs or simply a different vantage point, all without ever taking their eyes off the game. Berm seating — popular for years in Arizona — was still a relatively unknown phenomenon in Florida when Bright House opened. The festive Clearwater lawn extends nearly from foul pole to foul pole across the outfield, interrupted only by the dark hitter's backdrop in center and the tiki bar in left. Vendor carts line the walkway at the back of the berm, while palm trees trace the border of the stadium grounds. The front of this lounging lawn is level with the top of the outfield fence, providing a great view for those reclining on the grass in front. Meanwhile, the relatively steep incline of the hill allows people lazing about farther from the wall to enjoy a view that is unobstructed by those fans in front of them.

The berm offers a block-party type atmosphere. Young ladies sport bikini tops while they sun themselves on blankets. Parents toss balls to sons and daughters. Members of the twenty-something crowd retrieve frozen drinks and bottles of beer from the tiki bar, carrying them by the ice-filled bucketful back to their blankets. As for those feeling guilty about skipping work to attend a ballgame, well, there's something to readjust their attitude too: professional chair-massages on the left field walkway.

More than just providing a place for sunny revelry, the berm also affords close up views of the pitchers in the bullpens in left-center. The pens are tiered, running parallel to the outfield fence and to one another. The back pen, which serves the visiting team, is raised a few feet higher than the home pen, allowing fans a clear view of both areas.

Behind the video board on the left field berm, and behind the iron gates that line the back of the stadium, Philadelphia's minor leaguers refine their skills on the practice fields of the Carpenter Complex. Four of the five diamonds are arranged in a cloverleaf pattern; the configuration allows coaches and trainers to easily shuttle between the fields. The Complex—which names its four diamonds after Phillies legends Richie Ashburn, Steve Carlton, Robin Roberts and Mike Schmidt—has served the Phillies since 1967.

The 50-foot-wide thatch-roof tiki bar in left field home run territory is set behind a pavilion seating area that offers 60 barstools facing the field in five tiered rows. The tiki seats rise steeply, offering an effect similar to the one created by the Green Monster seats at Fenway Park in Boston. These comfortable stools are available on a first-come, first-served basis and are usually claimed well before the first-pitch when the ballpark first opens.

In Clearwater a day at the ballpark is just that—a full day. Fans sip margaritas before the game while watching batting practice. After the game, they sing along to the incantations of the live bands that play on the berm. A baseball game is played amidst the fun, while tasty cheesesteaks are consumed, and the kids are entertained at a colorful playground on the left field concourse.

As for the playing field, the dimensions replicate exactly the irregular expanse of the fence at Citizens Bank Park. The fence measures 329 feet from home plate to the left field foul pole, 385 feet to the power alley in left field, 381 feet to the triangle in left-center, 409 feet to straight-away center, 398 feet to the alley in right-center, and 330 feet to the right field foul pole. The nooks and crannies created by the sudden retreat of the wall in left-center pay tribute to Shibe Park, the longtime home of the Phillies and Philadelphia A's. The wavering outfield fence at Shibe maximized the size of the field by tracing the property boundaries of the homes on Philadelphia's 20th Street.

Bright House's exterior is nearly as impressive as its interior. At the ballpark's West Gate entrance a bubbly fountain is topped by a sculpture entitled "The Ace" that depicts the left-handed Carlton in mid-pitch. A practice infield and practice bullpen reside to the left of the plaza, treating fans to glimpses of players and coaches preparing for the game.

The Mediterranean style architecture of the stadium showcases attractive brown and tan arches. The stucco facade is adorned with decorative tiles that feature palm fronds as well as the four different style "P's" that the Phillies have used as their logo since joining the National League in 1883. Construction of the $30 million facility began in January of 2003 — funded jointly by the Phillies, City of Clearwater, Pinellas County, and the State of Florida. On the heels of an economic impact study in 2000 that indicated the Grapefruit League made a $450 million economic impact on Florida annually, then-governor Jeb Bush and the Florida legislature offered $75 million in matching funds for improvements and new additions to the Grapefruit League landscape. Florida's generosity came after several major league teams had begun to look at the Cactus League as a viable alternative to training in the Sunshine State. Clearwater received $7 million from Florida for the Bright House project, while the Phillies chipped in $12 million. Other ballpark renovations funded by the Florida legislature's bill that year included the ones in Dunedin (Blue Jays), Kissim-mee (Astros), Lakeland (Tigers), St. Lucie (Mets) and Vero Beach (Dodgers). Of those, all retained their teams except for Vero Beach, which lost the Dodgers to the Cactus League in 2009 despite the remodeling the state had funded.

Local cable company Bright House Networks struck a ten-year, $1.7 million, naming rights agreement with the Phillies in early 2004, and originally the ballpark was known as Bright House Networks Field. In 2010, however, the word "Networks" was dropped from the park's official name. The company retains two five-year options to extend the relationship at the end of the initial term.

The stadium officially opened on March 4, 2004, and the sell-out crowd of more than 8,000 people went home happy, after the Phillies defeated the Yankees 5–1. The highlight of the day for many came when the Phillie Phanatic mashed an

Fans enjoy the relaxed atmosphere of the finest outfield seating berm in Florida.

apple on a Yankees cap in front of the visiting dugout, then stepped back to watch as a flock of seagulls swooped down to fight over the mealy bait. All the while, Yankee owner George Steinbrenner looked on with mock disdain from behind the Yankees' dugout.

Opening Day 2004, was certainly not the Phillie Phanatic's first appearance in Clearwater. The Phillies have trained in Clearwater since 1947 without interruption. Only the Detroit Tigers who have trained in Lakeland every year since 1946 enjoy a longer consecutive tenure in their spring city. Philadelphia's connection to the Tampa Bay area actually dates back even further. The Phillies trained in St. Petersburg from 1915 to 1918 and in Bradenton from 1925 to 1927. In 1915, at a time when many teams still prepared for the season up north, the Phillies proved the merits of training in Florida, winning 14 of their first 15 regular season games en route to the National League pennant.

The Brooklyn Dodgers (1923–1932, 1936–1940) and Cleveland Indians (1942, 1946) trained in Clearwater before the Phillies established residence in the town. Prior to arriving in Clearwater, the Phillies trained in Hershey, Pennsylvania, in 1943 and in Wilmington, Delaware, in 1944 and 1945. Those not-so-southern spring sojourns were taken in an era when all of the MLB teams trained east of the Mississippi and north of the Potomac. Baseball commissioner Kenesaw Mountain Landis had struck an agreement with the U.S. Office of Defense Transportation to limit baseball travel during World War II, in order to free the railways for troops and supplies. After the war, in 1946, the Phillies set up camp at Miami Beach, which had been their spring home in the three years before the travel restrictions. The next year they moved to Clearwater.

From 1955 to 2003 Jack Russell Stadium was the Phillies' Clearwater home. From 1947 to 1954, they had played on a small field that would later serve as Jack Russell's left field parking lot. Located in downtown Clearwater, four miles from where the Phillies now play, Jack Russell had fallen into disrepair in its later year and the economically depressed neighborhood around it had become uninviting to tourists. Consequently, attendance at Phillies games had waned. In 2003, the Phillies averaged just 3,400 fans per home game, compared to the average crowds of more than 9,500 that fill Bright House today. Nonetheless, Jack Russell was a quaint and intimate place to watch a game. It offered palms beyond its outfield fences and a warning track of crushed white seashells (similar to the track that still exists at the community-use Joe DiMaggio Field across the street from Bright House).

The old stadium was also endowed with an array of quirky anecdotes that it earned through the years, like the story of its dedication day. Jack Russell Stadium was dedicated on March 10, 1955, before the Phillies opened the exhibition season with a 4–2 win against the Tigers. Baseball Commissioner Ford Frick and league presidents Warren Giles and Will Harridge took part in the ribbon-cutting ceremony, as well as Clearwater Mayor Herbert Brown. Jack Russell, a former big league pitcher who had won 85 games and lost 141 in a 15-year career with several teams, was on the field to introduce the guests of honor. Russell, who had settled in Clearwater after retiring in 1940, had played a leading role in the effort to build the new stadium, and had volunteered to serve as master of ceremonies. Reportedly none of the 4,209 fans in attendance were as surprised as Russell himself, when, at the end of the ceremony, the Mayor said that he had a few more words to say. Mayor Brown seized the microphone and announced that the new stadium would be named after Jack Russell.

Another surreal ballpark moment occurred at the stadium on the evening of June 26, 1985, when an umpire ejected ballpark organist Wilbur Snapp from the press box during a Florida State League game. When a close call at first base went against the Clearwater Phillies, Snapp launched into a rendition of "Three Blind Mice." The umpire immediately pointed at the press box and demanded that Snapp be removed. Snapp wasn't forced to leave the ballpark, just the press box, so he spent the remainder of the game in the grandstand making balloon mice for the children in attendance to throw onto the field. In the ensuing days Snapp's story was documented on *Good Morning America*, in *National Geographic*, and on the *Paul Harvey Show*.

Today, Bright House Field continues to host the Phillies' Florida State League affiliate during the summer months, but the team is called the Clearwater Threshers. The club adopted the new name in 2004. A thresher is a species of shark common to the Gulf waters. It feeds on other fish, crustaceans, and occasionally seabirds.

GETTING TO THE PARK. Bright House Field is on Old Coachman Road, which runs parallel to U.S. 19, one block west of the highway. From U.S. 19, take the Drew Street Exit and follow Drew Street west to the parking lot at the corner of Drew and Old Coachman. The ballpark is visible from Route 19. Late arrivals often have difficulty finding parking near the ballpark as there are only about 1,200 spots in the dirt lot of Joe DiMaggio Field and 300 spots at the Carpenter Complex to the north of the stadium.

The seating options surround the entire field, keeping fans close to the action.

SEATING. The ballpark "officially" lists 7,700 fixed seats and room for another 1,500 fans on the outfield lawn. In actuality, however, the Phillies put about 3,000 berm and standing room tickets on sale for each game. The Phillies average more than 9,500 per home date, thanks to a steady influx of fans who visit from the "City of Brotherly Love." One extremely full house turned out on March 22, 2010 to watch the Phillies beat the Yankees, 9–7. The announced attendance for the 2009 World Series rematch was 10,724. Then, the very next spring on March 21, 2011, a Red Sox versus Phillies game drew a whopping 10,912. The home team prevailed that day too, besting the Bostonians 4–1.

Aside from the nine luxury suites that hang over the concourse on the first base side and the three sections of club seating a bit further down the first base line, all of the seats are below the concourse. As a result, pedestrian traffic does not disturb any of the sight lines.

The seating bowl begins with Section 101 in deep right field near the foul pole, continues around the infield to Section 111 behind home plate, and ends with Section 120 in medium depth left. The seating bowl would be completely symmetrical if not for the picnic area between Section 120 and the left field foul pole. The stadium offers 23 rows of seats with all of the rows angled nicely toward home plate.

The Premium Box seats are located between the on-deck circles. Section 108 is situated at the inside corner of the Phillies' dugout on the first base side, while Section 114 is located at the inner corner of the visiting dugout. The Field Box sections begin behind the dugouts on either side of the field and continue into outfield foul territory (Sections 103–107 on the first base side; Sections 115–120 on the third base side). The seats at many regular season ballparks are not angled as well as the ones in Clearwater.

Sections 101 and 102 in deeper right field sell for the same price as the Field Boxes despite being labeled Baseline Boxes. Apparently, the Phillies wanted to achieve some truth in advertising even if they weren't willing to knock a few dollars off the ticket price to account for the seats being the farthest from the infield.

As for the three Picnic Terrace sections in left field, P1 is the closest to the infield, while P2 is a bit deeper, and P3 is tucked next to the foul pole. The seating in these sections consists of metal picnic tables with benches. This is a good place to sit down and have lunch before the game, but the outfield lawn provides a better overall viewing location for less money.

The Berm extends across the entire right field side and across half of left field home run territory due to the space occupied by the tiki bar and bullpens. Most fans look for blanket space in right-center where they can enjoy both a view of the game and a view of the scoreboard in left field.

THE BALLPARK EXPERIENCE. For many reasons, arriving at the ballpark early and staying late is central to the Bright House experience. First, there are the advantages to avoiding the pre- and post-game traffic logjams. Next, the line on the left field concourse to access the Phillies' clubhouse store is often 50 people

The unique left field tiki bar has inspired replicas in other spring cities like Sarasota and Fort Myers.

long by game-time. Additionally, swarms of glove-toting fans head for the outfield lawn shortly after the park opens to claim good spots to spread their blankets before the park becomes overrun with the throngs that turn out to watch the Phillies play. After the game, the party continues on the lawn as fans sing along with Jimmy Buffet type songs and catch some sunrays.

During the game, fans find it hard not to notice the ball attendants in the outfield corners. Hooters Girls race out to pick up loose balls wearing skimpy orange bikini bottoms and little else. In most towns this would play like just another shameless marketing ploy, but in Clearwater it is a bit more legitimate. The original Hooters is located just a mile and a half away.

As the Phillies take the field in the top of the first inning, the public address system blares "Eye of the Tiger," pumping up the team and its fans with the song that inspired Philadelphia underdog Rocky Balboa to win heavyweight glory in the *Rocky* movies.

Bright House offers four main food courts: the Bullpen Grill in left field, the Short Stop Grill — which serves a kids menu — on the concourse above third base, the Strikeout Café in right field, and the Home Run Grill behind home plate. The full array of traditional ballpark favorites are prepared fresh at these locations while mobile carts on the concourse sell frozen treats and specialty items. The trademark food — the Steak Sandwich — is only available at the Home Run Grill. This is one hoagie that doesn't disappoint. While the sandwich doesn't quite match the sliced rib eye subs served at Philadelphia landmarks like Pat's Steaks and Geno's Steaks, it comes pretty close. Pennsylvania favorite Yuengling is the premium beer on tap.

ON THE TOWN. Clearwater is home to some of the most beautiful coastline in the United States. The Gulf waters are blue-green, crystal clear, and usually about 70 degrees Fahrenheit during spring training. Unfortunately, college spring breaks coincide with baseball's spring training, often making it nearly impossible to access **Clearwater Beach**. Because the beach is situated on a barrier island, the access roads must cross the water and the bridges become very congested on sunny days. Gulf to Bay Boulevard (Route 60) should be avoided, especially on weekend dates. Those who do choose to wait for an hour or more to cross a bridge may be disappointed to find the beach parking lots completely full and closed for the day. A better option is to visit the shores of **Indian Rocks Beach** a few miles to the south. The area is not as commercialized but every bit as beautiful.

As for the rest of Clearwater, the town was once quaint and quintessentially Floridian, but today it consists of one strip mall after another. Visitors find just about every major chain restaurant in the country on U.S. 19, as well as some local favorites.

The Original Hooters is located at 2800 Gulf to Bay Boulevard. Fans may be disappointed to find that it is remarkably similar to the 57th Hooters or 120th Hooters that is located in their hometown.

Those who enjoy the Steak Sandwich at the ballpark and find themselves hankering for another before heading north can visit **Delco's Original Steaks and Hoagies** (1701 Main Street, Dunedin), which has its fresh Amaroso rolls flown in each day from Philly and serves Hank's Root Beer and Tastykakes too. **Capogna's Dugout** (1653 Gulf to Bay Boulevard) and **Philly's Famous Cheesesteaks** (4375 East Bay Drive) are also solid choices.

Phillies fans who reluctantly leave the Bright House tiki bar when the ballpark closes, can head to **Frenchy's Saltwater Café** (416 East Shore Drive) at Clearwater Beach to continue the fun.

For breakfast the next morning, Phillies fans and players flock to **Lenny's Restaurant** (21220 U.S. 19 North), which is just a ten-minute walk from Bright House Field. Not only does the joint have delicious cheesesteaks, sweet rolls and home fries, but it also serves scrapple — the mystery meat of choice in Philadelphia. It also features plenty of memorabilia. Framed photographs of famous Phillies Larry Bowa and Tug McGraw hang on the walls, as well as a signed jersey of Hall of Famer Mike Schmidt, who managed the Clearwater Threshers in 2004 before hanging up his coaching shoes. Lenny's does get a bit overrun with baseball fans during spring training, so visitors should arrive early if planning to eat before the game.

Florida Auto Exchange Stadium

(DUNEDIN) Toronto Blue Jays

Florida Auto Exchange Stadium
373 Douglas Avenue, Dunedin
727–733–0429
http://www.dunedingov.com/home.aspx?page=departments/LeisureSer
    vices/dunedinstadium
http://toronto.bluejays.mlb.com
Opened: 1930. Renovated: 2002. Seating Capacity: 5,510
• 8 miles southeast to Clearwater (Phillies)
• 21 miles east to Tampa (Yankees)
• 49 miles south to Bradenton (Pirates)
• 60 miles east to Lakeland (Tigers)

JUST EIGHT MILES north of the crowded tourist magnet that is Bright House Field in Clearwater, tiny Florida Auto Exchange Stadium sits in a residential neighborhood in sleepy little Dunedin. Here, fans enjoy spring ball in much the way one imagines the forefathers of the Grapefruit League did. The stadium is the most intimate one in either of today's spring circuits. The seats are close to the field, the façade is low and understated, the aisles and stairways are narrow, and the ballpark staff members are extremely friendly. The stands are cozy and the field has barely any foul territory. The right field foul pole stands just 327 feet from home plate, while the left field pole measures just 335 feet away. The right field power-alley checks in at 363 feet, while the left field gap measures a slightly deeper 380 feet, and center field measures 400 feet. Of course these dimensions are posted on the outfield wall in both feet and their metric equivalents, so that Blue Jays fans visiting from Canada — and there are always quite a few — feel at home. Similarly, both the U.S. and Canadian flags fly beyond the fence in right-center field. And both countries' anthems are performed prior to each game, just like at Rogers Centre in Toronto.

Like the stadium itself, the light banks above the field contribute to an old-

Members of the grounds crew put the finishing touches on the field before the game.

time atmosphere, with just a few scant rows of bulbs appearing atop each tower. While these lights might be useful for recreational purposes during the park's summer season, they are not utilized during the spring when the Blue Jays play all of their home games during the day. Until the early 2000s the park had a delightfully old-timey manually-operated scoreboard, too, but it was replaced by an electronic board above the left field wall as part of a 2002 renovation.

The ballpark ushers are pleasant retirees from the local community who seem more interested in snapping photos for road-tripping fans than in demanding that people sit in their assigned seats or stand behind some arbitrary line on the concourse. Outside the park, Dunedin's grandfathers and grandmothers double as parking attendants on days when their sleepy little seaside town is transformed into a bustling baseball village. The Dunedin Public Library, Dunedin Veterans of Foreign Wars Post, and Cornerstone Christian Church all open their parking lots to fans, charging small fees.

For the most part, the 4,500 or so people who turn out for games at Florida Auto Exchange Stadium are quiet and polite observers. Perhaps this is because many are visiting from Canada where the Blue Jays' regular season dome has grown notoriously quiet in the years since the Blue Jays' halcyon days of the early 1990s. The Canadians and genial elders filling the stands seem content to calmly watch the events of the game unfold without screaming, hollering, or even very often clapping en masse. Games sell out when the Red Sox, Yankees, or Phillies visit, but rarely otherwise.

The ballpark in this tranquil coastal town has been known by several names through the years, and has undergone many renovations. But the fact remains that hardball has been played at this location since 1930 when Mayor Albert Grant championed the construction of a baseball field. The field was expanded in 1933 when the city received a $250 federal grant to clear additional land.

The diamond was dedicated Grant Field on November 22, 1938, shortly before

Mr. Grant stepped down from his second stint as mayor. Aside from being a city official, the "Old Man of Dunedin" as Grant was affectionately known until his passing in 1956, was also the founder of the Bank of Dunedin, today known as Sun-Trust Bank. The bank was one of only two Florida financial institutions to remain solvent through the Great Depression. According to local lore, during one bank crisis, Grant tricked customers into believing there was no reason to panic by holding up stacks of newspaper clippings cut into the dimensions of dollar bills. Of course Grant put a few real bills on the outside of each bundle to mask the truth.

During its long life as an amateur field, Dunedin's ballpark was known simply as Grant Field and it still bore that name when the Toronto Blue Jays joined the American League in 1977 and decided to make Dunedin their spring home. The expansion team won its first spring game at Grant Field on March 11, 1977, posting a 3–1 victory against the New York Mets before 1,988 fans. The stadium's seating capacity at that time was just 3,417, with most of the seats appearing in the form of metal bleachers. The playing field was even smaller than today. The right field foul pole measured just 301 feet from home plate, while the left field pole rose 345 feet away. The outfield fences were adjusted prior to the 1984 spring season to account for the park's present dimensions. In 1985, Blue Jays players like George Bell, Tony Fernandez and Jesse Barfield returned to Dunedin to find a brand new home clubhouse awaiting them beneath the third base grandstand. Today this clubhouse serves the visiting team.

In 1990 the stadium underwent a major renovation as the city of Dunedin footed the bill for $2.5 million of work. The new stadium was dedicated "Dunedin Stadium at Grant Field" during a pre-game ceremony on March 3, 1990. Fans were happy to find new seats in right field that increased capacity to 5,500. Members of the media, meanwhile, were happy to find a new enclosed press box — unlike the previous one that had consisted of a few open-air boxes painted blue at the top of the seating bowl behind home plate.

In 2000, Toronto signed an agreement to remain in Dunedin for another 15 years, contingent on the completion of a $13.5 million upgrade to the facilities. The contract also offered the Blue Jays two five-year options to extend the relationship, which could keep the team in Dunedin through 2025. The largest funding source for this latest project came from the State of Florida, which contributed $6 million. Pinellas County pitched in $3 million, and the Blue Jays and city of Dunedin funded the remainder. Completed in time for the 2002 season, the project added a two-story building beyond the fence in right field. The building provides the Blue Jays with administrative space and a second floor deck from which team employees can watch the ballgame. It also provides Blue Jays players with a spacious clubhouse, a training room and a weight room.

The ballpark's exterior façade was also remodeled to its current beige brick appearance as part of this project. A pale blue metal roof runs along the top of the stadium and a brick tower rises above the small building in front of the stadium that houses the ticket office. At ground level outside the park, brick pillars hold up a black iron gate that encircles the concourse that runs behind the seating bowl. Other pillars hold up the seating bowl itself. Concessions, souvenirs, rest rooms and tidbits of Blue Jays history are located on this concourse. From the concourse, fans walk up narrow sets of steps to the mid-level walkway inside the stadium. The seats are all pale blue and the railings are bright red, giving the facility an inviting appearance that reflects the home team's colors.

As part of the 2002 project, the Blue Jays also received a new minor league complex in Dunedin just north of their previous one. Named after a former city commissioner, who was instrumental in bringing the Blue Jays to Dunedin initially, the Cecil P. Englebert Recreational Complex is a ten-minute drive from Florida Auto Exchange Stadium. It offers major and minor league clubhouses, five full practice fields, a practice infield, and administrative offices for the Blue Jays' minor league personnel. Four of the practice fields are arranged in a cloverleaf pattern with an observation tower in the center that allows instructors to watch over all four diamonds at once.

On the heels of this work, Dunedin officials decided to sell the naming rights to Dunedin Stadium at Grant Field. Just before the start of the 2004 spring season, a task force of Dunedin officials that included Englebert and Dave Eggers, chairman of the Dunedin Chamber of Commerce, announced that a deal had been struck with Knology Incorporated, a Georgia-based communications company. But the five-year, $400,000 naming rights agreement paled in comparison to the ten-year, $1.7 million deal that Clearwater had agreed to with Bright House Networks a few months earlier. Dunedin's deal was actually only worth $340,000 in cash, while the remaining $60,000 was scheduled to come in the form of free advertising that the stadium would receive through Knology cable services. After seven decades, the field that Albert Grant had envisioned and then developed was stripped of his name in 2004. Chalk up another one to the new economic realities of baseball — even

The small seating bowl barely extends past third base.

spring training baseball! In another sign of the times, though, the Knology moniker didn't last long. In November 2010, Dunedin officials struck a new seven-year $181,000 naming rights deal with the used car dealership after which the park is currently named.

In addition to having welcomed every single Blue Jay who has played spring training ball for the Toronto club through the years, the venerable field in Dunedin has also served as the home of the Blue Jays' Class-A affiliate in the Florida State League since 1977. The Dunedin High School Falcons have made the park their home for decades too.

GETTING TO THE PARK. From U.S. 19, follow Sunset Point West, then turn right on Douglas Avenue and follow it north to the stadium. The parking lot behind the home plate grandstand is small and fills up early. At $15 per spot in 2012, it was more expensive than most other Grapefruit League lots. Season ticket holders park in this lot for free and also enjoy exclusive access to the VIP Lounge under the third base grandstand inside the park. But most fans park at the privately operated lots in the neighborhood, which are considerably less expensive. The largest of these is directly across the street from the stadium, as Veteran's Memorial Park is transformed into a parking lot on game day. There are a limited number of free street spots north of the stadium on Douglas for those who don't mind a half-mile walk.

SEATING. In a throwback to an earlier era, the seats all appear in foul territory, behind the plate and along the baselines. On the right side of the diamond the seating extends into medium depth right field, while across the field the grandstand ends just past third base. From overhead, therefore, the stadium would resemble a backwards "L" with home plate serving as the locus where the two lines form a right angle. The 1990 renovation, which added two extra right field seating sections in both the 100- and 200-levels, created this asymmetry.

The seats all take the form of fixed blue plastic seats. In other words, the seat bottoms don't flip up or down. The seats are just fixed in place, with narrow metal armrests separating them from one another. Below the narrow mid-level walkway fans find the 100-level's Box seats, while above the walkway are the 200-level's Reserved seats. There are just seven rows throughout most of the 100-level and 16 in most of the 200-level.

The best seats can be found between Section 103, behind the Blue Jays' first base dugout, and Section 109, behind the visiting team's dugout. Section 106 is directly behind home plate. In Sections 103 and 109 the first row is Row 3 due to the protrusion of the dugouts.

The best Reserved sections are 205, 206 and 207. Section 206 is directly behind the plate, while 205 is just to the right of the plate, and 207 is just to the left. Due to the presence of the press box, the sunroof does not extend overhead. On the left field side of the diamond, pretty much any seat is a winner, seeing as even Section 111 at the very end of the grandstand is situated just past the third base bag. On the

Favorite Blue Jays who played in Dunedin are remembered with colorful banners on the Florida Auto Exchange concourse.

right side, Sections 100 and 100A are located in medium depth foul territory, making them less desirable than the other Box sections. The same can be said for Sections 200 and 200A of the Reserved.

For fans seeking rain relief or shade, the blue metal sunroof covers Rows 9–16 of the Reserved. On hot days fans in Rows 15 and 16 enjoy a cool breeze that blows through an opening at the top of the seating bowl. Behind Row 16 there is a small standing room area that often comes in handy for those seated down below wishing to escape the sun for a few innings. Here, fans will notice the basketball-sized porcelain baseballs that decorate the railing behind the last row of seats.

THE BALLPARK EXPERIENCE. Upon passing through the turnstiles and entering the concourse that runs at ground level behind the stadium, fans encounter colorful banners that honor great Blue Jays players of the past and present. Each player's name and uniform number appears on his oversized baseball card, along with a color photo. Among those honored are Roy Halladay, Devon White, Ernie Whit, George Bell, Dave Stieb, Shawn Green, Tom Henke, Joe Carter, Carlos Delgado, Tony Fernandez and former Blue Jays manager Cito Gaston, who guided the team to back-to-back World Championships in 1992 and 1993.

The concourse also houses a "Dunedin to the Show" exhibit beneath Section 210 on the left field side. A baseball-shaped blue plaque honors each member of the Dunedin Blue Jays who later went on to play in the big leagues, colloquially known as "the Show." Each plaque features the player's name and the year or years that he spent playing Class-A ball in Dunedin. The balls honor such Dunedin veterans as Mark Hendrickson (1999–2000), Vernon Wells (1999), Billy Koch (1997–1998), Chris Stynes (1993), Steve Karsay (1992), Mike Timlin (1989–1990) and Lloyd Moseby (1979).

The ballpark gates open two and a half hours before the first pitch, allowing fans the chance to watch both squads take batting practice. The Blue Jays always hit first. The best places to obtain autographs are at the ends of the concourse in left and right field. In these spots, a short chain-link fence separates fans from the players in the bullpens. The Blue Jays' pen is in right field, behind the outfield fence, while the visiting team's pen is in left field, parallel to the foul line. Neither bullpen is particularly visible from inside the park, but the pitchers do sometimes take a few moments to mingle with fans before the game. Fans who wait in the box seats near third base can chat with the visiting players as they access the field from the clubhouse.

As game time approaches, road-trippers wondering what percentage of the crowd hails from the Great White North gain a decent indication of this after the singing of the U.S. National Anthem. The visiting and transplanted Canadians in attendance boisterously sing along with "Oh, Canada."

Local retirees, who are members of the Blue Jays Dunedin Booster Club, staff the concession stands. What these men and women may lack in speediness, they more than make up for with their friendliness. The Barbecue Pulled Pork is quite good as is the pizza provided by Jet's Pizza. A small bar on the left field concourse provides a comfortable area to sit down, but lacks a view of the game. Appropriately, LaBatt's Blue is the beer of choice for visiting Canadians.

ON THE TOWN. Founded in 1870, Dunedin is the oldest town on Florida's Gulf Coast. The town received its name in 1882 when a pair of Scottish settlers petitioned the government to open a post office named "Dunedin." In Scottish, the word *Dun* means "rock" and *Edin* means "castle." Combined, the words mean "Castle on the Rock."

Although it is not far from bustling Clearwater and Clearwater Beach — where most of the Blue Jays stars rent luxury condos during the spring, Dunedin maintains a quaint village-like atmosphere. The only thing a bit discordant with this vibe is the shop advertising "Guns and Ammo" within shouting distance of the ballpark on Douglas Avenue.

Those looking for a classic diner experience, either for breakfast or lunch, will find **Iris's Grill** (234 Douglas Avenue) just to their liking. Located across the street from the ballpark, Iris's has been serving scrumptious omelets, open-faced sandwiches and pies for more than two decades. Many Dunedin locals never go to a game without stopping into Iris's first, and more than a few Blue Jays players and coaches have stopped in through the years too.

Downtown Dunedin is just a mile north of the ballpark at the intersection of Douglas and Main Street. There, a beautiful mural on the side of a tavern chronicles Dunedin's colorful history. From Douglas, a left turn on Main leads to a strip of pastel colored one-story buildings in the Mediterranean architectural style; these house boutiques and restaurants. Favorite pre- and post-game spots on Main Street include **Skip's Bar and Grill, Casa Tina Gourmet Mexican Grill, The Dunedin Smoke House** and **Delco's Steaks and Hoagies**. At the end of this delightful little stretch, Main Street empties into a marina parking lot.

When the Blue Jays big leaguers aren't in action, fans visit the **Cecil P. Englebert Recreational Complex** (1700 Solon Avenue) to watch the minor leaguers play.

The ferry landing for **Caladesi Island State Park** is also only a ten-minute drive from the ballpark. The beach on this scenic island a mile from shore has appeared on many lists ranking the most breathtaking beaches in America. The beach is accessible via ferry from a landing at **Honeymoon Island State Park** (1 Causeway Boulevard). The ferry boats leave every hour, beginning at 10:00 A.M.

McKechnie Field

(BRADENTON) Pittsburgh Pirates

McKechnie Field
1611 Ninth Street West, Bradenton
877–893–2827
http://mlb.mlb.com/spring_training/ballpark.jsp?c_id=pit
http://pittsburgh.pirates.mlb.com
Opened: 1923. Rebuilt: 1992. Renovated: 2008. Seating Capacity: 6,562
• 13 miles south to Sarasota (Orioles)
• 43 miles north to Clearwater (Phillies)
• 46 miles north to Tampa (Yankees)
• 50 miles south to Port Charlotte (Rays)

NOT MUCH WENT right for the Pittsburgh Pirates in the 1990s and first decade of the twenty-first century. By 2012, the once mighty Bucs had suffered through nineteen consecutive losing seasons. The ignominious streak dated all the way back to the team's National League Championship Series loss to the Braves in 1992. After that team lost many of its stars to free agency, there was woefully little for the team to celebrate in the two decades to follow. Sure, the team opened beautiful PNC Park in Pittsburgh in 2001, but the unveiling of that gem did little to enhance the team's performance and many locals soon took to boycotting the new park to send Pirates management a message — "Improve the team, or we won't pay to watch it!" Despite the long stretch of futility, however, one thing did go right for the Black and Gold during this otherwise gloomy period. While the Pirates were busy losing games, the good folks in Bradenton were taking measures to ensure that their quaint little yard would endure the changing times and survive to host Grapefruit League action well into the new century. Bradenton made some subtle but necessary improvements to its ballpark, and as it celebrated the fortieth anniversary of its affiliation with the Pirates in 2008, it inked the team to a new thirty-year lease that should keep the Pirates in town through 2038.

A town cut from much the same cloth as working class Pittsburgh, Bradenton has supported the Pirates through good times and bad. Though many Bradenton

The arching home plate façade was built in 1992.

residents have never visited the Steel City, the small town south of Tampa Bay boasts a fan base that closely follows the Pirates all summer long. These folks remember fondly the days when Pirates managers like Danny Murtaugh and Chuck Tanner forecast great things for their teams during the spring trainings of 1972 and 1979, respectively, and then returned as World Champions the next years to see their joyous faces honored on the billboard above the DeSoto Bridge, which spans the Manatee River.

The feelings of affection have been mutual through the years. Not only have the rooters in Bradenton loved the Pirates, but the Pirates have loved them back. Because Bradenton is a small town and because the Pirates are not one of the game's glamour teams that attract swarms of media types and hordes of traveling fans, the Bradenton locals and Pirates players have mingled, perhaps, a little more than the players and fans do in other spring cities. Appropriately, this friendship has been cemented at inviting little McKechnie Field.

The ballpark originally opened in 1923 as spring home to the St. Louis Cardinals. It is named after Bill McKechnie, a Hall of Fame manager who made Bradenton his retirement home. While the field remains on the same plot of land where Babe Ruth, Jimmie Foxx, Hank Aaron, Eddie Mathews and Roberto Clemente once played, the stadium has been rebuilt several times. The current incarnation of the park debuted in the spring of 1993.

McKechnie Field offers old-time charm and plenty of it. The cream-colored exterior façade behind the home plate grandstand reflects the Spanish Mission architecture common to the area. The structure rises in several arches to a rounded nexus in the middle. At street level, a green iron gate separates the sidewalk from the concourse behind the seating bowl. The decorative green metal sunroof provides a distinctive finishing touch. Inside, the grandstands on the first and third base lines exist in separate structures entirely from the impressive facade behind home plate. These base-line seating structures sit like the old-fashioned ballpark grandstands that appear in period video reels of players like Ruth and Foxx in action. The bleacher sections in right and left field foul territory help boost the park's seating capacity to 6,562.

The roofs above the first and third base seating structures are white with green trim facing the field. They are adorned with white pennants that proudly fly the green letter "M," spread evenly around the stadium's top rim. Down at field level, meanwhile, the home dugout is on the first base side, while the bullpens account for the park's only blatant instance of asymmetry. The Pirates' pen is located in right field where the seating bowl ends, arranged so that the pitchers throw from near the foul line to catchers who squat facing the field. On the other side of the diamond, the visiting relievers throw parallel to the left field foul line to catchers who squat facing, more typically, the outfield wall.

Pirates relievers watch the game from the right field bullpen (courtesy The Gup Collection).

The dark green outfield wall stands 335 feet from home plate down the lines, 370 feet away in the power-alleys and 400 feet away in center field. Flag courts on either side of the dark green hitter's backdrop in center honor each of the Pirates' championship teams with gold, black, and white flags. The different colors distinguish between Pittsburgh teams that merely qualified for post-season play, that claimed the National League pennant, and that captured the World Series title. The scoreboard in left field is topped by a face-clock reminiscent of the timepiece that once existed at Ebbets Field in Brooklyn and of the one that currently resides above the scoreboard at Baltimore's Oriole Park at Camden Yards. Palm trees rise behind the outfield fence. The trunks are spaced evenly allowing for perfect intervals of usually blue sky to appear between their lush canopies.

As for the ballpark light towers, they are a relatively new addition. They were added in 2008 as part of a renovation that cost the State of Florida $15 million. Prior to that, McKechnie Field was the only spring venue in current use that had never hosted a night game. Although the Pirates typically play only one or two evening affairs per spring, the lights were important because they made the park suitable for minor league play during the regular season. Thus, the Pittsburgh Marauders of the Florida State League now use the park, enabling it to generate revenue for Bradenton during more than just one month per year. Also added in 2008 was a new visiting team's clubhouse. Renovations were also made to Pittsburgh's Pirate City minor league complex.

In 1992, the Pirates and the City of Bradenton teamed up to completely rebuild McKechnie Field at a cost of $3.5 million, which seems like a paltry figured compared to some of the more recent spring training constructions, and considering the beauty of the facility in Bradenton. The previous incarnation of McKechnie Field, which consisted of rickety wooden bleachers capable of accommodating just 4,200 fans, had been built in 1953. That incarnation of the park had served as the spring home of the Milwaukee Braves (1953–1962), Kansas City Athletics (1963–1967), Oakland Athletics (1968), and Pirates who arrived in 1969. The ballpark featured a manual scoreboard in left field that for years was operated by Hall-of-Famer Edd Roush, who retired to Bradenton after an 18-year playing career during which he batted .323 for five different teams. Perhaps it was fitting, though bittersweet, that Roush died at McKechnie Field on March 21, 1988, after collapsing in the press room before a game. He was 94 years.

In earlier days, Bradenton's ballpark served as home to the St. Louis Cardinals (1923–24, 1930–1936), Philadelphia Phillies (1925–1927), Boston Red Sox (1928–1929), Boston Bees (1938–1940) and Boston Braves (1948–1952). Cardinal pitcher Dizzy Dean was one of the most popular players to ever pass through Bradenton, and locals still talk about the gas station that he bought one spring on the corner of Tenth Street and Fourth Avenue. Dean spent more time pumping gas that first spring than he did working on his curveball, and soon the Cardinals were being referred to as "The Gas House Gang." Because Dean often had difficulty staying out of trouble in St. Louis during the off-season, each year the Cardinals would

Most fans would rather stand during pregame warm-ups than sit in the plastic bucket seats (courtesy The Gup Collection).

send him to spring training in Bradenton months before the rest of the team reported. The team even went so far as to hire a Bradenton sports writer named Brack Cheshire to look after its fun-loving hurler one spring.

Like Roush, who settled in Bradenton in 1952, Bill McKechnie chose to live in Bradenton after his career and remained a resident from 1946 until his passing in 1965 at age 79. "The Deacon" as he was known, played the game for 11 seasons, mostly with the Pirates, then launched a 25-year managerial career that saw him guide the 1925 Pirates to the World Championship. Prior to being dedicated "McKechnie Field" in 1962, the ballpark at the corner of Ninth Street and 17th Avenue had gone by many different names including Fairgrounds Field, City Park, Cardinals Field, Ninth Street Park and Braves Field.

As for the Pirates, Bradenton is the 16th different site they have used as a spring training base. The team trained at four other Florida sites before arriving in Bradenton: Jacksonville (1918), Miami Beach (1947), Fort Pierce (1954) and Fort Myers (1955–1958). Pittsburgh also spent springs in such far-away places as Havana, Cuba (1953), Hollywood, California (1948), and San Bernardino, California (1935, 1937–1942, 1946, 1949–1952). The Pirates' tenure in Bradenton is by far the team's longest stay in any spring town and ranks second-longest in all of the Grapefruit League, trailing only the Tigers' long relationship with Lakeland, which dates to 1946.

As wonderful as McKechnie Field is, apparently Bradenton recognizes that it could still use a bit more modernizing. In 2012 plans were afoot to pursue another round of renovations—this one estimated to cost $7.5 million. The work would expand the grandstand, replace the metal grandstand roofs, create a Bradenton Walk of Fame on the concourse, and add a tiki bar in right field. Here's hoping they don't modernize McKechnie Field too much. Its old-time charm is what makes it special.

GETTING TO THE PARK. McKechnie Field is located half a mile west of U.S. 41 on the corner of Ninth Street West and 17th Avenue in a commercial neighborhood consisting mostly of auto repair shops. Just west of the ballpark, visitors will find Bradenton's "Village of the Arts," which houses a plethora of galleries and studios. To access the ballpark, take U.S. 41 South, turn right on 17th Avenue, and follow it directly to the ballpark. There are several independently owned parking lots on Ninth Street where local businesses charge a small fee. Another option for those staying in town is to make use of the local bus system. Both Route 2 and Route 10 of the MCAT (Manatee County Area Transit) service the ballpark.

SEATING. The crowds have continued to grow larger in Bradenton in recent years. Today, the Pirates average more than 5,000 fans per home date. Tickets are

Light towers were finally installed as part of the 2008 renovation (courtesy The Gup Collection).

affordably priced and most seats provide excellent views of the action. The odd numbered sections are on the left field side of the diamond, while the even numbered sections are on the right field side. Sections 1 and 2 are behind home plate. Section 22 is in far right field and Section 21 is in far left field.

The metal seats are all one-piece units that don't flip up like most stadium chairs. These are more similar to the fixed seats one might expect to find in a bus terminal lobby. Thankfully, yellow seat cushions emblazoned with the Pirates logo can be rented for a small fee on the concourse.

The Box sections represent the first six rows, extending nearly from foul pole to foul pole in Sections numbered 1–22. Rows 8–22 of Sections 1–4 behind home plate are also considered Box seats, even though they are above the concourse. Box seats in Bradenton sell for less money than the cheap seats at many other spring venues.

The Reserved seats consist of Rows 1–16 behind the concourse on the first and third base lines. The roof covers everyone in Row 4 and higher. The small price to pay for the luxury of sun relief and rain protection is the presence of steel support poles rising up at the front of each section. These poles are too thin to significantly obstruct sight lines and manage to give the grandstand an old-time feel similar to Fenway Park in Boston.

The Reserved Bleachers are located in outfield foul territory, with four sections appearing in right field and three in left. There are 16 rows in each section. The best views are to be found in the sections closest to the infield: Section 16 in right field and Section 15 in left field. There is no protection from the sun or rain in these sections and the Bleachers do not provide any form of back support for fans.

THE BALLPARK EXPERIENCE. In recent decades the Bradenton Pirate Boosters have helped to further fuse the Pirates' identity with Bradenton's. Members of the club pay a small annual fee for the privilege of serving as volunteer ushers and concessionaires at the ballpark. In turn, Boosters receive a complimentary picnic hosted by the Pirates each spring, and an offer to travel to Pittsburgh during the summer to be the Pirates' guests in one of the PNC Park luxury suites. During the spring season, these congenial men and women play an integral role in helping to ensure that everyone's day at McKechnie Field is enjoyable.

Upon entering the ballpark fans are greeted by Pirate Boosters renting out yellow seat cushions. Other Boosters sell ballpark treats, direct fans to their seats, or work the speed-pitch booth on the right field concourse. All of these tasks are performed by men and women who wear wide smiles, offering a marked contrast to the attitudes displayed by some of the mercenary staffers at other spring ballparks.

The Pirate Parrot, a colorful mascot, roams the grandstand posing for pictures and entertaining the children in attendance.

Aside from the distinctive grandstand boxes on the first and third base lines, the next most eye-catching aspect of McKechnie is the outfield flag display. On gold flags, the years representing the franchise's World Series winning teams

Spanish moss hangs from the trees outside the Pirates' minor league complex on Roberto Clemente Memorial Way.

appear—1909, 1925, 1960, 1971 and 1979. Black flags mark the years in which the Pirates won the National League pennant but not the World Series—1901, 1903 and 1927. White flags connote seasons in which the Pirates made the playoffs but lost before reaching the World Series—1970, 1972, 1974, 1975, 1990, 1991 and 1992. There is also a flag that flies the Pirates' buccaneer and crossed-bats logo.

As for the ballpark concessions, the concourse behind the seating bowl includes a stand operated by Demetrios' Pizza. The pizzeria has operated on Bradenton's Cortez Road since 1976. Clearly, this is the highlight of the Bradenton spread. In addition to excellent tomato pies, Demetrios' sells Greek salads and Baklava. The Pirates Cove stands, meanwhile, offer ballpark basics, including a foot-long all-beef Hebrew National Hot Dog. The freshly made Fruit Smoothies provide the per-fect late-inning treat on a warm spring day.

Pirate fans will get a kick out of visiting the "Marauders in the Majors" display on the concourse. Here, photos honor current Pirates who once played their regular season ball in Bradenton.

ON THE TOWN. The relationship between Bradenton and the Pirates seems as solid as any enjoyed by a spring training town and its team. Many former Pirates choose to make Bradenton their home after their playing career concludes. Some, such as Mike LaValliere and Don Robinson have even coached the local high school baseball team at Saint Stephen's Episcopal High School. This type of involvement between former Pirates and the local community is nothing new, and in part, is what led author William Zinsser to focus his 1989 book *Spring Training: The Unique American Story of Baseball's Annual Season of Renewal* on the Pirates and their camp in Bradenton.

A few hours before each home game, the Pirates take batting practice at their **Pirate City** complex at 1701 27th Street (also known as Roberto Clemente Memorial Way) four miles from McKechnie Field. These sessions offer fans the chance to snag batting practice balls that sail over the outfield fences and to ask players for autographs. The crowds are usually small, allowing just about every fan in attendance a shot at claiming a ball that bears the signature of Florida State League President Chuck Murphy. An hour before the game, the Pirates file onto a bus and head to McKechnie Field. The four-field Pirate City facility was originally built in 1969 when the Pirates first arrived in town. During the winter of 1999 it underwent a major renovation at a cost of $5 million. Then it was renovated again in 2008.

Another attraction worth checking out in Bradenton is the **River Park Hotel** (Third Avenue and Ninth Street). On the shores of the Manatee River, just a mile north of McKechnie Field, the seven-story pink stucco building is a retirement home today. But in its heyday, back in the 1930s, this was a thriving hotel that housed the Cardinals players and coaches each spring. Dean's service station was located across the street from the hotel on the corner of Fourth Street and Tenth Avenue where a parking garage for the SunTrust Bank now stands beside a towering broadcast antenna. An old advertisement for Dean's station still hangs in the cafeteria of the River Park Senior Residence. The piece displays Dean wearing his Cardinals uniform and a gas station attendant's cap. The caption reads "Dizzy Dean's service station on Tamiami Trail in downtown Bradenton: Specialized lubrication, complete service and standard oil products."

While they may not enjoy quite the long history that the River Park Hotel/Senior Residence does, there are several establishments where baseball fans congregate to enjoy post-game meals and beverages in Bradenton. Popular joints not too far from the park include **Fanatics Sports Bar and Grill** (4669 Cortez Road), **The Roadhouse Grill** (5051 14th Street) and **Joey D's Chicago Eatery** (4304 14th Street). Those looking for great pizza need look no further than **Demetrios' Pizza House** (1720 Cortez Road West), a Bradenton favorite that has won many local readers' choice awards. Fans in search of a late breakfast or an early lunch before the game funnel into **Popi's Place** (818 17th Avenue West). The sign in front of the diner features a baseball player swinging at an oversized baseball. The player is wearing a *red* cap, making it obvious that the "P" above the bill stands for "Popi's" rather than "Pirates." But make no mistake, the folks inside Popi's are Pirates fans through and through, as is just about everyone who lives in Bradenton.

Ed Smith Stadium

(SARASOTA) Baltimore Orioles

Ed Smith Stadium
2700 12th Street, Sarasota
941–893–6300
http://www.scgov.net/ballpark/default.asp
http://baltimore.orioles.mlb.com
Opened: 1989. Renovated: 2011. Seating Capacity: 8,500
• 13 miles north to Bradenton (Pirates)
• 39 miles south to Port Charlotte (Rays)
• 54 miles north to Clearwater (Phillies)
• 57 miles north to Tampa (Yankees)

FOR YEARS Ed Smith Stadium was one of the most uninspired Grapefruit League ballparks. Between the springs of 2010 and 2011, though, it received an extensive makeover that transformed it into one of Florida's most charming baseball havens. Wisely, the Orioles, who moved to Sarasota in 2010 after the Reds left for Arizona, commissioned their former vice president for planning and development, Janet Marie Smith to oversee the remodeling. Ms. Smith is often credited as being the visionary behind the retro-classic design of Oriole Park at Camden Yards. Although she'd left the Orioles in 1994, she returned to the Baltimore organization to work with Washington, D.C.–based David Schwarz Architects and Sarasota-based Hoyt Architects to design and implement the $31.2 million project in Sarasota. Ms. Smith had gotten some practice in ballpark makeovers in the years since she'd last worn Oriole orange in a position with the Red Sox, for whom she led the endeavor to install seats atop Fenway Park's fabled Green Monster.

The work in Sarasota involved endowing hitherto nondescript Ed Smith Stadium with more character and making it more fan-friendly. It was funded by Sarasota County, which evidently saw the value in maintaining Sarasota's presence as a Grapefruit League bastion. The charming Gulf Coast town has been hosting spring ball since the 1920s with very few interruptions through the years. By all accounts, the Ed Smith Stadium remodeling effort was a huge success. While once the stadium

façade resembled a gray concrete block plopped down on
the sidewalk, now it reflects
the Mediterranean arches
and seashell earth tones
famous throughout Florida's
Sun Coast. Awnings in the
Orioles' signature orange
accent the warm and wel-
coming structure. As fans
pass through these arches
and into the main entrance-
way, the runway to the interior concourse opens nice
and wide to allow a view of
the entire field from behind
home plate. Up above, a

The 2011 renovation gave Ed Smith Stadium a Mediterranean style façade (Wikimedia Commons).

The stadium façade as it appeared before the 2011 renovation.

massive ring of linked baseball bats serves as the scaffolding from which decorative
orange, white, and black banners hang, commemorating the Orioles' championship
seasons.

An additional concourse, atop the last row of seats, was also added as part of
the remodeling. This new walkway includes concession stands, bathrooms and
shaded space where fans can stand and watch the game. It's an open-air concourse
too, meaning that it doesn't seal in the back of the stadium, but rather allows a nice

breeze to blow into the park on either side of the two-story press box. The press box is still on the small side, but it's quite attractive now with its orange and black letters that read "Spring Home of the Baltimore Orioles," and its orange and white plates display the Orioles' retired numbers. From left to right these numbers are: 20 (Frank Robinson), 5 (Brooks Robinson), 4 (Earl Weaver), 22 (Jim Palmer), 33 (Eddie Murray) and 8 (Cal Ripken, Jr.). Finally, a blue and white plate bearing a 42 honors the universally retired digits once worn by Jackie Robinson.

Behind the seating bowl, an expanded concourse at ground level offers a lot more shade than the previous incarnation of the ballpark did. The bullpens are in foul territory between the end of the grandstand and the nearest foul pole. Above and behind the pens, festive orange patio umbrellas provide cool spots from which fans can peer at the game or at the relievers warming up. Beautiful palm trees also loom over the concourse down the lines in right and left, to provide some additional shade.

In addition to these improvements, the entire ballpark was reseated as part of the work. The gaudy bright blue and red stadium chairs that once filled Ed Smith Stadium were replaced by comfortable plastic seats cast in the Orioles' trademark ballpark color, Camden Green. More than 1,500 of these chairs, in fact, once filled the grandstands of Oriole Park at Camden Yards.

Still another product of the well-thought-out ballpark makeover is the fan pavilion in left field home run territory. It offers five rows of wall-top seats and an area where those wishing to stand and mingle may enjoy the game as well. Upon its unveiling, the pavilion immediately became the most sought-after part of the park. More than just adding a fun place to sit, the pavilion adds to the Mediterranean flavor of the park. The concession stand that rises at its back is nicely flanked by palms and is itself, no mere food shack. It sports the same attractive arches as at the stadium's home plate entrance, regal columns, and a Mediterranean-style tile roof.

A previous effort to remodel Ed Smith Stadium nearly took place in 2008, but Sarasota voters rejected a ballot measure that would have funded the proposed project with municipal bonds. As a result, the Cincinnati Reds, who had been tenants at Ed Smith from 1998 through 2009, pulled up stakes and headed west to Goodyear, Arizona.

The most heart-warming anecdote from the Reds' years in Sarasota occurred in the home locker room of Ed Smith Stadium during the spring of 2003. Reds third baseman Aaron Boone was dressing at his locker before workouts in the early spring when he noticed that reporter Hal McCoy was practically in tears. McCoy, a Hall of Fame writer who was in his thirty-first season of covering the Reds for the *Dayton Daily News*, had suffered a serious stroke during the off-season that had damaged his optic nerves in both eyes and left him nearly blind. The scribe explained to Boone, with whom he had always enjoyed a friendly relationship, that he was no longer able to do his job and that he would be leaving camp soon. Boone told McCoy that he was one of the best writers in the business, then spent the rest of spring training leading him around both the home and visiting locker rooms so he could conduct interviews. With his lifelong passion for the game restored, McCoy overcame his disability and remained with the *Daily News*. He was one of the first media members to report to spring training in Sarasota in March of 2004.

Prior to that, the White Sox had made Sarasota their spring home from 1960 through 1997, before embarking on their own trek to the Cactus League in 1998. The Chicago team's tenure in Sarasota is recalled most often today for the sideshow that was the Michael Jordan baseball experiment. After leading the Chicago Bulls to the NBA championship in 1994, the best basketball player in history retired from the sport and decided to test his athleticism and coordination on the baseball diamond. Although Jordan's single greatest previous accomplishment in the game had come in 1975 when he was named "Mr. Baseball" of North Carolina by the Dixie Youth Association at age 12, on February 7, 1994, Jordan signed a free-agent contract with the White Sox. A short time later he reported to Sarasota to begin workouts with White Sox hitting coach Walt Hriniak. Jordan's presence attracted throngs of fans to White Sox workouts that had previously been observed by crowds of fewer than 100. And a Nike van set up shop outside the gates of Ed Smith Stadium, selling Air Jordan apparel.

Jordan played in his first Grapefruit League game when he entered an early March contest against the Rangers in the sixth inning as a defensive replacement in right field. He wore uniform number 45. More than 7,000 fans and more than 100 media members witnessed the occasion. In the bottom of the sixth inning, Jordan came to bat with one out, no one on base, and the White Sox trailing 7–0. He tapped a meek grounder down the first base line, which pitcher Darren Oliver fielded. Oliver swiped a tag onto Jordan as he ran to first. But not knowing that home plate umpire Drew Coble had signaled an out, Oliver tossed the ball to the first baseman anyway. As Jordan ran through the base, first base umpire Chuck Meriwether signaled that the lanky runner was safe. Coble overruled Meriwether, as it was his right to do, causing the crowd to boo lustily. After the game Jordan spoke to reporters about the confusing play. "As much as I wanted to be safe," he said, "I knew I was out. The ref at first confused me."

In the coming months Jordan got better acquainted with baseball's umpires and players. He batted .202 with 51 RBI, 30 stolen bases and 114 strikeouts in 127 games for the Class-AA Birmingham Barons of the Southern League. He also set a new league record by committing 11 outfield errors. In the winter of 1994 Jordan played for the Scottsdale Scorpions of the Arizona Fall League, batting a more respectable .252 in 35 games.

As for Ed Smith Stadium's current tenants, the Orioles, they played their spring games in Fort Lauderdale from 1996 through 2009, before signing a 30-year lease with the City of Sarasota that should keep them at Ed Smith until 2040. For the most part, the Orioles' tenure in Fort Lauderdale was pleasant, though a tragic incident that occurred in 2003 will forever link the team and city. After workouts at Fort Lauderdale Stadium on February 16, 2003, Orioles pitcher Steve Bechler collapsed in the Orioles clubhouse. Bechler, whose body temperature had risen to 108 degrees Fahrenheit, experienced massive organ failure. He died the next day. An herbal dietary supplement containing ephedra was linked to his death. The U.S. Food and Drug Administration shortly thereafter banned the sale of ephedra.

Prior to playing in Fort Lauderdale, the Orioles had spent four years at Al Lang Field in St. Petersburg (1992–1995). From 1959 to 1988, they trained exclusively in Miami, but in 1989 and 1990 they spent only part of each spring in that city. Toward the end of their stay in the Southern Florida hot spot, they had difficulty filling out a full slate of home games. Other teams, many of which trained in central Florida or on the Gulf Coast, didn't like the long drive to Miami. For that reason, the Orioles split their camp in 1989 and 1990, spending half the spring in Miami and half in Sarasota. Finally in 1991, the team severed ties with Miami's Bobby Maduro Stadium and moved its camp to Twin Lakes Park in Sarasota.

Twins Lakes Park (6700 Clark Road) was the centerpiece of a minor league complex that the Royals had used before the Orioles arrived to spend one spring working out there. The Orioles played two games at Ed Smith Stadium in 1991, while playing the rest of their games on the road. Despite the fact that it wasn't suitable for major league games, Twin Lakes Park has remained the Orioles' minor league complex to this day, and its use by the team helped paved the way for the

The low seating bowl places most fans close to the action.

lease agreement the Orioles and Sarasota eventually signed in 2009 to bring the O's big leaguers to Ed Smith Stadium on a permanent basis.

While Baltimore's minor leaguers toil in relative anonymity ten miles from Ed Smith Stadium each spring at Twin Lakes Park, the major leaguers get ready for the start of the Grapefruit League on the four practice fields that lie beyond the outfield fences of Ed Smith. The 53-acre Sarasota Sports Complex is nicely decorated with trees sporting Spanish moss and with a smattering of palms. The site also includes 35,000 square feet of clubhouse space and offices for the Orioles coaches and staff.

The Sarasota Sports Complex was originally built by the city of Sarasota at a cost of $9.5 million after the 1988 spring season. Previously, the city's tenants at the time, the White Sox, had played at Payne Park, three miles southwest of the current complex. Payne Park was a wood-plank ballpark constructed during the height of the Florida real estate boom in 1923 to accommodate John McGraw's New York Giants. The park was built along with a community fair ground after Sarasota Mayor E. J. Bacon convinced Calvin and Martha Payne to provide the city with 60 acres of land at the bargain price of $18,000. McGraw, who guided his teams to ten World Series appearances in a 32-year managerial career, was lured to Sarasota by prominent residents Samuel W. Gumpetz and John Ringling. Upon bringing his Giants to town in 1924, McGraw invested more than a million dollars in a Sarasota real estate development known as Pennant Park.

For four seasons Sarasota residents filled the 2,400-seat Payne Park. And when the ballpark was full, they improvised. Future Negro Leagues star and Major League Baseball goodwill ambassador Buck O'Neil, was a child in Sarasota in the 1920s. According to O'Neil, he and his friends converted a pine tree behind the center field fence at Payne Park into a ladder by nailing two-by-fours onto its trunk. They would climb the boards, and sit in the tree bows to watch Babe Ruth, Ty Cobb and other stars of the era play.

When the Giants chose not to return to Sarasota in the spring of 1928, McGraw cited the town's insufficient lodging as the main reason. Because there was no hotel in town large enough to accommodate the entire team, the notoriously rigid manager said he found himself constantly venturing from one establishment to another to make sure his boys were behaving. Other people blamed the team's departure on McGraw's superstitious nature, pointing out that his perennial pennant contenders were in the midst of a three-year World Series drought when they opted not to return to the Sun Coast.

Fortunately for the hardball fans in Sarasota, it was not long before the Red Sox arrived in the spring of 1933. Boston played its pre-season games at Payne Park until 1958, excepting the war years of 1943 through 1945. Then, the White Sox arrived in 1960 and stayed for nearly four decades. Mr. Ed Smith was the president of the Sarasota Sports Committee, which brought the White Sox to town in 1960. Today there is a plaque honoring him on the right field concourse of the stadium that bears his name.

The Orioles have averaged more than 7,000 fans per game since their return to Sarasota in 2010 and the crowds appear as though they will keep growing in the years ahead. Ed Smith Stadium is a fine venue for spring training baseball. And it does just fine by fans in the summertime too. It sees use from June through August as home to the Gulf Coast League Orioles.

GETTING TO THE PARK. From I-75 South, the Ed Smith Stadium is accessible from Exit 213. Follow University Parkway west to Tuttle Avenue and turn left. From I-75 North, Exit 210 is the best option. Follow Fruitville Road west, and then take a right on Tuttle. The grass field across the street from the stadium on 12th Street accommodates about 2,500 cars.

SEATING. There are 7,500 seats at Ed Smith Stadium. The Orioles also sell 1,000 standing room tickets per game, bringing the stadium's capacity to 8,500. Games are likely to sell out when the Red Sox, Yankees or Phillies visit, so plan accordingly.

The Infield Boxes (Sections 105–121) consist of rows 1–12 along the baselines. Section 105 is just past first base, Section 113 is behind home plate, and Section 120 is just past third. Fans looking to sit behind the home dugout on the first base side should aim for seats in Sections 107–110.

The Lower Boxes begin where the Infield Boxes leave off — where the infield dirt meets the outfield grass along the first and third base lines — and continue into medium depth foul territory. Sections 101–104 trace the right field foul line, while Sections 122–125 trace the line in left.

The Reserved Grandstand sections are raised above the interior walkway, where they are elevated enough to allow seat-holders clear views over the aisle traffic. Section 201 is in relatively deep right field, Section 213 is behind the plate, and Section 225 is in relatively deep left field. The roof, which was expanded as part of the remodeling effort, provides sun relief to those in Row 7 and higher in most Reserved Grandstand sections. As a rule, the first base side offers more shade than can be found across the diamond.

The Left Field Pavilion seats are modeled loosely after the home run territory seats atop the Green Monster in Boston and the tiki seats in Clearwater. Fans sitting in this part of the park enjoy ample leg room and have a nice shelf on which to place their ballpark treats. There is also room in back for standing room patrons to take in a view of the game. A special concession stand serves some delicious treats at the back of the pavilion too.

THE BALLPARK EXPERIENCE. Between just about every half inning, the public address announcer introduces a kitschy contest or promotion sponsored by a local company. These stunts keep fans laughing. One of the funniest routines has the announcer say something like, "Attention fans. We have an important announcement. Would the owner of silver Toyota Camry, with Ohio license plate … 845 RDU … please report to the press box? We regret to inform you that your car has been ... (long and dramatic pause) ... selected the dirtiest car in the lot. You receive a $25 gift certificate to have your car detailed at the number one auto center in Sarasota."

During the middle of the sixth inning, a lucky female fan is designated the "Sweetheart of the Game." A stadium employee delivers a bouquet of flowers to the winner's seat, as a gift from Beneva Flowers. For one game each year—usually at the start of the spring—the local florist also orchestrates a special "Bird Night" when the first thousand or so ladies to arrive at the park receive Bird of Paradise flowers.

Baltimore Crab Cakes are the trademark food at Ed Smith Stadium, just like at Oriole Park in Baltimore. Esskay brand hot dogs are available, too, for visiting Baltimoreans. Fans watching back home on MASN, meanwhile, will be happy to see an oversized sign behind the right field fence touting the signature Baltimore hot dog brand. Another sure winner is the barbecue stand behind the Pavilion in left, where fans find slow-cooked barbecued beef, brats and bison burgers. There is also a small sit-down restaurant near the home plate entrance.

Roaming the grandstand, a favorite beer vendor is the large gentleman who wears a bulbous green and orange hat that comes complete with a flashing headlight. He also blows a whistle all afternoon, to make sure thirsty fans know he's coming.

In addition to seeking out the trash cans topped by Orioles batting helmets on the concourse, it's also worth fans' time to take a stroll on the concourse to check out the colorful map of Florida that marks each Grapefruit League team's home city with a pennant bearing the team's colors and name. The many "Watch Out for Batted Balls" signs, meanwhile, portray cartoon style orioles (birds, not players) dodging baseballs.

Outside the park, a campy sign lists the distance to every Orioles outpost throughout the game, along with the distance to each city from Sarasota. For example, the sign notes that it's 893 miles from Sarasota to Baltimore, and 917 miles to Aberdeen, Maryland, where the New York–Penn League Aberdeen Iron Birds play.

As for the best place to collect autographs, the home clubhouse sits beyond the right field fence. Accordingly, fans line up down the right field line to catch players as they head to the showers.

ON THE TOWN. Sarasota is an old-money resort town. The year 1927 was an important one in the city's history as it saw the development of two of Sarasota's most popular current attractions. In the same year that Babe Ruth hit 60 home runs for the Yankees and Charles Lindbergh flew the first solo nonstop flight across the Atlantic, John Ringling constructed a $2.5 million museum to house his $16 million art collection. Meanwhile, golfer Bobby Jones—fresh off his victory in the U.S. Golf Association Amateur Championship—cut the ribbon on Sarasota's new municipal golf course, which would later be named in his honor. Today, the **John and Mable Ringling Museum of Art**—located two miles north of downtown Sarasota on U.S. 41—draws visitors from around the world. And the **Bobby Jones Golf**

Club offers two 18-hole courses on Circus Boulevard. Sarasota also features white sand beaches, upscale downtown boutiques and a vibrant arts community.

The sports complex at **Twin Lakes Park** (6700 Clark Road) accommodates the Orioles minor leaguers in the spring. The facility includes nine diamonds of varying sizes and nine carpeted batting cages. The Central Sarasota County Little League and Senior League programs also use the complex.

The Sports Page (1319 Main Street) is a popular fan hang-out before and after games. For a slightly more refined dinner experience, players and fans visit the **Columbia Restaurant** (411 St. Armand's Circle). This Columbia is a satellite franchise of the original Columbia that opened in Tampa's Ybor City in 1905. The Columbia's Mediterranean-inspired dining rooms and patio are delightful and the Spanish/Cuban cuisine is really something special. After dinner, guests visit the gift shop where they find fine cigars and Spanish pottery. Clearly, this Florida institution is the highlight of St. Armand's Circle, which features more than 130 shops and restaurants, and makes for a wonderful evening out.

Charlotte Sports Park

(PORT CHARLOTTE) Tampa Bay Rays

Charlotte Sports Park
2300 El Jobean Road, Port Charlotte
727–825–3250
http://charlottecountyfl.com/CommunityServices/ParkPages/SportsPark/
http://tampabay.rays.mlb.com
Opened: 1988. Renovated: 2009. Seating Capacity: 6,823
• 35 miles south to Fort Myers (Red Sox and Twins)
• 44 miles north to Sarasota (Orioles)
• 55 miles north to Bradenton (Pirates)
• 88 miles northeast to Lakeland (Tigers)

DURING THE FINAL years of the Texas Rangers' tenure in Port Charlotte, the facility then known as Charlotte County Stadium was not very highly regarded among spring fans. It was infamous, in fact, for being an excessively hot place to watch a game, for being too cramped, and for being poorly maintained. Thus, when the Rangers left in 2002, setting their sights on a brand new park awaiting them in Surprise, Arizona, not many tears were shed by spring travelers. At that time, it appeared Port Charlotte, which had entered the spring game in 1988 with the stadium's opening and the Rangers' arrival, had outlived its time as a Grapefruit League hub. Fortunately, though, the game has been reborn in this rustic Gulf Coast outpost. Since 2009, the home-state Tampa Bay Rays have made an extensively remodeled version of what is now known as Charlotte Sports Park their home. The park is still small, but thanks to its makeover it is now more "cozy" than cramped, and it features the fan-friendly amenities today's ballpark aficionados expect.

The signature design element of the new-and-improved Charlotte stadium is its 19,000-square-foot Baseball Boardwalk. The arcing wooden walkway traces the course of the outfield fence, providing a festive place for fans to mingle and watch the game. Out by either foul pole, the Boardwalk meets the wide concourse that runs up to and then behind the infield grandstand, allowing fans to walk laps around the entire field should they so choose. The approach taken by the ballpark

The stadium entrance received a full makeover during the 2009 renovation (courtesy The Gup Collection).

designers at HOK Sport, who oversaw the $27 million renovation — which was funded by the State of Florida, Charlotte County and the Rays— was to build unique viewing locations *around* the entire field, rather than building a large grandstand *behind* it. They kept the small original grandstand, and gave it a major sprucing up and reseating, rather than demolish it. Today, the grandstand provides room for about 5,000 people, who sit in "Rays-blue" plastic seats that are as attractive as they are roomy and comfortable. And thanks to the new grandstand roof, the fans in the seats enjoy more shade than they did at the previous incarnation of the park. There are also large blue canopies and tents on the concourses to similarly provide sun relief.

The grandstand extends only a bit past the corner bases, then grass seating berms appear along the outfield foul lines. The berm in right field ends just before the foul pole, but the one in left wraps around the pole and provides a limited amount of berm seating in home run territory. There, fans can get down nice and low to the field and watch the game through a chain-link stretch of the outfield fence. Similarly, the relievers, who warm up in right (home) and left (visitors) field home run territory, watch the game through chain-link.

Aside from offering plenty of free space for fans to stand in groups and watch the game while sipping a beer or soda, the Boardwalk also houses three picnic areas where fans sit along the railing atop the fence, and a thatched-roof tiki bar that resembles the one at Bright House Field in Clearwater. The Boardwalk also allows fans to look down into the bullpens.

Outside the park, the three-story cream façade makes a far less dramatic impression on the landscape than the two nearby stadiums in Fort Myers do on theirs. Nor does the façade have the architectural appeal of the old-timey ballpark in Bradenton. It is just a cream block with some blue trim and some large windows. Inside the park, the tiny press box is similarly unobtrusive. The top level is for the press, while the lower level houses indoor/outdoor luxury suites. The same cream color as outside appears on the structure inside the park, while the press box is adorned only by the names of the park's two home teams: the spring training Rays, and the regular season Charlotte Stone Crabs of the Florida State League. The seating counter for the press is so small that a special area is set up in the grandstand seats outside the press box during spring training to accommodate the overflow of media members. If only the press were granted two levels within the tiny structure, there might be room to fit all of the scribes, but it's understandable that the ballpark's regular season tenants would prefer to have a high-end group seating area behind the plate. After all, it's rare that more than a handful of reporters turn out to cover Florida State League games.

The dugouts are as notable for being wide as the press box is for being small. Amazingly there are two rows of wooden benches inside each dugout. And there's room for players and coaches to stand along the protective screen at the front of each dugout too. It's not uncommon, therefore, to see three rows of uniformed personnel inside each dugout during spring training. If there's another professional park in North America with dugouts big enough to house players three-deep, this writer has yet to find it.

The outfield view is sealed in nicely by the Boardwalk and by a wall of trees beyond the field in left. Although there are two small ponds beyond the Boardwalk in left, they aren't visible from most seating locations. In center, the batter's-eye is a semi-transparent black screen, dark enough to provide the hitters with a good backdrop, but porous enough so that fans walking on the Boardwalk behind it may still view the action on the field. Immediately behind the Boardwalk in right, a Rays clubhouse that was added as part of the 2009 renovation offers a stretch of raised balconies from which team personnel watches the games. The facing of this structure, which appears in the same cream color as the press box, sports a painted blue and white pennant commemorating each of the years the Rays have qualified for post-season play.

While some of the other spring parks have added monstrous scoreboards, the approach at Charlotte Sports Park is still more Bush League than Big League. Beside the tiki hut in left, a small board rises to display the line score and game situation (balls, strikes, outs). On the face of the outfield fence in right, meanwhile, a small high-definition diamond vision screen displays a headshot of whichever batter is at the plate, along with his stats for the day.

The ballpark's Boardwalk is what sets it apart from practically every other park in the land. Interestingly, this stroke of genius came about more by accident, or perhaps we should say "necessity," than anything else. Early in the design process, the thinking was that the renovation would add a seating berm across the outfield. But environmental concerns related to the two ponds beyond the field in left made carrying out that vision untenable. Rather than giving up on creating the sort of festive outfield lounging location that has become a staple of the spring game in so many other Florida and Arizona cities, the folks in Port Charlotte scaled back the stadium footprint and built a standing deck. By good fortune, or grand vision, or maybe just because it's so novel, the Boardwalk looks like it was always meant to be there: fans love it and it makes the park unique.

Just as the construction plans had to be modified, the name of the facility has traveled a circuitous route to arrive at its present destination. The park was dubbed Mosaic Field at Charlotte Sports Park for a short while in 2010, after the Rays struck a 15-year naming-rights agreement with the fertilizer company. But Charlotte County, which had fought a lengthy legal battle throughout the early 2000s to limit Mosaic's ability to open potentially environmentally harmful phosphate mines in the watershed that feeds into Charlotte Harbor, nixed the deal. Nonetheless, Mosaic

The large roof shades the upper portion of the grandstand on the first base side (courtesy The Gup Collection).

The large seating lawn begins just beyond third base and wraps around the foul pole into left field home run territory (courtesy The Gup Collection).

has infiltrated the park with its large advertising signs on the outfield fence and atop the dugout roofs.

More than likely, the Rays and Charlotte County will eventually find a corporate namesake that meets both their criteria and the stadium will be rechristened. But as of 2012, no such suitor had been found. One thing is for certain, though, the Rays will be staying in this rustic setting 75 miles south of their regular season home for some time to come. The team's spring lease to use Charlotte Sports Park and its five and a half abutting fields runs through 2029.

Previously (1998–2008), the Rays had played their Grapefruit League games at Al Lang Field (a.k.a. Progress Energy Park) on the St. Petersburg waterfront. No doubt there were benefits to playing spring games a mile from their regular season home stadium, such as being able to use the regular season weight room, batting cages, and training facilities at Tropicana Field. But the thinking in the Rays front office was that the players would benefit from making their spring camp a bit farther from their regular season homes and condos. The experience in Port Charlotte is more immersive and, one would think, more conducive to the sort of team-building and bonding that is an important part of each year's camp. Along those lines, during the spring of 2012, some seventy members of the Rays organization shaved their

Fans along the third base line watch members of the visiting Red Sox warm up. In the background, fans stake out standing room on the outfield boardwalk (courtesy The Gup Collection).

heads to raise money for the Pediatric Cancer Foundation and the Vincent Lecavalier Pediatric Cancer and Blood Disorders Center at All Children's Hospital. Leading figures in the effort were Rays manager Joe Maddon and All-Star players Evan Longoria and David Price. Team owner Stu Sternberg and executive vice president Andrew Friedman also shed their locks to show solidarity with the cause and its brave cancer survivors. The shaving ceremony took place on the right field portion of the Charlotte Sports Park Boardwalk.

Prior to the Rays' arrival in Port Charlotte, the city had hosted the Rangers from 1988 through 2001. The Rangers' time in Port Charlotte is today recalled most often for two monumental press conferences that took place at County Stadium. In the spring of 1993, Nolan Ryan announced from a podium in the home clubhouse that he would be retiring after the upcoming season. After an injury-marred 5–5 campaign, Ryan held true to his word and made his 27th season in the big leagues his last. Then, in the spring of 2000, County Stadium was the site of the press conference to announce the Rangers had signed Alex Rodriguez to a 10-year $252 million deal. Because the media room at the ballpark was too small to accommodate the media horde, A-Rod was introduced on the dugout roof and fielded questions from reporters who sat in the first base seats.

Although big league ball left town from 2001 through 2009, the yet-to-be-renovated ballpark in Port Charlotte hosted a professional team during the summer of 2007, when the Charlotte County Redfish of the independent South Coast League debuted at County Stadium. Managed by retired slugger Cecil Fielder, the Redfish went 22–64 to finish in last place. Then the league, which also had an outpost in Bradenton and four other southern cities, went out of business. Today, Ripken Baseball owns and operates the Charlotte Stone Crabs, who have made Charlotte Sports Park their home since 2009. The Stone Crabs are a Rays affiliate.

GETTING TO THE PARK. From the north, take I-75 South to Exit 179 and turn right onto Toledo Blade Boulevard. Turn right onto El Jobean Road and the ballpark will appear on the left. It's about an eight mile ride in total from I-75 to the ballpark. From the south, take I-75 North to Exit 164. Follow U.S. 41 North to El Jobean Road. Turn left on El Jobean and follow it to the park. Parking is available in a large grass lot on the first base side of the park, while overflow lots can be found across the street at the Charlotte County Fairgrounds and at a nearby motorcycle dealership.

SEATING. The grandstand is bisected by a narrow walkway. Below the walkway are seven to ten rows of seats depending on the section, except for in the sections behind the dugouts where the dugout roofs protrude into the seats, leaving room for just three rows. The two outermost sections on either side of the diamond — Sections 101 and 102 just past first base, and Sections 114 and 115 just past third — compose the Lower View Level and sell for a few dollars less than the Home Plate Boxes (Sections 103–113) between the corner bases and home plate. Section 108 is directly behind home plate.

Above the interior walkway, fans find 16 rows of View Level Terrace seats. Section 201 is above the spot where the infield dirt meets the outfield grass behind first base, Sections 208–211 are behind the plate, and Section 218 is at the spot where the infield dirt meets the left field grass. Fans seated in the second level on the first base side enjoy more shade than fans across the diamond do.

A General Admission ticket allows access to either of the berm seating areas or to the Boardwalk. Both berms are close to the field and nicely sloped. The smaller one, on the right field line, is preferred by most fans since it doesn't require rooters to look into the sun to watch the game. The nice thing about a General Admission pass is that it allows its holder to take in the park from many different angles. While standing on the Boardwalk for a full nine innings may not sound too appealing, it is well worth the achy knees to stand in home run territory for a few innings, just for the experience of taking in the action from a unique vantage point.

THE BALLPARK EXPERIENCE. Both berms see their share of incoming foul balls, so ball-hounds expecting to buy General Admission tickets should plan on bringing their gloves. After the game, the front of the right field berm is a nice place to catch Rays players for autographs as they head to the clubhouse in right field.

Long home runs to right clank down on the two-story clubhouse facility that looms behind the Boardwalk. Such shots are something of a rarity, but there are a few each spring. Long balls to left, meanwhile, sometimes carry over the berm and Boardwalk to splash down in the two muddy ponds.

Another scenic aspect of this park is its nesting ospreys, which can often be observed building large nests in the light banks. Bring a pair of binoculars to the game and you'll be able to see the large branches—too large to be deemed sticks—with which they compose their lofty abodes.

The trash cans topped by oversized Rays batting helmets are a very nice touch. What little leaguer wouldn't want just such a can in his bedroom!

Atop the berm in right field, young fans delight in finding two play areas—one for tykes and one for older kiddos. Raymond the Manatee, the mascot whose antics charm and perplex fans all season long at Tropicana Field, makes occasional appearances in Port Charlotte too.

There is also a special concession stand on the right field concourse that features a kid-friendly menu. The adults, meanwhile, find an array of stands behind the grandstand. The First Base Fiesta serves **Barbecue Pork Nachos**, **Cuban Sandwiches** and tasty **Tacos**. Fans also find stands manned by local vendors dishing **Beer-Battered Grouper Sandwiches** and **Gyros**.

ON THE TOWN. Port Charlotte will not soon be confused with one of the more developed Grapefruit League destinations like Tampa or Fort Myers. Travelers who enjoy the great outdoors and have grown weary of the busy highways and urban sprawl throughout much of the Sunshine State, however, may find it to their liking.

In the early spring each year, the practice fields on the right side of Charlotte Sports Park offer an ideal up-close-and-personal setting for fans to watch the big-leaguers getting ready for the Grapefruit League season. Once the spring games begin, these fields are still worth a visit for anyone interested in scouting the Rays' perennially stellar minor league prospects.

A short drive north brings fans to **North Charlotte Regional Park** (1185 O'Donnell Boulevard), which offers amateur baseball and soccer fields, a golf course, nature trails and a fishing pond. South of the Rays' complex, meanwhile, gorgeous **Tippecanoe Bay** is surrounded by a 350-acre nature preserve that offers walking trails and a canoe launch.

Traveling fans looking for a comfortable atmosphere, delicious food, and TVs showing big league baseball or NCAA basketball games need to head only two and a half miles from Charlotte Sports Park to where **Joe Cracker Sportsgrille** (1020 El Jobean Road) awaits. This island-themed sports bar serves homemade burgers, pizzas, island specials, and daily drink specials. It even offers a trolley service that brings fans to and from Rays' games. The trolley runs in a continuous loop all game long. For almost the same price fans pay to park at the ballpark, Joe's patrons get parking, a hot dog, and transportation to the game and back. For those looking to avoid the traffic logjam after the game, this is a great option. On Friday nights, Joe's also has live music.

Another popular choice among local connoisseurs is **Big Geroy's BBQ** (2395 Tamiami Trail). Located in Bell Plaza, where its smiling pig logo welcomes hungry lunch and dinner guests, Big Geroy's serves absolutely scrumptious barbecue favorites. The ribs are excellent, while the sliced beef and sliced pork are also just about as good as Southern barbecue can get. It's no wonder that spring baseball fans fill the place each March.

Jet Blue Park

(FORT MYERS) Boston Red Sox

Jet Blue Park at Fenway South
11581 Daniels Parkway, Fort Myers
888–733–7696
http://boston.redsox.mlb.com
Opened: 2012. Seating Capacity: 11,000
• 6 miles south to Fort Myers (Twins)
• 35 miles north to Port Charlotte (Rays)
• 75 miles north to Sarasota (Reds)
• 90 miles north to Bradenton (Pirates)

THE 2012 SEASON BROUGHT the Red Sox and their fans an interesting convergence of ballpark milestones. A month before the team and its fans would celebrate the one-hundredth anniversary of Fenway Park's opening in Boston in 1912, they toured, admired and thoroughly enjoyed themselves during spring training at the nearest facsimile yet built in honor of the Red Sox's hallowed regular season yard. And yet, as closely as it mirrors the playing dimensions and trademark features of Fenway Park, Jet Blue Park stamps its presence on the Grapefruit League map with some Floridian design features and unique characteristics of its own as well.

From the outside, the centerpiece of the seven-field, $77.8 million Fenway South complex projects a chic modern design. The several overlapping white roofs that provide the grandstand and concourse with 59,000 square feet of rain and sun protection are the dominant features. Built to withstand up to 130-mile-per-hour hurricane gusts, these roofs are ultra-modern looking; with their slanted white support pillars, they look like a New Age sculpture. They also combine to bear some resemblance to Marlins Park in Miami, which also opened in 2012. And each of the roof tiers, when observed individually, looks something like the beveled wings of a jumbo jet.

Jet Blue, which ferries snowbirds from Boston's Logan International Airport to nearby Southwest Florida Airport, paid $1 million for naming rights to the Fort Myers ballpark in a deal with Lee County and the Red Sox that runs through 2020.

The Green Monster in Fort Myers has seats inside the wall, protected by netting (courtesy The Gup Collection).

Outside Jet Blue Park, in further tribute to the airline, a tail fin from an actual Jet Blue jet rises like a monument to welcome fans to the grounds.

Once fans enter the park, the modern façade and layered roof no longer dominate the view. Rather, it is the very specter of Fenway Park that fans behold as they walk from the concourse into the seats. The field dimensions replicate Fenway's. The Green Monster begins its ascent just 310 feet from home plate in left, while Fenway's trademark center-field triangle measures 420 feet from the batter's box in deep right-center, the bullpens in right lay 380 feet from home, and the Pesky Pole in right rises just 302 feet from home. Just like at Fenway, fans have taken to scribbling their names and personal messages on the bright yellow paint of the foul pole named in honor of longtime Red Sox player and coach Johnny Pesky. During a 2012 visit, graffiti from fans representing all six New England states could be quickly identified. The stretch of foul pole that rises atop the Fort Myers Monster in left field also sports magic marker messages.

While Jet Blue Park comes much closer to mirroring Fenway than any of the other ballparks that have been designed to pay tribute to "America's Most Beloved Ballpark," it does not copy Fenway exactly. Nor does it endeavor to. At field level, for example, the manually operated scoreboard on the left field wall is the very one that displayed the ongoing game's line-score and the American League scores at Fenway from the 1970s until 2001 when a new Fenway board was installed. While the slate board in Fort Myers is a Fenway original, it's not identical to the one at Fenway currently, nor is the manner in which the score is updated the same as at Fenway. At Fenway, the attendant has room inside the wall to change the scores. At Jet Blue, the attendant sits inside the wall, but due to the limited space inside must emerge onto the warning track with a six-foot step ladder to change the scores as game-events warrant. One of the very first games ever played at Jet Blue was an exhibition between the Red Sox and Northeastern University baseball team. After the Red Sox won 25–0, scoreboard attendant Kevin Walsh estimated that he had dragged his ladder out of the wall some 100 times over the course of the evening!

While the green paint on the wall above the black scoreboard is the same shade as at Fenway, the wall itself is not identical to Fenway's. The Monster in Boston tops out at 37-feet, six-inches above field level, before giving way to pavilion style seats. The Fort Myers Monster rises approximately 20 feet before giving way to a stretch of netting behind which three rows of fans sit inside the wall watching the game. Batted balls that hit the netting and carom back down onto the field are in play. Balls that sneak through the netting are ground-rule doubles. Above these

The Green Monster begins its ascent 310 feet from home plate just like in Boston but rises six feet higher than Fenway Park's 37-foot-high original (courtesy The Gup Collection).

unusual seats another stretch of green wall brings the towering edifice's full height to some 43 feet. At the very top, in home run territory, fans find more seats and a wide concourse for standers to utilize.

In the centerfield triangle, fans find a blue and yellow advertisement for Giant Glass, just like at Fenway. Then the bullpens appear in straightaway right, only instead of rising bleacher seats at their back, fans find a small grass seating area and some bleacher benches from which to watch the game. After the bullpens and seating lawn, the facing of the right field grand stand seats is decorated with the Red Sox's retired numbers in their familiar Fenway location and order. They appear from left to right: 9 (Ted Williams); 4 (Joe Cronin); 1 (Bobby Doerr); 8 (Carl Yastrzemski); 27 (Carlton Fisk); 6 (Johnny Pesky); 14 (Jim Rice); 42 (Jackie Robinson).

The curvature of the wall in right field fair territory also rings familiar to fans who have visited Jet Blue's sister park in Boston, but the fence is not exactly the same as at Fenway. The angles seem sharper than in Boston and the railing separating the fans from the field is higher. Down the left field line, meanwhile, the Fenway-replica is more exact, right down to the inconvenience of fans sitting in Sections 112–118 being unable to see into the left field corner behind them.

In 2008, the Lee County Board of Commissioners voted 3–1 in favor of building the new field in Fenway's likeness. The vote came after the Red Sox had threatened to leave City of Palms Park in Fort Myers to move to Sarasota's Ed Smith Stadium. The land acquisition costs for Fenway South totaled $20 million, while the cost to design the complex and park cost $8 million. Then the actual construction totaled about $50 million. Amazingly the lion's share of the work took place in less than a year. After an official ground-breaking ceremony on March 4, 2011, 900 construction workers and tradesmen worked to build the main stadium according to the specs provided by the noted ballpark experts at Populous, as well as to build the six practice fields, and the 60,000 square-foot clubhouse behind the left field wall.

The clubhouse walls are decorated with inspirational quotes from Williams and Yastrzemski. The words from Williams read, "Ballplayers are not born great. They're not born great pitchers or hitters or managers, and luck isn't a big factor. No one has come up with a substitute for hard work."

A tunnel that runs beneath Jet Blue's third base seats connects the clubhouse to the home dugout on the third base line. This is another aspect of the park that is not exactly like Fenway; in Boston, of course, the Red Sox's dugout is along the first base line. The tunnel is, however, a colorful one. It is adorned with murals and pictures of great moments in Red Sox history, such as ones displaying the team's 2004 and 2007 World Championship celebrations.

More accessible to the common fan, a timeline of great moments and players in Red Sox history can be found on the stadium's main concourse. And red and blue pennants painted onto the facing of the press box honor championship seasons in Red Sox history.

The Red Sox's retired numbers are represented by monuments outside the park (courtesy The Gup Collection).

The Fenway South complex also includes soccer fields. Soon it may also include a hotel and retail complex; both were in the planning stages as the Red Sox played the 2012 Grapefruit League season.

After Jet Blue Park hosted a Red Sox fantasy camp in February of 2012, and then exhibition games between the Red Sox and the Boston College and Northeastern University baseball teams, the first official Grapefruit League game at Jet Blue Park occurred on March 4, 2012. The Red Sox beat the Twins 8–3 that day, but not before a quartet of Red Sox legends brought the crowd to its feet during the pregame ceremony. Luis Tiant, Dwight Evans, Rice and Yastrzemski emerged from the door in the left field scoreboard to thunderous applause. They slowly walked to the infield to deliver four game balls to Fort Myers and Lee County dignitaries who tossed them to current Red Sox players. Next, former Red Sox left fielder and Fort Myers native Mike Greenwell stepped onto the field and announced "Play ball!"

The Red Sox's previous facilities in Fort Myers, including City of Palms Park, had been built in 1992 at a cost of $24 million. Unfortunately, though, four of the five practice fields the team utilized were two miles from the main ballpark. This made it difficult for the Red Sox coaches to oversee the action on all of the fields early in spring training when camp was still bustling with minor leaguers. This task was made markedly easier by the opening of Fenway South in 2012. That year, new Red Sox manager Bobby Valentine used his bicycle to shuttle between the six fields surrounding Jet Blue Park.

Fort Myers is the eighteenth different spring home the Boston Red Sox have used since 1901. Previously the team trained in Winter Haven (1966–1992) where it seemed like one scandal unfolded after another. In the spring of 1987 Roger Clemens pitched an exhibition game against Harvard University then left camp in a huff when his contract was renewed at $400,000 for the upcoming season. He held out for more money for the remainder of camp. A few days after Clemens left, Winter Haven police apprehended Boston pitcher Dennis "Oil Can" Boyd in the home clubhouse of Chain of Lakes Park to inform him that he had a number of video rentals overdue at a local video store. The titles, which appeared in the local newspaper the next day, included *Nudes in Limbo* and *Sex-Cetera*. Wade Boggs stole the headlines a few years later when he fell out of a moving jeep that his wife was driving in Winter Haven. Although the vehicle ran over the third baseman's elbow, leaving an imprint of tire marks on his skin, Boggs suffered no serious injuries. Another year, Boggs found himself answering questions in Winter Haven about his illicit relationship with Margo Adams who had shared details of their relationship with *Penthouse*.

Prior to their time in Winter Haven, the Red Sox trained in Scottsdale, Arizona, from 1959 to 1965. The team's history in Florida also includes stops in Tampa (1919), Bradenton (1928–1929), Pensacola (1930–1931) and Sarasota (1933–1942, 1946–1958). Tragedy struck in 1907 after the Red Sox broke camp in Little Rock, Arkansas, when player-manager Chick Stahl returned to his home in West Baden, Indiana, and committed suicide on March 28. Stahl's Red Sox had finished last in the American League in 1906 with 49 wins and 105 losses, and his friends and family members said the pressure of managing had become too daunting.

Baseball's history in Fort Myers dates back to 1925 when legendary manager Connie Mack's Philadelphia Athletics spent their first spring at Terry Park. Since then, every team that has trained in Fort Myers—including the city's current tenants, the Red Sox and Twins—has won a World Series during its affiliation with the city. Originally built in 1906 and named after Tootie McGregor Terry who donated the land for the facility, Terry Park was the spring home of the Athletics through the 1936 spring season. Later the Cleveland Indians (1939–1941), Pittsburgh Pirates (1955–1968) and Kansas City Royals (1968–1987) utilized the park, which was renovated through the years. During the Kansas City years, the park featured an artificial playing surface just like Kauffman Stadium (then known as "Royals Stadium") in Kansas City. In 1989 and 1990, the Fort Myers Sun Sox of the short-lived Senior Professional Baseball Association used the field, and in 2003 the Golden Eagles of Florida Gulf Coast University called the park home while waiting for their new park to be built in Fort Myers. Terry Park continues to see use as an AAU and amateur baseball field today, although the structure that once seated spring fans

The wavy roof atop the grandstand is reminiscent of the roof at Dodger Stadium (courtesy The Gup Collection).

no longer exists. The 5,000-seat grandstand was destroyed by Hurricane Charley in 2004, and rather than rebuild it entirely, the Lee County Sports Authority decided to haul away the wreckage and erect a small bank of metal bleachers around the infield. Nonetheless, the facility celebrated its centennial in 2006.

As the Red Sox unveiled Jet Blue Park and readied for Fenway Park's centennial in 2012, one could only wonder how many decades the team would spend at the shiny new Fenway-replica in Fort Myers. Clearly, given the park's many nods to Fenway, it would be discordant for any other big league team to ever host spring games on the grounds. As for the traveling Bostonians expected to fill the park each spring, they couldn't get enough of Jet Blue in its first season, and the team's lease with Lee County and the City of Fort Myers runs through 2032. So, it would seem the marriage between the Red Sox and Fort Myers is built to last.

GETTING TO THE PARK. From I-75 North or South, take Exit 131 and follow Daniels Parkway east through the intersection of Ben. C. Pratt Highway. The ballpark will appear on the left, a mile and a half after the intersection.

SEATING. Tickets to Jet Blue Park are among the most coveted and expensive in the Grapefruit League. Aside from the $5 lawn seats and $10 bleacher seats in

Red Sox fan George Gratto poses beside the monument honoring Ted Williams (courtesy The Gup Collection).

distant right field home run territory, tickets cost between $15 and $46. In total, the park places 5,300 seats on the infield, 4,600 in the outfield, and has standing room, berm and bleacher accommodations for about 1,500 more.

The Dugout Box/Field Box seats are in the rows below the midlevel walkway on the infield. Section 100 is right behind home plate, while the even-numbered sections continue along the third base line to Section 110, which is even with the third base bag, and the odd-numbered sections continue along the first base line to Section 111, which is a bit past first base. The Left and Right Field Box seats continue into the outfield, extending much deeper into right than left. Clearly, the better seats are on the left side of the diamond, even if they don't allow for a view into the nearest outfield corner.

Above the midlevel walkway, the steeply rising Grandstand offers Section 200 directly behind the plate, then continues to Section 213 just past first base, before pausing for a gap, and then beginning again to offer Right Field Grandstand seats in Section 215–229. Just like at Fenway, the farther fans travel into the right field corner, the worse the vantage point becomes, although it should be noted that there are no view-blocking roof support pillars for fans to contend with at Jet Blue Park, nor are the seats angled toward centerfield instead of home plate, as is the case at Fenway. Down the left field line, the Grandstand pauses for a gap between Section 212 and 214, before continuing to Section 224, which abuts the Green Monster. These seats are much better than their counterparts in right field.

The three rows of Green Monster seats inside the left field wall appear in Sections M1-M9. This is a well-shaded and entirely unique spot from which to enjoy the game. Every one of the 258 seats comes with a nice wide shelf for fans to rest their drinks, and offers plenty of legroom. Above, the 215 Green Monster Deck Seats appear in a single long row that's 43-feet above the field.

The Seating Lawn in right field doesn't provide much of a view due to its distance from the infield, which is made even greater by the bullpens that sit between it and the field. The Reserved Bleachers behind the Lawn provide a slightly improved vantage point, because they're raised, but should be avoided if possible.

THE BALLPARK EXPERIENCE. For transplanted Bostonians living in Florida who haven't been to Fenway in a while, seats on the first base side of the field will allow them to feel almost as if they've returned. With the only-slightly-bizarre version of the Green Monster serving as the backdrop for the game to those watching from this side of the field, it's almost possible to pretend the game is being played in the Fens. Traveling members of Red Sox Nation, meanwhile, will identify many aspects of the Fenway experience at Jet Blue Park. Wally the Green Monster entertains fans in the stands, wearing his Number 97 jersey and flashing his mischievous grin. Meanwhile, the ballpark P.A. system cranks Neil Diamond's "Sweet Caroline" during the "eighth inning stretch."

The ballpark music also distinguishes itself for having a 1970s or 1980s bent. Fans arriving early to take in the park and watch pregame workouts should brace themselves for "Crocodile Rock" and other "bad" tunes of the era.

The apparel shop sells clothes and merchandise bearing the logos of every Red Sox minor league affiliate. A favorite item each spring is the green St. Patrick's Day Red Sox hat.

The ballpark concessions are managed by Aramark. Just like at Fenway there are some tents outside the park manned by local companies that serve treats too. Inside the park, the Fenway Franks and Fenway Sausages are solid choices, along with the Sam Adams Beer. Outside, the Crab Roll made by Pincher's Crab Shack is a nice homage to the Lobster Roll served at Fenway Park, and the Pulled-Pork Sandwich and Rack of Ribs at the Rib City stand are also delicious.

At the start of each spring the Red Sox Foundation hosts a "Dancing with the New Stars" competition at the ballpark to raise money for charity. Usually the team's rookies show off their moves on this special night in pairings with smooth-stepping local residents. The Red Sox veterans serve as judges. Bobby Valentine made quite the impression in 2012, as the new skipper wore a pink vest and showed off some flashy dance moves before finally stepping aside to let the rookies do their thing.

An extra special game each spring is the one at which the Red Sox host forty or so young patients from the Dana-Farber Cancer Institute in Boston. The Jimmy-Fund-sponsored program treats the youngsters to a game in one of the Jet Blue Park luxury suites and gives them a chance to meet several of the Boston players at an event earlier in the day. The Red Sox's affiliation with the Jimmy Fund dates back to Ted Williams' time with the team. The Splendid Splinter was one of the first and most vocal advocates for the charity. A statue outside Jet Blue Park depicts Williams placing his oversized cap onto the head of an adoring young fan, reminding visitors of the Jimmy Fund and the important work it does.

A nice tribute to Red Sox history outside the park is the monument garden in which each of the Red Sox's retired numbers—1, 4, 6, 8, 9, 27, 42 — takes the form of a giant stone monument. Fans enjoy posing beside these for photos and then reading the text on the side of each that memorializes the player it represents. In fact, fans don't find any tribute quite like this in Boston around Fenway Park. These are more similar to the monuments that stand outside Oriole Park at Camden Yards in Baltimore to honor famous Orioles like Cal Ripken and Jim Palmer.

City of Palms Park hosted the Red Sox from 1993 through 2011.

ON THE TOWN. Located in southwest Florida on the Gulf Coast, Fort Myers features beautiful beaches and interesting historic sites. In 1886 the great inventor **Thomas Edison** built a winter home on McGregor Boulevard in Fort Myers. Not long after, **Henry Ford** moved in next door. Today the homes of both men — including Edison's laboratory and Ford's workshop — are on display.

Red Sox fans make the short ride from Fort Myers to neighboring Cape Coral where **Mike Greenwell's Family Fun Park** (35 Pine Island Road) is located. Greenwell, who claimed to wrestle alligators with his bare hands in the off season, was known to Red Sox fans as "The Gator" during his time in Boston (1985–1996). In 1992, the slugger opened the amusement center, which houses a fish-feeding dock, an 8,000-square-foot maze, bumper cars, a playground, a mini golf course, go-cart tracks, a massive arcade, and batting cages. It also features the **Dugout Sports Bar and Grill**. The park is open year-round from 10:00 A.M. to 10:00 P.M. on Sunday–Thursday and until 11:00 P.M. on Fridays and Saturdays.

Terry Park, which was awarded National Historic Landmark status in 1995, is located on Palm Beach Boulevard between Terry Avenue and Palmetto Avenue. The old field is part of a community sports complex that also includes three practice fields.

City of Palms Park (2201 Edison Avenue), where the Red Sox previously played their spring games, still stands. It remains to be seen how the Lee County Sports Authority will utilize the park now that both of the city's spring teams play elsewhere. The prospect of a third big league team moving to Fort Myers would seem remote, but rumors along those lines were circulating at the time this book went to print. The Nationals and Astros were thought to be possibilities. Even if another team doesn't arrive to inhabit City of Palms Park, it's worth a visit during a spring training tour, if only to see the gorgeous royal palms that border its façade along the intersection of Edison and Broadway.

The Twins' **Hammond Stadium** is located about six miles from Jet Blue Park on Six-Mile Cypress Parkway. Each spring fans take advantage of special dates when favorable scheduling allows them to catch a Red Sox game in the afternoon and a Twins game at night, or vice versa. During spring training, the Red Sox and Twins enjoy a friendly rivalry, competing against one another for the Mayor's Cup, which is awarded annually to whichever team wins more games in head-to-head competition. Usually the teams play a best-of-five or best-of-seven-game series over the course of the spring.

The **Hideaway Sports Bar** (1418 Dean Street) is the perfect place for traveling Red Sox fans to watch spring baseball or NCAA basketball after a day at the ballpark. The Hideaway features a jumbo TV, the tastiest Maryland-style Crab Cakes south of Baltimore, and an atmosphere that's comfortable and friendly.

Hammond Stadium

(FORT MYERS) Minnesota Twins

Hammond Stadium at Lee County Sports Complex
14100 Six Mile Cypress Parkway, Fort Myers
800–338–9467
http://www.leeparks.org/facility-info/facility-details.cfm?Project_Num=
0225
http://minnesota.twins.mlb.com
Opened: 1991. Seating Capacity: 8,010
• 6 miles east to Jet Blue Park (Red Sox)
• 51 miles north to Charlotte Sports Park (Rays)
• 86 miles north to Sarasota (Reds)
• 140 miles east to Jupiter (Marlins & Cardinals)

IN 1991 THE MINNESOTA TWINS severed ties with the city of Orlando—the only city the franchise had ever called its spring home — and moved to Fort Myers where brand new Hammond Stadium awaited them. It is easy to imagine how ecstatic the Twins and their fans must have felt upon arriving in Fort Myers that first spring and approaching the team's new Grapefruit League stadium. It is also easy, however, to imagine the slight sense of disappointment those same folks must have felt upon entering Hammond Stadium. From the outside, it is one of the most stunning ballparks on the Florida landscape. The wide palm-adorned path leading to the main entrance is as majestic as it is long, and the stadium at the end of the path rises to such heights as to suggest the impressive monument to the spring game outside is but a harbinger of an even more magical baseball venue waiting inside. Once fans pass through the turnstiles, however, Hammond Stadium is rather plain. And it's not the most comfortable of the spring parks, either, owing to an entire second level composed of aluminum bleachers. While a small seating berm was added down the right field line in 2007, the lawn is only large enough to accommodate about 200 fans. And there is no lawn seating area beyond the outfield fences as at many of the other spring parks. Hammond Stadium also lacks the walk-around or 360-degree concourse that fans enjoy at other spring parks these days.

That said, the stadium's interior is functional and the Twins draw quite well each spring, perennially averaging more than 8,000 fans per home date and surpassing the 100,000 mark in spring attendance. The ballpark food is a cut above the fare at most of the Grapefruit League yards. And the fact that the Red Sox play just six miles away at Jet Blue Park enables fans to easily complete a spring doubleheader by watching an afternoon game at one of the city's venues and then an evening game at the other.

As fans approach Hammond Stadium on Six-Mile Cypress Parkway, a fountain sprays water into the air in the middle of a pond that lies beyond the ballpark's right field fence. Having been thus welcomed to the 80-acre complex, fans pull into a grass parking lot where each row is sentimentally named after a famous former Twin. The complex includes such streets as Puckett Avenue, Blyleven Lane, Beatty Boulevard, Mauch Manor, Oliva Avenue, Perry Parkway, Kaat Avenue, Hrbek Road, Carew Court, Pohlad Drive, and so on. A pre-game stroll through this unique memory lane gets fans thinking about baseball as they head toward the stadium and also provides an easy way for them to remember where they parked.

The main entrance to Hammond Stadium is more awe-inspiring than any other stadium façade in the Grapefruit League. Royal palms extend high into the

The stadium façade is said to resemble Churchill Downs.

sky, lining either side of the 200-foot-long footpath that leads from the parking lot to the stadium. At the end of the path, a waterfall cascades down the front face of the stadium, splashing into a Twins wishing well. The high beige façade was designed in the Old Florida Style and was intended to resemble Churchill Downs, the racetrack where the Kentucky Derby is held.

To the left of the stadium lies a full-sized practice field. Bleachers accommodate early-arriving fans who watch the Twins prepare for the game. Near this field, and built into the underside of the stadium, batting cages allow fans an up-close view of big leaguers working the cobwebs out of their swings.

Fans can also take a moment to review the plaques mounted on the stadium façade honoring members of the Professional Baseball Scouts Hall of Fame. This Hall to honor baseball's oft-under-appreciated "birddogs" was established in 2008 by the Goldklang Group, which owns the Fort Myers Miracle — the Florida State League team that makes Hammond Stadium its summer home. The group is owned and operated by legendary baseball promoter Bill Veeck's son, Mike Veeck, among other individuals.

To enter Hammond Stadium, fans ascend a large concrete stairway that empties onto a concourse beneath the grandstand, midway up the seating bowl. A plaque at the top of the stairway displays a bust of William H. Hammond. The plaque reads, "In recognition of the many years of leadership and service to Lee County by one of the county's finest citizens, the Lee County Board of Commissioners hereby dedicates this facility as of March 19, 1994, the William H. Hammond Stadium." Hammond was the assistant county administrator who led the effort to bring the Twins to town. Nearby, another plaque reads, "Lee County Florida: Winter home of the Minnesota Twins."

The spacious concourse offers multiple bathrooms, plenty of concession stands and a beer garden behind the seats on the third base side. Fans enter the seating bowl using runways that connect the main concourse to the interior walkway that runs between the Box and Reserved seats.

Inside the stadium, unpainted concrete and silver aluminum are the most prominent design features. The concrete press box is decorated with pennants commemorating the years that the Twins have made the playoffs, as well as with the team's retired numbers: 3 (Harmon Killebrew); 6 (Tony Oliva); 14 (Kent Hrbek); 28 (Bert Blyleven), 29 (Rod Carew); and 34 (Kirby Puckett). Above this, the peak of the tower that rises between third base and home plate lights up at night to offer a nice decorative touch.

Large palm trees that have continued to grow more impressive as the ballpark and surrounding complex have aged appear in two distinct clusters, in straightaway left and straightaway right field. The pond beyond the fence in right is barely visible from most locations inside the park. Long home runs do occasionally splash down there, though. There is a flag court in right-center and a scoreboard in left-center. As for the field itself, it is a symmetrical 330 feet down the lines and 405 feet to center. The Twins' bullpen is located after the seating bowl ends in left field. The

The exterior façade includes a fountain and wishing well.

five-mound pen is separated from the field by a high fence. The visiting bullpen occupies the same area in right field, providing two mounds.

Just about all of the seats are on the infield, as the seating bowl extends only to where the infield dirt meets the outfield grass on either side of the diamond. The small berm and accompanying party deck appear in shallow right, immediately after the seating bowl. Fortunately for fans in the grandstand behind home plate, the once-obtrusive screen that protected fans from foul balls at the expense of good sightlines has been replaced by a thinner, much less view-blocking one that extends from Sections 104–112. Unfortunately, more than half of the seats in the stadium — all of the ones above the midlevel walkway — take the form of metal bleachers with backs. They're not very comfortable, especially when they heat up in the sun.

The stadium and surrounding complex were completed in 1991 at a cost of $16 million, supported in part by a Lee Country tourist tax. The complex includes four full practice fields, two practice infields, ten indoor batting cages, and 30 practice pitching mounds. It also has soccer fields, softball fields, jogging trails, and an eight-acre manmade lake stocked with bass and crappie.

From April to September, the Fort Myers Miracle, a Twins affiliate, uses Hammond Stadium. The Miracle typically draws about 2,000 fans per game to its 70 home dates. Along with Mike Veeck, actor Bill Murray and songwriter Jimmy Buffett are part owners of the team, and both have been known to appear at Hammond Stadium. Each year at the end of the spring season, the Twins play an exhibition game against the Miracle. Then, the big leaguers head north, while the minor leaguers move into the home clubhouse.

The Twins' relationship with Fort Myers began on a high note and has remained strong ever since. The team started the 1991 season by winning a team-record 21 games during its inaugural camp at Hammond Stadium. Seven months later, the Twins won their second World Championship in four years. Previously the franchise had trained in Orlando dating to the 1936 season when an earlier incarnation of the club — known as the Washington Senators — debuted at Tinker Field. Other than the war years of 1943 to 1945 when the Senators trained in College Park, Maryland, the franchise remained loyal to Orlando until leaving for Fort Myers.

The Twins' relocation came about after the team petitioned Orlando for improvements to Tinker Field in the late 1980s, asking for $5 million in improvements that would enlarge the grandstand and provide new clubhouse facilities. The city demurred. At the same time, Fort Myers was declining similar requests by the Kansas City Royals to renovate its Terry Park, where the Royals had trained since 1968. After the Royals announced they would be leaving for what would turn out to be a short stay in Davenport, Florida, Fort Myers took advantage of the rift between the Twins and Orlando and jumped into the fray. Lee County offered Minnesota a more lucrative deal than the team had even been seeking, and suddenly Fort Myers was on the fast track to becoming a spring training destination once again. All that remained was to construct a $16 million facility. Local residents wondered why the county hadn't offered the Royals a deal like it offered the Twins, but most embraced the newcomers.

Hammond Stadium is a decent place to watch a game. The sightlines are clear, but the bleachers in the second level just aren't that comfortable. And there isn't much standing room for those looking to escape their seat. Fans should make every effort to secure a box seat or seat on the right field lawn.

GETTING TO THE PARK. From I-75 take Exit 131 and follow Daniels Parkway West. Take a left on Six-Mile Cypress Parkway, which leads to the Lee County Sports Complex parking lot. The county offers a courtesy shuttle service for fans before and after games, transporting those in need of a lift between their cars and the ballpark entrance.

SEATING. Fans enter the seating bowl on a mid-level walkway that separates the 16 rows of Box seats from the 16 rows of Reserved bleachers. The chairs in the Box sections are dark green, while the metal benches of the Reserved sections are silver. The lower bowl rises steeply, allowing plenty of leg room between rows and enough height between rows so that fans never have to peer between the heads of those in front of them.

A full house watches the Twins host the Red Sox (courtesy The Gup Collection).

Box 101 is located just beyond first base. Box 108 is directly behind home plate, and Box 115 is about ten feet past third base. Boxes 112–114 are behind the Twins' third base dugout, while Boxes 102–104 are behind the visiting team's dugout.

Due to the protrusion of the fences that separate the ends of the seating bowl from the bullpens, fans seated in the outfield-most Box seats cannot see into the nearest outfield corner. For example, those seated in Box 115 have no view of the left field corner, and those seated in Box 101 have no view of the right field corner.

Reserved Section 201 is located in shallow right field, while Section 209 is behind the plate, and Section 217 is in shallow left. The roof does not offer much protection from the rain, as it covers only the last four rows of the Reserved sections. But because the roof protrudes toward the sky at an upward angle, it offers a significant amount of shade. For the first hour of 1:00 P.M. games, the roof shades the Reserved sections on the first base side. Later in the afternoon, the shade shifts to the Reserved sections on the third base side, causing fans to migrate as they follow the shadow.

The Lawn seating area is reminiscent of the one at Roger Dean Stadium in Jupiter, in that it is only a tiny parcel in right field foul territory. The grass is lush and steeply sloped. But there's only room for about 200 people. There are also two rows of barstools atop the berm on the concourse. These chairs are sold as Drink

Metal bleachers fill the upper half of the grandstand.

Rail seats. They offer a decent view of the action, more comfort than practically any other seat in the park, and easy access to the Twins Territory concession stand on the right field concourse.

General Admission tickets are sold in advance once the rest of the seats have sold out. General Admission amounts to standing room. The problem is that there really isn't any free space to stand at Hammond Stadium. As a result, General Admission ticket holders wind up standing in the midlevel walkway where they block the aisles and make it difficult for other fans to access the concession stands and bathrooms.

THE BALLPARK EXPERIENCE. Every March, Lee County officials designate one special home date "Minnesota Day." Fans arrive at the park a few hours early and set up hibachis in the parking lot for a tailgate. Bratwurst and other Midwestern delights highlight the celebration.

The best place to wait for autographs outside the park is in the picnic area located on the third base side of the stadium. Fans are separated from players only by a four-foot-high rope that lines the path players follow to get from the main stadium to the practice field. Inside the park, the best spots to get autographs are in Sections 101, 102, 114 and 115. In these sections, only the low field wall separates the fans from the players. In all other Box sections the protective screen that rises behind home plate limits fan and player interactions.

The daily lineups for both teams are posted on the concourse behind Section 214. Usually a crowd of fans watches with rapt attention as a stadium employee fills out the batting orders on a white board an hour or so before the game.

The concession stands sell Grilled Brats, Hamburgers, Chicken Sandwiches and Philly Cheese Steaks. Much of the fare is cooked over hot charcoal. The Brat is delicious, but it's not the only treat that will remind fans of the experience at Target Field in Minneapolis. Fans on the prowl at Hammond Stadium will also find State Fair favorites like Cheese Curds, Sweet Potato Fries, Funnel Cake Fries, Mini Corndogs, and the ever-popular Sweet Potato Sundae, which is a bed of sweet potato fries, topped with vanilla ice cream and caramel syrup. The Ale Battered Shrimp Plate and Boneless Buffalo Wing Basket are other favorites. Afterwards, a Cherry or Blue Raspberry Slushy washes it all down.

On the concourse behind Section 215, the beer garden provides a sitting area for adults, serving a Yuengling Black and Tan as well as imported bottles. From this location, fans can look out the back of the stadium and watch minor league players working out on the practice field.

Long home runs to right field splash down into a pond.

In between the fifth and sixth innings, a local dairy bar sponsors a daily race that takes place behind the stadium's outfield fence. The race begins behind the wall in center, and ends at the right field foul pole. Large colorful pictures of an ice cream cone, a key lime pie, and an orange compete in the race, the pictures held above the fence by the people (presumably) who participate in the race at ground level.

ON THE TOWN. Fort Myers is a fairly large coastal city that has its Club Med type areas as well as its stretches of strip malls and urban sprawl. The area around the Twins complex was once rather sparsely populated but has continued to be developed in recent years. The local High School is nearby as is a strip of places to shop and eat on Daniels Parkway. Those looking for a meal before the game can visit **Potts Sports Café** (6900 Daniels Parkway, No. 26) or **Nino's Italian Restaurant** (6900 Daniels Parkway, No. 37). **Bistro 41** (Bell Tower Shops) is reportedly a popular dinner choice among players, while spring training fans assemble at **Shoeless Joe's Café** (13051 Bell Tower Drive). **Rib City** (12575 Cleveland Avenue) and **The Prawnbroker** (13451 McGregor Boulevard) are also fan hangouts.

Fort Myers is home to a number of excellent public golf courses such as **Whiskey Creek Golf Club, Hideaway Country Club, Eastwood Country Club** and **Fort Myers Country Club.**

Fort Myers Beach Park is located on Estero Island about twelve miles from Hammond Stadium. It features clean white sand for sunbathing. Meanwhile, **Sanibel Island** (15 miles away) makes for a nice day-trip. The islands are home to nearly 300 species of birds, alligators, conches and other types of unique coastal creatures. Nature trails and beaches present visitors with opportunities to view these Gulf Coast locals in their natural environment.

In 1998 minor league ice hockey found a home in Southwest Florida and in 2012 Arena Football did too. The **Florida Everblades** of the East Coast Hockey League play at Fort Myers' Germain Arena (11000 Everblades Parkway), as do the **Florida Tarpons** of the Ultimate Indoor Football League.

For college baseball, Fort Myers is home to Division II **Florida Gulf Coast University** (10501 FGCU Boulevard), which plays at Swanson Stadium. There, the outfield view showcases a large grove of beautiful palm trees.

Roger Dean Stadium

(JUPITER) St. Louis Cardinals
and Miami Marlins

Roger Dean Stadium
4751 Main Street, Jupiter
561–775–1828
http://www.rogerdeanstadium.com/
http://stlouis.cardinals.mlb.com; http://florida.marlins.mlb.com
Opened: 1998. Seating Capacity: 7,200
• 41 miles north to Port St. Lucie (Mets)
• 113 miles north to Viera (Nationals)
• 134 miles west to Fort Myers (Red Sox)
• 134 miles west to Fort Myers (Twins)

FROM MARCH TO SEPTEMBER, Roger Dean Stadium hosts more professional baseball games than any other ballpark in America. During spring training, the Cardinals and Marlins combine to play approximately 32 Grapefruit League contests at the park. Then, during the regular season, the park hosts about 140 Florida State League games, as it serves as home to both the Jupiter Hammerheads and the Palm Beach Cardinals. The stadium also houses the Gulf Coast League Cardinals and GCL Marlins, who play another 30 home games apiece each summer. Additionally, Roger Dean Stadium and its 12 surrounding fields host amateur baseball tournaments during the fall and winter.

Roger Dean Stadium is the only Grapefruit League stadium that hosts two teams each spring, whereas in Arizona five different Cactus League stadiums host two teams. The stadium opened in 1998 as the centerpiece of a 110-acre, $28 million baseball complex located within the master-planned community of Abacoa. The complex provides each team with six practice fields, a two-story clubhouse, and batting cages. The Cardinals' facilities and fields are on the right field side of the main stadium, while the Marlins' facilities are on the left.

Roger Dean Chevrolet, a local auto dealership, paid $100,000 per year for the naming rights to the stadium from 1998 through 2008, then renewed its deal with

The stadium sports a Mediterranean flair.

Palm Beach County to keep the name unaltered through 2017, which also happens to be the year the Marlins' and Cardinals' leases are set to expire. It remains to be seen if the Marlins and Cardinals will remain in Jupiter when those deals run out.

Originally the Cardinals shared the complex with the Expos. But in 2002 Jeffrey Loria sold the Montreal franchise to Major League Baseball and purchased the Marlins, and shortly later it was announced that the Marlins—who had been training at Space Coast Stadium in Viera—and the Expos would swap spring sites. The switch made sense for Loria who owns a home in nearby Palm Beach. It also made sense for Jupiter, since the Expos were rumored to be on the brink of big league extinction at the time, and city officials wanted to ensure two teams would continue using the complex each spring. After the Expos avoided contraction, but wound up being relocated and rechristened the "Washington Nationals," they settled into Space Coast Stadium, where they continue to make their spring home.

Billing itself as a "smart growth" community, Abacoa provides a neighborhood environment along with space for professional and recreational activities. The community's Town Center is located a few miles south of downtown Jupiter on land that previously belonged to the MacArthur Foundation. In addition to the baseball complex, Town Center includes office buildings, an outdoor amphitheater, parking garages, apartments, townhouses, specialty restaurants, and retail space. One of Florida Atlantic University's seven campuses is also located in Abacoa, and there's a public golf course too.

All of Town Center's buildings were constructed after the ballpark opened in 1998, and all share the same earth tone color scheme. Soft yellow, blue, tan and red hues mark the buildings, which all look remarkably alike. Green aluminum roofs cap each structure. Driving on Main Street en route to Roger Dean Stadium it feels almost as if one is entering an elaborate utopian movie set or perhaps Disney World. The sidewalks are impeccably clean, the grounds immaculately maintained, and the buildings all match.

Outside Roger Dean's Gate A, royal palm trees encircle an attractive brick courtyard. The bricks are inscribed with the names of donors who supported the stadium's development. Some bricks bear names, while others include brief messages, such as: "No. 1 Cardinals Fan," or "For the Love of the Game." Not surprisingly the façade of Roger Dean Stadium blends in perfectly with the community around it. Cream colored stucco rises above a four-foot-high red brick foundation. A green aluminum roof covers the top rim of the ballpark, while green aluminum also caps the many decorative towers that rise at regular intervals as part of the park's exterior. At the main entrance, the cream stucco gives way to dark red stucco. Two 20-foot-high archways serve as the ballpark entrances. The Marlins' logo is mounted above the left arch, while the Cardinals' logo is mounted above the right arch. The logos of both clubs also appear on many of the exterior towers, as do the logos of the Palm Beach Cardinals and Jupiter Hammerheads.

Inside, the stadium is fairly generic, but both big league teams enjoy equal representation. The home teams' logos appear on the left-center-field message board, right-center-field scoreboard, and outfield fence. Beyond the fence, the logo of each team appears on the team's clubhouse — the Cardinals' in right field and Marlins' in left field. The St. Louis dugout is on the first base line, while the Miami dugout is on the third base line. The Cardinals' bullpen is in right field, and the Marlins' bullpen is in left.

The concession concourse is behind the seating bowl at ground level. The part of it that runs below the press box is covered, but it is open to the sky down the base lines. Along the same idea as the brick program outside the park, small metal plaques on the concourse behind home plate pay tribute to season-ticket holders from Roger Dean's inaugural 1998 campaign. The logo of either the Cardinals or Expos appears on each plaque to denote which team the season-ticket holder supported. Cardinals logos outnumber Expos logos by a ratio of nearly two to one. The concourse also houses the Palm Beach County Sports Hall of Fame. Banners pay tribute to men and women like golfers Jack Nicklaus and Mark Calcavecchia, football players Heath Evans and Fred Taylor, and baseball icons like Hank Aaron and Bucky Dent.

The concourse also offers an interactive kids area behind the right field seats where fans use batting cages, a Wiffle ball field and speed pitch booths. Upon leaving the concourse and entering the seating bowl, the lack of a sunroof above the grandstand is noticeable in its absence. The roof covers only the press box and luxury suites above the grandstand on the first base side. The low seating bowl extends well into the outfield on both sides of the diamond, ensuring that every seat is close to the playing field. Unfortunately, there is nearly twice as much foul territory along the baselines as at most spring training parks, though, so sitting near the field doesn't necessarily constitute sitting near the action. Farther down the lines, a covered party deck sits near the foul pole in right behind a small grass berm. In deep left field, a bank of metal bleachers angles nicely toward the infield.

The field measures 335 feet to the left field foul pole, 380 feet to left-center, 400 feet to center, 375 feet to right-center, and 325 feet to the right field foul pole. A large black screen rises above the center field wall to provide a favorable backdrop for hitting, while advertising signs cover the outfield walls except in straight-away center. The foul poles are also covered with advertising banners as well.

The clubhouse buildings behind the outfield fences reflect the ballpark's color scheme and design. Each provides a second-story deck from which team personnel can watch the game. A home run by Mark McGwire in Roger Dean's very first game — played between St. Louis and Montreal in 1998 — put a scare into sunbathers on the left field deck, knocking loose a chunk of stucco from the upper levels of the building. The 450-foot dinger was a prelude to McGwire's record-setting 1998 season during which he smashed 70 steroid-fueled home runs to break Roger Maris's single-season record. The Cardinals won that inaugural game, incidentally, by a score of 5–0. Another highlight of the day for the 6,899 fans in attendance

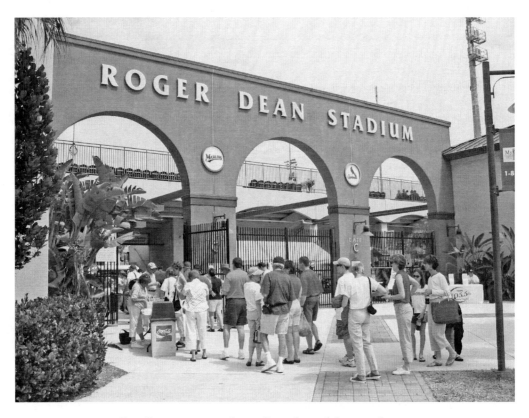

Fans line up to enter the stadium through large arches.

came during the seventh-inning-stretch when Stan Musial played "Take Me Out to the Ballgame" on his harmonica.

While the folks in Jupiter still talk about the McGwire clout, Marlins slugger Giancarlo Stanton hit a batting practice homer before a game against the Red Sox in 2012 that sailed completely over the building off of which Big Mac's shot clanked. The Stanton ball sailed right over the peaked roof of the tower on the left side of the structure, before touching down nearly 500 feet away.

Roger Dean Stadium suffered some serious damage in the summer of 2004 as Hurricanes Frances and Jeanne delivered a one-two punch that caused more than $3 million in losses to the facility. The two storms knocked down seven of the eight light towers surrounding the field, and ripped off parts of the press box and club-house roofs.

For the Cardinals, sharing a spring training complex with another team is actually nothing new. St. Louis coexisted with the New York Mets at St. Petersburg's Al Lang Field from 1962 to 1987. Later, the Cardinals split time at the park with the Baltimore Orioles from 1992 to 1995. The Cardinals trained in St. Petersburg from 1938 through 1997, discounting the war years of 1943 to 1945 when they stayed closer to home, training in Cairo, Illinois. When the Tampa Bay "Devil Rays" entered the big leagues and expressed an interest in training in their home city, the Cardinals gracefully stepped aside. The team's Grapefruit League history also includes stops in Bradenton (1923, 1924, 1930–1936) and Daytona Beach (1937).

As for the Marlins, Roger Dean Stadium is the third spring park they've used. The newcomers to the National League trained in Cocoa Beach during the 1993 Grapefruit League season, then resided at Space Coast Stadium from 1994 to 2002. The stadium in Viera had been constructed specifically to suit the Marlins, as its teal seats attested.

As for Palm Beach County's Grapefruit League history, spring baseball has been played in these parts for more than half a century. West Palm Beach's 5,000-seat Municipal Stadium provided striking outfield views of bridges arching over the Intra-coastal Waterway for years. That ballpark served as home to the Braves from 1963 to 1997 and home to the Expos from 1969 to 1972 and 1981 to 1997. After both teams left, the ballpark was razed, making room for a Home Depot.

GETTING TO THE PARK. From I-95, take Exit 83 and follow Donald Ross Road East. Turn left on Central Boulevard and then right on Main Street, which appears after a rotary. Once inside Town Center, follow the signs to the ballpark. There is ample parking on the grass lot beyond left field. Early arrivals also park for free on the streets surrounding the park. The parking garage at the intersection of University Boulevard and Parkside Drive is another option.

SEATING. The Cardinals and Marlins both average close to 7,000 fans per game at Roger Dean Stadium. For years the St. Louis club outdrew the Miami one, but in 2012 the Marlins—fueled by renewed interest in the team sparked by its signing of several free agents and the impending opening of Marlins Park—averaged more fans per game than the Cardinals. When the two teams play one another—which occurs approximately four times per spring—games almost always sell out. The Red Sox, Mets and Braves also draw well as visitors, no matter which home team they're playing. Due to the long drive between Jupiter and their spring camps, those teams have been visiting Roger Dean Stadium with decreasing frequency in recent years.

Roger Dean Stadium offers Field Box seats below the mid-level walkway, Loge Box seats above the walkway, Bleacher seats in deep left field and Berm seats in right. Once these sections have completely sold out, Standing Room tickets are offered. The cost for Field Box and Loge Box tickets varies depending upon the anticipated demand for tickets, as games are slotted into one of three different pricing tiers. In general, prices in Jupiter are on the high side compared to other spring cities.

The Field Boxes appear in Sections 102–124. Section 102 is in deep right field, Section 113 is behind the plate, and Section 124 is in deep left. While there are 14 rows in most sections, Sections 106–110 and 116–120 offer only eleven rows (4–14), due to the protrusion of the dugouts into the stands.

The Loge Boxes appear in Sections 201–213. Section 201 is the deepest of these in right field, while Section 213 is the deepest in left. Section 207 is behind home plate. Loge Box seats on the infield (204–210) provide better views of the game than Field Box seats in the outfield (102, 103, 121–124). There are 12 rows of Loge seats in most sections. Sections 204 and 205 offer only Rows 1–8, as the five luxury suites steal space from them. Sections 206–209 offer only Rows 1–11, as the press box claims the last row. The back rows of Sections 204–209 are shaded by the rise of the press box but otherwise there isn't much escape from the sun (or rain) at this stadium.

The Marlins (left) and Cardinals (right) clubhouse buildings loom beyond the outfield fence.

The low press box casts very little shade on the seats.

There are 16 rows of Bleachers in left field. The silver metal benches don't offer anything in the way of back support, but they are angled toward home plate.

The small Berm in right field also aims fans toward the infield from its location behind the Cardinals' bullpen bench. Three hundred Berm tickets are sold on game day. The Berm usually sells out well before the Bleachers. This is a coveted location for kids and families and the best spot in the park for autograph seekers.

Standing Room ticket holders are allowed to loiter at the back of the mid-level concourse and in the open area between the end of the seating bowl and the start of the bleachers in left field. A game is deemed an official sell-out after all of the 6,700 Box and Bleacher tickets, 300 Berm tickets, and 200 standing room tickets have sold.

THE BALLPARK EXPERIENCE. Each January, Roger Dean Stadium gets ready for spring training by welcoming area fans to a Fun Fest event that includes ballpark foods, games and a preview of the teams that will soon be arriving in Jupiter. Once workouts begin in February, the complex's twelve practice fields give wandering fans the chance to visit two big league camps in one morning. It's an easy walk from the Cardinals' part of the complex to the Marlins' part. And afterwards there are plenty of places within walking distance where fans can have lunch in Town Center.

Once the games begin, the crowds in Jupiter tend to be younger than at many of the other Grapefruit League stadiums. Abacoa residents and professionals are apparently not averse to the idea of playing hooky to catch an afternoon game in March.

A tent on the left field concourse provides shaded picnic tables for fans. The ballpark concession stands offer a Bratwurst steamed in beer, and a Roger Dean Dog that weighs one-third of a pound and comes topped with grilled onions and peppers. Local merchants set up on the concourse too, offering Pulled Pork Sandwiches and Shrimp Po' Boys.

Autograph collectors enjoy better access at this park than at most. Before and during games, fans line up near the bullpens in deep right and deep left. The relievers are usually pretty accommodating.

ON THE TOWN. Located on Florida's Treasure Coast, Palm Beach County protrudes farther into the Atlantic Ocean than any other expanse of Florida shore. For more than a century the 105-foot-tall Jupiter Lighthouse has stood atop a 46-foot-high hill on the northern shore of Jupiter Inlet guiding ships to harbor. The town was not officially incorporated until 1925 but the origin of its name — Jupiter — dates back much further. When Spanish explorers initially landed at the area now known as Jupiter Cove, they discovered Jega Indians living on the banks of what is now known as the Loxahatchee River. The Native Americans called the river the Jobe River. Later, when English settlers arrived in the 1760s they mistook the name Jobe for the mythological Roman god Jove, also known as Jupiter. And the name stuck.

In the 1980s several thousand acres of land in Jupiter that were previously controlled by the MacArthur Foundation were freed for development. Today, the town continues to grow, spurred by the Abacoa project. It's easy to see why Jupiter is a popular bedroom community for West Palm Beach. With **Bowling Rocks Beach**, **Jupiter Beach Park** and **Carlin Park Beach** nearby, and golf courses like **Jonathan's Landing**, **Jupiter Dunes**, **Jupiter Hills**, and **Riverbend Golf Club**, the area offers not only affordable housing but a wealth of recreational activities.

For baseball fans, Abacoa hosts lively pre- and post-game get-togethers at **J.J. Muggs Stadium Grill** (1203 Town Center Drive). The sports pub specializes in Black Angus burgers, grilled pizzas, Buffalo wings and cold drafts. A mural on the exterior wall depicts the faces of famous sluggers — Stan Musial, Babe Ruth, Ted Williams and Willie Mays — providing a scenic place for fans to pose for pictures. Other Town Center restaurants include **Jumby Bay Island Grill** (1203 Town Center Drive), **Costello's Trattoria and Pizzeria** (1209 Main Street), and **Pineapples Tropical Food and Fun** (1200 Town Center Drive). There used to be a 16-screen movie theater across the street from the ballpark, but it closed in 2006 and was demolished in 2010.

Outside of the Town Center complex, the Jupiter dining scene also offers the open-air and tropically inspired **Guanabanas** (960 North Highway 1A), which features lush banyan trees, tiki huts, hand-carved stone pathways and live music, along with a gourmet menu specializing in seafood. Guanabanas is a savvy pick for those traveling the spring baseball circuit with their significant other and looking for a memorable evening out. The **Dive Bar Restaurant** (318 South Highway 1) and the **Square Grouper Tiki Bar** (111 Love Street) are also local hotspots.

Tradition Field

(PORT ST. LUCIE) New York Mets

Tradition Field
525 NW Peacock Boulevard, Port St. Lucie
772–871–2115
http://www.stlucieco.gov/parks/trad_field.htm
http://newyork.mets.mlb.com
Opened: 1988. Renovated: 2012. Seating Capacity: 7,800
• 40 miles south to Jupiter (Cardinals/Marlins)
• 75 miles north to Viera (Nationals)
• 110 miles northeast to Lake Buena Vista/Kissimmee (Braves and Astros)
• 135 miles east to Fort Myers (Red Sox and Twins)

THE NEW YORK METS' Tradition Field was built a few years before the Camden-Yards-inspired revelation in baseball park design that soon transformed the game's parks at both the major and minor league levels into fan-friendly paradises. As such, Port St. Lucie's stadium will never be confused for one of the more scenic or architecturally distinctive Grapefruit League yards. That said, Tradition Field has been renovated on two separate occasions since its debut in 1988, and the work has gone a long way toward endowing the park with the sort of seating options and character that today's fans expect.

The highlight of an $8.7 million remodeling effort prior to the 2004 spring season was the addition of a well-manicured, well-sloped seating berm in right field home run territory. The atmosphere on the lawn is noticeably more relaxed than in the steep grandstand behind home plate and along the infield baselines. For most games—excepting ones that are expected to be very highly attended—fans are even permitted to bring lawn chairs onto the berm just like people used to do 30 miles north in Vero Beach until Dodgertown closed in 2009. What's more, the berm in Port St. Lucie is nicely decorated with small palms. The trees create a tropical paradise for those sitting on the embankment that spans from the foul pole to deep right-center, and also create a scenic outfield view for fans watching from the grandstand.

The grandstand rises steeply, placing many fans high above the field.

Another nice improvement to the ballpark brought about by the first renovation was the removal of the uncomfortable and unsightly aluminum bleachers along the left field foul line to make way for three rows of field level seats. Just behind the seats, the work added a festive terrace that provides picnic tables facing the field for group use. The field and terrace seats are all close to the action and they're nicely accented by a long blue canopy that gives the park some character. In addition to offering a look into the Mets' left field bullpen, the terrace seats allow access to a nearby tiki bar.

Eight years later, a $2.5 million renovation in 2012 sought to replicate the same effect along the right field foul line, by removing the last remaining banks of aluminum bleachers in the park, adding six rows of field level seats, and adding a 16,000-square-foot party deck behind the seats. This most recent project was clearly an improvement to the park's seating grid. Behind the new seats, the work installed a walkway that connects the deck to the berm area so that fans holding berm tickets are no longer required to use a separate entrance than other ticket holders. The work also added a high-def video screen to the scoreboard in left field. Finally, it added administrative space that St. Lucie County officials hope will enable them to attract a second big league team to Tradition Field to join the Mets.

The 2004 renovation was probably the more transformational one to the ballpark, though. It changed the whole look of the facility's exterior, replacing the concrete with red brick and blue steel. That work also began the movement to outfit the park with comfortable field level seating all the way down the outfield lines, rather than just in the high-rising structure behind home plate. That initial project also added a much-less obtrusive protective screen behind home plate than had previously existed, and added open-air luxury suites between the top of the grandstand and the press box. The Mets footed $7.25 million of the project, with the rest of the funding coming from a tourist tax on hotel and motel rooms in St. Lucie. As for the $2.5 million 2012 renovation, it was funded largely by the restructuring of a preexisting municipal bond at a lower interest rate.

The stadium's name, like its physical face, has changed through the years. From the time of its opening in 1988 through the 2003 season, the stadium had been known as "Thomas J. White Stadium," in homage to the developer who donated the 100 acres of pine forest and swampland upon which the $11 million stadium was built in 1987. White's motives were not purely philanthropic, as the developer had a vested interest in helping St. Lucie lure a big league team to town. White owned an additional 4,500 acres of land surrounding the parcel that he gifted, and he was in the process of developing it into a commercial and residential moneymaker.

Upon the completion of the 2004 renovation, the stadium was renamed Tradition Field. While it would be nice to think that the Mets and St. Lucie County were paying tribute to the Mets' fine tradition of excellence in choosing such a name, nothing could be further from the truth. In fact, Core Communities, a local developer building a master-planned community in St. Lucie named Tradition, had bought the naming rights. The deal was supposed to fetch $1.5 million over ten years for St. Lucie County, but by 2009 Core was either unable or unwilling to make good on its commitment for the upcoming season, and so a new naming deal was struck. Digital Domain Holdings, a media production company based in St. Lucie, paid $75,000 to name the park in 2010. The annual fee escalated each season after in increments tied to the Consumer Price Index. The Park was known as Digital Domain Park until 2012, but after the company filed for bankruptcy and backed out of the naming deal, Port St. Lucie and the Mets resumed their naming affiliation. The park was re-christened Tradition Field in 2013.

In an attempt to do right by the stadium's original benefactor, Thomas J. White, the county placed a bronze plaque on the front of the stadium bearing an etching of his face. The plaque reads: "Thomas J. White Plaza, dedicated March 5, 2004. In 1986 in order to bring the New York Mets spring training program to this area, visionary builder Thomas J. White constructed and donated this facility to the fans of St. Lucie County."

Not far from the White marker, a row of five granite monuments resides at the base of two flagpoles, one that flies the Stars and Stripes, and one that flies the Florida State Flag. From right to left, facing the stadium, the monuments read:

- Saint Lucie County Sports Complex: Florida Home of the New York Mets. Opening Day, March 5, 1988. Made possible by the people and governing bodies of St. Lucie County and Port St. Lucie whose support of the Pennies for Progress tourist tax referendum in St. Lucie West was a vital contribution. "Make no little plans, for they have no magic to stir men's blood."— Daniel H. Burnham, 1846–1912.
- Investment for the future, $1 million improvement completed February 1999.

- In memory of George McClelland, St. Lucie Mets director of public relations, 1988–2000. Will be forever remembered for his love of the game of baseball.
- In memory of Andy Kaplan, first general manager of the St. Lucie Mets baseball club — Florida State League. "Flourishing here, his joyful love of youth and the game —1988.
- In memory of Joe McShane, New York Mets project coordinator for the building of Thomas J. White Stadium in 1988. Will be forever remembered for his hard work and dedication to the New York Mets organization.

Not far from these markers, an eight-foot-tall sculpture commemorates the horrific events of September 11, 2001, that saw the Twin Towers of New York's World Trade Center reduced to rubble by a terrorist attack. The piece was created by a local sculptor named Pat Cochran. It portrays the two proud towers, while incorporating an actual piece of steel salvaged from the Trade Center buildings by New York City firefighters. This exceptionally well-done piece debuted at the end of the 2005 spring season at a dedication ceremony attended by Tom Glavine and other dignitaries.

Because of its steep grandstand and massive roof that stretches ever-skyward, Tradition Field falls short of providing the quintessential Grapefruit League experience that fans enjoy in cities like Bradenton and Dunedin. Fortunately, though, it has some distinguishing features that make it unique. The berm provides a nice backdrop for the game in right, while pines and palms rise behind the fence and scoreboard in left-center. The complex's six practice fields sit farther in the distance, beyond the wall in left. The outfield dimensions still mirror those once found at Shea Stadium, measuring 338 feet down the lines, 371 feet to the power alleys, and 410 feet to center field. The outfield wall and seats are appropriately Mets' Blue. All that's missing is a big Home Run Apple — like the one at Citi Field in New York — behind the outfield fence.

In 2012, the Mets marked the twenty-fifth anniversary of their arrival in St. Lucie by announcing they had agreed to extend their lease with St. Lucie County through at least 2023. Prior to moving to St. Lucie, the team had camped in St. Petersburg from its inception as a franchise in 1962 through 1987. For 26 years, the Mets shared Al Lang Field with the St. Louis Cardinals. In 1987, New York's final Grapefruit League home-opener in St. Petersburg was made all the more memorable when the reigning World Champions squared off against the Red Sox. The game was a rematch of the previous October's World Series. In the very first inning, Boston starter Al Nipper plunked New York's Darryl Strawberry with a pitch in retaliation for a home run Strawberry had hit against him in Game Seven of the World Series. Strawberry charged the mound, and a bench-clearing brawl ensued.

The next spring the Mets arrived in St. Lucie. At the time, their complex was surrounded by undeveloped swampland. Since then, a vibrant town has sprung up around the park. Tradition Field is not perfect, but it makes Mets fans feel right at home in March. Then, during the summer months the Florida State League's St.

A view from behind the palm trees on the right field berm.

Lucie Mets play at the park. The team enjoys a good following; the Single-A Mets team set a franchise record in 2012, drawing 105,379 fans.

GETTING TO THE PARK. Tradition Field is about half a mile from I-95. Take Exit 121 (St. Lucie West Boulevard), go east for about a quarter of a mile, then turn left on Northwest Peacock Boulevard East. The ballpark appears almost immediately. Most people park in the large grass lot in front of the stadium, but some thrifty fans park in the shopping plaza a quarter mile away on Peacock.

SEATING. The park holds about 7,000 fans, including the 500 or so who sit on the right field berm. During March, the typical game draws between 5,500 and 6,000 people. When the Red Sox, Yankees or Cardinals visit, however, it's not uncommon for games to sell-out. The ticket options include Premium Box, Field Level Terrace, Upper and Lower Reserved, and Berm admission.

The Mets dugout and bullpen are on the third base side. The first base seats enjoy more shade than the seats across the diamond do. By the later innings, though, most of the grandstand seats are shaded by the large roof. The roof also serves as an umbrella for those in Sections 201–207 on rainy days.

The original stadium designers took the approach of providing a high-rising seating bowl around the infield, instead of a low seating bowl around the entire field. As a result, the lower seats in the grandstand are quite good, while the upper seats feel a bit removed from the game. Section 101 is directly behind home plate below the mid-level walkway, and Section 201 is behind the plate above the walkway. The odd-numbered sections continue down the first base line, and the even-numbered sections continue down the third base line.

The Premium Boxes represent the first three rows of field level seats behind home plate in Sections 101–105. Fans in the first row find that their feet are actually below field level and that their knees are level with the field. As well as enjoying a great view of the game, the people in these seats can look into the dugouts through glass panels that prevent them from leaning — literally — right into the dugouts. The Premium Boxes are labeled Rows AA–CC.

The Field Level Terrace seats, as their name might suggest, are located at field level in even-numbered Sections 114–124 down the left field line and odd numbered sections 115–119 down the right field line. These position fans right along the bullpens, which are in foul territory.

The Lower Reserved ticket designation encompasses the rest of the seats below the grandstand walkway. So these seats aren't quite as good as the Premium Boxes

A sunscreen on the berm provides shade for fans.

and Field Level Terrace seats, but they're still good. The seating bowl stretches only so far as the infield dirt beyond first base (Section 113) and third base (Section 112). Most sections offer Rows A–K, except for where the first row is C due to the intrusion of the dugouts.

The Upper Reserved consists of the grandstand seats above the walkway. These are marked Rows L–X. Fans seated above Row P will be forced to identify their favorite players by the tops of their caps rather than their faces. This is a park where savvy fans pay a little more to sit down low.

Berm ticketholders enjoy their own concession stand, bathrooms, and picnic tables where they can sit and eat while still keeping an eye on the game.

THE BALLPARK EXPERIENCE. As fans arrive at the ballpark and peruse the monuments on the entrance plaza, "Meet the Mets" fills the air outside the park, delighting nostalgic visitors.

Prior to the start of each game, the Mets' lineup is announced in a most unique fashion. After the playing of the National Anthem, the public address announcer reads the home team's batting order and, as he does, each Mets starter sprints to his position in the field. Once all of the players are in their proper spots, they begin tossing warm-up balls around the infield and outfield, and the pitcher — who takes the mound last — begins warming up.

The concession stands serve knish and Nathan's Famous Hot Dogs, just like at Citi Field. The pretzels are grilled on hot coals. The tiki bar behind the left field terrace has a wide selection of beers.

For autograph seekers, the best bet is to head down the lines to where fans enjoy close access to the bullpens. For batting practice balls, the berm is the place to be. The front of the sloped lawn is elevated and actually begins about six feet behind the right field wall. The gully between the field and berm is fenced off, preventing fans from accessing it. And of course, many batting practice homers fly right into this no-man's-land. After batting practice, though, a ballpark employee collects the balls and usually tosses at least a few to the fans on the lawn.

The glassed-in luxury boxes atop the grandstand are flanked by outdoor luxury seating areas where VIPs can get some fresh air when the mood strikes them. Special spring training instructors like original Mets player Al Jackson, who visits St. Lucie each year to work with the team's pitchers, can sometimes be spotted in this area.

One unique feature of the practice complex beyond the stadium is its bat house. You may be jogging your memory to recall what rarely turned to page of the baseball encyclopedia may have defined this term for you at one point or another. Rest assured, your baseball vocabulary isn't lacking. This bat house is a place where living, breathing, flying bats live. That's right, those winged rodents that can often be observed circling the light towers high above minor league ballparks. Back in the mid–1990s, a flock of Free-Tailed Bats decided to roost at the ballpark. The bats sneaked into the press box, infiltrated the concourses, and even got into the bat racks in the dugouts. Accordingly, the St. Lucie County Commission voted to bring a "bat exclusion expert" to town all the way from Wisconsin. Then, in 1998, the County constructed a four-foot by eight-foot bat house adjacent to the stadium. The house is 14 feet off the ground, supported on stilts. It can house 10,000 bats. To check out the bat house from ground level, head to the east entrance of the stadium and follow the signs directing fans.

ON THE TOWN. St. Lucie is centrally located on Florida's eastern coast, a reasonable morning's drive from West Palm Beach to the south or Melbourne to the north. Tradition Field is northwest of downtown Port St. Lucie in an area known as St. Lucie West. This seaside community offers the scenic white sand beaches of **Hutchinson Island**, opportunities to observe nature at the **Savanas State Preserve**, and scuba diving access to shipwrecked Spanish galleons just off shore.

The sunken pirate ships, which date back to the early 1700s, account for the area's "Treasure Coast" nickname. In addition to Spanish warships, the warm Atlantic waters also contain the remnants of Civil War and World War II vessels— some located just 200 yards off shore. Many divers set out for these ruins from **Blue Planet Dive & Surf** (1317 St. Lucie West Boulevard).

St. Lucie is also home to **PGA Village Golf Resort** (1916 Perfect Drive) which welcomes players of all skill levels and houses the PGA Museum of Golf.

From 1953 through 2008, the Dodgers played at Holman Stadium in Vero Beach.

For a taste of New York, baseball road-trippers head to **Val's Tomato Pies** (7240 U.S. Route 1), which makes a delicious New York style pie. Fans will be hard pressed to find a tastier pizza during their time in Florida. The **St. Lucie Draft House** (6630 U.S. Route 1) is also quite popular, and once you've tasted the ribs, buffalo wings, and fries you'll understand why. This is the sort of place where a group of fans can sit and order appetizers off the expansive menu all night long.

A ride from Port St. Lucie to Viera, where the Nationals play, provides the opportunity to make a quick stop in Vero Beach to pay respects to **Dodgertown** (4001 26th Street), where the Dodgers trained from 1949 through 2008. Today, the complex that Branch Rickey envisioned and Walter O'Malley built is known as **Vero Beach Sports Village**. It hosts amateur baseball and football tournaments and the occasional summer concert. Those wishing to recall a simpler time for the spring game should visit the centerpiece of the historic complex where Holman Stadium sprouts live oak trees growing right between the ballpark seats. Other highlights include the streets and walkways named after legendary Dodgers, the light posts sporting glass orbs painted white and stenciled with red stitching, and the heart-shaped pond that O'Malley built one year as a Valentine's Day gift to his wife.

Space Coast Stadium

(VIERA/MELBOURNE)
Washington Nationals

Space Coast Stadium
5800 Stadium Parkway, Viera/Melbourne
321–633–4487
http://www.viera.com/VieraOutdoors/SpaceCoastStadium.aspx
http.washington.nationals.mlb.com
Opened: 1994. Renovated: 2008. Seating Capacity: 8,100
• 54 miles west to Kissimmee (Astros)
• 63 miles west to Lake Buena Vista/Kissimmee (Braves)
• 75 miles south to Port St. Lucie (Mets)
• 113 miles south to Jupiter (Cardinals/Marlins)

PROVIDING AS PASTORAL a setting for baseball as any park in the Grapefruit League, Space Coast Stadium makes up for whatever it may lack in the way of modern-amenities by tying its identity to the U.S. Space Program and embracing a space theme. From the moment fans exit their cars and begin making their way toward the stadium, they encounter one design nod or tribute after another to America's pioneering and innovative history of space exploration.

Outside the park, a 13-foot-tall, 350-pound model of a space shuttle stands mounted in launch position. The orbiter is crafted from fiberglass while the external tank and rocket boosters are made of aluminum. The $15,000, one-fifteenth scale model was donated by the nearby Kennedy Space Center in March of 1997. Not far from this unique model, a fountain shoots water high into the air from amidst a man-made reflecting pond. On the shores of this scenic waterfront stands a 17-foot-tall statue of mythical Mudville slugger Casey, made famous by Ernest L. Thayer's 1888 poem "Casey at the Bat." A tiny baseball diamond beside the pond features stone bases and a red clay infield.

A long gradually-sloping ramp leads from ground level to the entrance of the ballpark and the concourse, which runs beneath the grandstand, midway up the seating bowl. The ramp is topped by a colorful sign that reads "Welcome to Space

Despite Viera's efforts to welcome Nationals fans, disappointingly few have visited since the team's arrival in 2005 (Wikimedia Commons).

Coast Stadium," and bears the logos of both the Washington Nationals, who call the park home during March, and the Florida State League Brevard County Manatees, who play at the park during the minor league season. Contrary to what one might expect, the Manatees are not a Nationals' farm club; they have been a Milwaukee Brewers affiliate since 2005. But rather than embracing the blue and gold of the Brewers' logo, the Manatees' emblem, like their uniform, reflects the darker blue and red of their home stadium and of the Nationals. As for the Nationals, their High-A team plays closer to home, in Potomac, Maryland.

Indeed, Space Coast Stadium has represented the Nationals' color scheme very well since a $2.6 million renovation in 2008 that stripped away the silver and teal paint and teal seats that were leftovers from the Marlins' time at the park. Until that facelift, the ballpark's exterior had been gray and blue. Now it consists of red, white and blue siding, which climbs high by Grapefruit League standards, but is visually appealing thanks to the patriotic coloration. Inside, red, white, and blue pennants fly atop the grandstand, while the ballpark seats are the same deep blue as the ones found at Nationals Park in Washington. The red railings and red trim complement the seats nicely, although down the lines the unpainted aluminum bleachers detract from the effect.

The space exploration theme prevails at concession stands like "the Loading Dock" and "Orbit Grill." The playing field pays tribute to the Space Program by remembering the two fallen NASA shuttles. A tall banner on the right field foul pole depicts the Challenger lifting off, with the date of its tragic explosion — 1/28/86 — at the bottom. On the left field pole, a similar banner remembers the Columbia, which was lost on 2/1/03. Prior to the installation of these majestic banners in 2004, the word "Challenger" had appeared vertically on both poles. In 2012, the shuttle tributes were temporarily replaced by vertical banners that read "Kennedy" to celebrate the 50th Anniversary of Kennedy Space Center. That spring the March 8th game between the Astros and Nationals was designated "Space Day." Beneath blue skies on a gorgeous 75-degree afternoon, the director of the Space Center, Bob Cabana, threw out the first pitch, the fans ogled a full-scale replica of NASA's new Orion Multi-Purpose Vehicle, and Ryan Zimmerman blasted a Livan Hernandez pitch into orbit in an 8–0 Nationals win.

As tempting as it might have been to conclude that day that all was well with baseball in the unincorporated master-planned community north of Melbourne known as Viera, the paltry crowd of just 2,800 on hand told another story. As the 2012 Grapefruit League season took place, it was no secret that the relationship between the Nationals and Brevard County, which owns Space Coast Stadium, had grown tenuous. Not only were the Nationals continuing to play at the most isolated camp in the Grapefruit League or Cactus League — one that leaves them with just three opponents within a seventy-five mile drive, but after eight seasons in Viera, Washington fans still had not taken to visiting Florida's Space Coast in large numbers. Nor were many local fans from the Melbourne area turning out to support the Nationals.

Since arriving in 2005 as the exiled Montreal Expos, the Nationals have averaged only about 4,500 fans per game. As such, the Nationals were reportedly mulling their options. Officially, the team's lease with Brevard County runs through 2017, but the Nat's have a relatively inexpensive out-clause in their contract that they could exercise sooner than that if the right opportunity to relocate presents itself. One possibility would have them moving to the Red Sox's former stadium in Fort

A 13-foot replica of a space shuttle outside the park pays tribute to the nearby Kennedy Space Center.

Myers—City of Palms Park—where they would compete with the Red Sox and Twins in that city's spring baseball economy. Another possibility would have the Washington team moving to Port St. Lucie to share Tradition Field with the Mets. While Washingtonians would surely find Port St. Lucie a more appealing March destination than Viera, such a move wouldn't solve the problem of the camp being too isolated. The Nationals would be farther, in fact, from the two teams in Kissimmee and would be resigning themselves to playing the majority of their spring games against the Mets, Cardinals and Marlins. The most likely scenario is that Osceola County will approve and build a two-team complex to house the Astros and Nationals in the Kissimmee area.

The reality is, today's big league players just aren't too keen on those three- or four-hour bus rides across the state that were once a common part of the spring training experience. Just as the Cactus League has centered its teams within an hour's drive of one another in the Phoenix Valley, it appears the Grapefruit League, which has already abandoned east coast bastions like Fort Lauderdale, Miami and Vero Beach, is in the midst of migrating to the Gulf Coast. If the Nationals do pull up stakes in Viera, it seems likely that the Marlins and Cardinals would leave Jupiter when their leases run out at Roger Dean Stadium in 2017. Otherwise, they and the Mets would be the only teams on Florida's Atlantic Coast.

In the meantime, Space Coast Stadium continues to sit amidst the Carl Barger Sports Complex, surrounded by pleasant green pastures north of Melbourne. The planned community of Viera is gradually being built around the complex's five practice fields and stadium, creeping ever closer with each passing spring. It's really a quite pleasant setting in which to watch a game.

The Nationals arrived in Viera in the spring of 2003, back when they were still known as the Expos. The Expos had previously played at Roger Dean Stadium, which they had shared with the Cardinals from 1998 through 2002. In 2003, the soon-to-be-relocated Canadians swapped sites with the home-state Marlins who had trained at Space Coast Stadium since its opening in 1994. The switch was precipitated by a deal that saw Montreal owner Jeffrey Loria sell the Expos to Major League Baseball and then buy the Marlins from John W. Henry, who then bought the Red Sox. After the swap, Loria backed out of an agreement that Henry had made with Viera to keep the Marlins at Space Coast Stadium through 2017, so he could take his new team to Jupiter where his old club had trained. Meanwhile, Major League Baseball assigned the Expos to Space Coast Stadium. Then the Expos became the Nationals two years later.

The stadium was built in 1993 at a cost of $6.5 million, while the surrounding complex cost another $3.5 million. The Viera Company, the developer of the planned community, donated the 80 acres on which the stadium and complex reside. Brevard County financed the stadium's construction with loans and a countywide hotel tax, while the Marlins paid for the practice complex.

Originally there was a manually-operated scoreboard on the grass hill behind the left field fence. The scoreboard operator watched the game from a raised platform to the right of the board. As an added attraction, whenever a member of the home team hit a home run, smoke spewed from a gigantic baseball that rose above the scoreboard, signifying a lift-off. The stadium's 2008 renovation replaced this board, though, installing in its place an electronic scoreboard and a small video screen. In addition to endowing the park with the Nationals' color scheme as discussed above, the project also upgraded the P.A. system, added new grandstand roofs, and improved the field drainage. A 2010 project added a tiki bar and picnic platform on the left field berm, though it should be noted that this rather basic party area lacks the charm of the similar structures in Clearwater and Sarasota.

In right field, palm trees loom over the forest green outfield fence, while home runs long enough to clear the trees clang onto the aluminum roof of a building that houses batting cages. The field measures a symmetrical 340 feet down the lines, and 404 feet to center. The outfield fence is twice the height in right field as in left. In right, there are two levels of advertising signs wallpapering the fence. In left, the shorter fence allows fans on the berm a view of the game. The home bullpen is largely out of sight for those in the stands, located parallel to the foul line in deep right, separated from the field by a wall. The visiting pen is behind a wall in deep left.

A two-level structure behind home plate houses the press box and 12 luxury boxes, which have sliding glass doors to provide fresh air on nice days. Compared to the uninspired blocks that serve as press boxes at many of Florida's spring parks, the home plate façade at Space Coast Stadium is unique. The small canopy roofs atop the first base and third base grandstands would appear to have been installed for mainly decorative purposes, as neither provides much shade.

As for the history of this franchise's spring sojourns, Jupiter was not the first Palm Beach County town to serve as the Grapefruit League home of the Expos. Prior to playing at Roger Dean Stadium, the Montreal team trained in West Palm Beach from 1969 through 1972 and from 1981 through 1997, sharing Municipal Stadium with the Atlanta Braves, for whom the stadium was built in 1962. The Expos also spent eight springs (1973–1980) ninety miles north of Melbourne at Daytona Beach's Jackie Robinson Ballpark. That park currently serves the Florida State League's Daytona Cubs. Mr. Robinson made history on the field while playing for the International League's Montreal Royals in 1946. While many Florida cities banned Robinson from games at their stadiums, he was allowed to play at City Island Ballpark in Daytona. After spring training, he led the International League with a .349 batting average and 113 runs scored. The next spring he trained with the Brooklyn Dodgers in Havana, Cuba, before claiming the National League Rookie of the Year Award.

According to baseball lore, City Island Ballpark is also where the Grapefruit League got its name. Long before Jackie Robinson would transform baseball, another future icon of the sport was instrumental in naming the spring league. The Brooklyn Dodgers were training in Daytona Beach in 1915, back when the team was still called the "Robins" in honor of its popular manager Wilbert Robinson. Airplanes were still relatively new and when one flew over the field one day outfielder Casey Stengel bet Robinson he couldn't catch a ball dropped from the sky. And so, after practice, Stengel went off to find a pilot, while Robinson practiced catching pop-ups. The next day, the groan of a plane slowly became audible during practice. Stengel said it was time to settle the bet, and "Uncle Robbie" scurried to get ready in the middle of the diamond. Then Stengel appeared to have second thoughts. He told his manager it wasn't too late to call off the wager and warned that a ball falling from such height might rip a hole through Robinson's glove and cause serious injury to him. But the proud manager wouldn't back down. The plane began circling. Then, the pilot ejected a small spherical object. Robinson staggered, waited, and ... splat. He began screaming when he realized he was covered with what could only be the pulpy chunks of his own hand! Then he realized he was only covered with pink grapefruit. According to some versions of the story, Stengel — who would go on to become one of the game's classic pranksters — substituted the fruit for the ball. According to other accounts, pilot Ruth Law forgot to bring a ball and used an object from her lunch instead. Whichever was true, soon players throughout the game were calling Florida's circuit the "Grapefruit League."

As for baseball's history in the Viera/Melbourne area, the Houston Astros played their spring games just north in Cocoa Beach from 1964 to 1984, and the

Marlins played in Cocoa Beach prior to their inaugural season of 1993. Both teams utilized a stadium called Cocoa Expo where large snakes were known to sun themselves on the outfield lawn, and outfielders tended to think twice about diving for balls hit into the gaps.

Whether the Grapefruit League will continue to maintain an outpost on the Space Coast is anyone's guess. Considering the migration west — to both Arizona and Florida's Gulf Coast — over the past decade, it seems entirely plausible that Space Coast Stadium will have gone the way of the spitball by the time this book is due for another edition. But for the benefit of a little variety, here's hoping the East Coast makes a comeback with Viera finding a way to stay in the game.

GETTING TO THE PARK. From the north, take I-95 to Exit 195. Turn left onto Fiske Boulevard and follow it to the stadium. From the south, use Exit 191 and turn left onto Wickham Road, then right onto Lake Andrew Drive, then right on Stadium Parkway. The parking lot is a dusty field on the right side of the stadium. Due to the complex's remote location there are no other parking options.

SEATING. Space Coast Stadium offers chair and bleacher seating for 7,200 fans and room for about another thousand on the left field party deck/berm. But this is one park where fans hardly ever have to worry about getting tickets in advance.

Fans ascend a long ramp to access the ballpark concourse.

There are almost always good seats available on game-day, with the possible exception of the one day each March when the Yankees come to Viera. In a typical spring, fans see the Nationals' home schedule larded up with games against the Astros, Braves, Marlins, Cardinals and Mets, with a Tigers and Yankees game thrown in for good measure.

The seating bowl rises steeply, but the seats—including the outfield bleachers—angle nicely toward the infield. The seats below the wide mid-level walkway comprise the 100-level, while the seats above the walkway comprise the 200-level. Sections 101 and 201 are in deep left field, while Sections 110 and 211 are directly behind home plate, and Sections 119 and 221 are in deep right field.

The Batter's Box price category represents the first two rows of seats in Sections 107–113. All of these are down at field level behind the plate. The rest of the 100-level consists of Box seats, including seven rows below the walkway and Row 8, which is actually on the front of the walkway. Sections 113–115 are behind the home dugout, while Sections 105–107 are behind the visiting team's dugout. The first row of seats is Row 3 in these sections.

The 200-level offers seats on the infield, while beyond the corner bags there are three banks of bleachers along either foul line. Fans should make every effort to get into the more comfortable Reserved seats (Sections 204–218). The rows number 9–24. At the outer extremes, Section 204 is even with third base, while Section 218 is even with first base. The canopy roofs protect fans in Rows 16–24 from rain. The best shade is found in the upper rows of the left field Reserved (Sections 204–206).

In outfield foul territory, the Reserved Bleachers offer 16 rows of silver metal benches. These are the type of bleachers that have metal backs on them, but the view is distant. Sections 201–203 are in left field and Sections 219–221 are in right. Sections 203 and 219 provide the best sightlines because they are the closest to the infield.

The berm and adjoining party deck in left field are usually reserved for private parties. By the time the third or fourth inning arrives, however, the ushers are not too stringent in guarding the ramp leading from the main seating bowl to the lawn. Most fans will agree, though, that their grandstand seat provides a superior view of the game than the berm does.

THE BALLPARK EXPERIENCE. A game at Space Coast Stadium does not offer the same energy that games do at some of the Florida parks. But the experience in Viera is unique. As the game approaches, the announcer calls out the names of the starters, allowing time for each player to run to his position on the field. This is similar to the pre-game ritual at Tradition Field in Port St. Lucie, but slightly different. Rather than introducing players by their place in the batting order, as in Port St. Lucie, in Viera the players are introduced according to their position in the field—first the left fielder, then the center fielder, right fielder, third baseman, shortstop, second baseman, first baseman, catcher, and finally the pitcher.

Because Space Coast Stadium is surrounded by open fields, games here are notorious for being played under windy conditions. If the wind is blowing out, expect the park to be a launching pad for homers.

The best foul ball location is directly behind home plate. The protective screen extends straight up and then abruptly stops, allowing pop-ups to bounce off the press box and fall into the seats. When the bleachers are sparsely populated (which is often), they are good spots to run down foul pops too.

The food is slightly better than average but a bit on the expensive side. The Caesar salads, Pizza and Taco-in-a-Helmet are solid choices. Fans also enjoy the Marinated Chicken Skewers and Barbecue Chicken Nachos.

As a final tune-up before the Grapefruit League season, the Nationals sometimes welcome the Georgetown University baseball team to Viera for an exhibition game. In 2012, Coach Pete Wilk's Hoyas held their own against the big leaguers, bowing by a respectable 3–0 score. That was a vast improvement over the previous year, when the Nats won 15–0.

In 2012 the best-selling item at the souvenir stand was a Number 37 Nationals T-shirt with the name Strasburg written across the back. After enjoying a stellar camp, Stephen Strasburg drew the team's Opening Day start against the Cubs, and then enjoyed a stellar first half of the season to make the NL All-Star team.

ON THE TOWN. Viera is slowly blossoming into a vibrant planned community. As such, it offers the familiar assortment of chain hotels and restaurants within a short drive of the ballpark. To cruise the dinner options, visit Town Center Avenue, North Wickman Road, or Colonnade Avenue.

Nearby **Cocoa Beach** is a popular spot for recreation and entertainment. This hopping beach town is situated on Merritt Island, a thin strip between the Atlantic Ocean and Banana River Lagoon. The town has a relatively low full-year population but is humming in March when spring break coincides with spring training. Cocoa Beach offers access to tropical cruises, casino boats, and deep-sea fishing tours. It also offers swimming, surfing, sunbathing, dining and clubbing. On the lagoon side of the island, Banana River tour boats offer glimpses of alligators, sea birds and turtles in their natural habitats.

Cape Canaveral is part of the northernmost tip of Merritt Island. **The Kennedy Space Center** (Route 405) is open daily from 9:00 A.M. until 6:00 P.M. The Visitor's Complex includes: The Astronaut Hall of Fame; two launch pads; live action theatrical shows; a Rocket Garden that includes rockets from all eras of American space exploration; a full-size shuttle mock-up; a five-story movie screen that plays IMAX films; and the actual capsules from the Gemini Program.

Eighty-five miles north of Cocoa Beach, **Jackie Robinson Ballpark** (105 East Orange Avenue, Daytona Beach) continues to see summer use as home to the Florida State League Daytona Cubs. FSL baseball has been played on this site dating back to 1920 when the Daytona Beach Islanders took the field for the first time. Originally called, "Daytona City Island Ballpark," the stadium opened in 1915 as spring home to the Brooklyn Dodgers as detailed above. In the 1920s a new wooden grandstand and press box were added. The ballpark was renovated again in 1951, but Hurricane Donna tore the improvements away in 1960. In 1962, the covered grandstand and press box that stand today were built. New clubhouses and bleachers were added in 1972 to accommodate the Expos. After Hurricane Floyd did heavy damage in 1999, a new roof was installed in time for the next minor league season. Today a statue of Robinson interacting with young children stands at the main entrance, and a historic exhibit on the concourse honors Robinson.

Osceola County Stadium

(KISSIMMEE) Houston Astros

Osceola County Stadium
631 Heritage Park Way, Kissimmee
321–697–3200
http://www.osceolastadium.com/
http://houston.astros.mlb.com
Opened: 1985. Renovated: 2003. Seating Capacity: 5,300
• 15 miles west to Lake Buena Vista/Kissimmee (Braves)
• 47 miles southwest to Lakeland (Tigers)
• 54 miles east to Viera (Nationals)
• 81 miles west to Tampa (Yankees)

BASEBALL'S SMALLEST spring training park sits not in some sleepy little town that time has conveniently forgotten, but in the bustling tourist town of Kissimmee. Highway 192, which funnels cars from the Florida Turnpike toward Disney's Magic Kingdom, is adorned by sprawling hotels and flashing neon lights. The landscape is anything but pastoral. In the midst of all the commercialism and commotion, the Astros longtime spring stadium sits at the far end of a grass parking lot, half a mile from the road. The ballpark is easy to miss on the first drive past on Highway 192. If Osceola County Stadium is nothing else, it is small. Even after undergoing a major renovation prior to the 2003 season, it accommodates just 5,300 fans. The next smallest Grapefruit League venue is Florida Auto Exchange Stadium in Dunedin, which holds 5,510. Considering this, it is ironic that Osceola County Stadium does not provide a particularly intimate setting for a game. Due to its uninspired design, the stadium seems larger than it actually is. Additionally, the tightly-fenced and closely-guarded practice complex adjacent to the park is not welcoming to fans in the way that many of the other spring complexes are. Osceola's four practice fields and two infields are completely off-limits to fans on game days. The cloverleaf of fields is open to the public only in February, before the spring games begin.

Osceola County Stadium is handsome enough from the outside. The exterior

The brickwork on the plaza features a giant baseball design.

façade projects a southwestern flare, which is appropriate given the facility's ties to Houston. Red stone blocks anchor the base of the stadium and rise to form arches spanned by iron gates. Above these arches, tan stucco meets an auburn aluminum roof. The plaza outside the ticket windows and main entrance consists of a patchwork of bricks that depicts an enormous baseball. Gray bricks represent the ball's white horsehide, while red bricks serve as the stitching.

Entering the ballpark, fans encounter an uncovered but roomy concourse, then a stadium that is about as basic as a professional park can be. Behind home plate, the one-level press box is adorned with pennants that honor the Astros teams that have claimed division titles through the years. The screen behind home plate does not allow foul pops to drop into the stands, but slants back at an angle to connect to the top of the press box. This design can be observed at many regular season big league parks, of course, but in those cities the press box is much higher. Because the press box is so low in Kissimmee, fans may feel as though they're watching the game from inside a giant net.

The view beyond the outfield fence does little to enhance the visiting fan's experience. The administrative building that wraps around the left field corner is palatable, blending in with the ballpark and spawning a tower that bears the Astros logo, but the tower is only visible from the seats on the right field side. A few scraggly pines rise behind the fence at various points and a small pond festers behind the right field foul pole. A very basic scoreboard looms in right-center. A simple black screen serves as the hitter's backdrop. Car and truck traffic passes continuously on a road behind the right field fence. In total, these surroundings fail to contribute much to the atmosphere.

There are only two runways that allow fans to access the seating bowl from the concourse behind the grandstand. One is on the first base side and the other is on the third base side. Fans can also access the seats from the open patios in the outfield corners. The field measures a symmetrical 330 feet down the lines, 390 feet to the power alleys, and 410 feet to center. The bullpens are located on either side of the field in foul territory. Though there is ample foul territory around the field, the outermost warm-up mounds are situated so that the bullpen catchers must straddle the foul line as they wait to receive pitches. Located out near the outfield foul poles, the home plates behind which the bullpen catchers squat are only about six inches from the nearest line. If the bullpens were moved closer to the infield, where there is more foul territory, this problem would be averted, but perhaps then the relievers would be more vulnerable to foul liners. The Astros' dugout, like the team's bullpen, is located on the left side. These dugouts aren't as big as the ones in Port Charlotte, but they do intrude quite far into the stands.

The ballpark received an $18.3 million renovation between the 2002 and 2003 spring seasons. The project was partially funded by a $75 million grant to improve ballparks across Florida that was endorsed by Governor Jeb Bush in 2000. The work was preceded by the signing of a 15-year lease extension between the Astros and Osceola County that will keep the team in Kissimmee through 2016. The renovation removed the bleachers that had previously filled the seating bowl and replaced them with comfortable green stadium seats. It also added two new luxury boxes, bringing the total number at the stadium to four. A 23,500-square-foot major league clubhouse was also added, as well as a new 30,000-square-foot minor league clubhouse. The visiting team's clubhouse was also remodeled. Additionally, the exterior façade and concourses received makeovers.

As hard to believe as it may be today, at the time of its original opening, the Astros' facility earned many accolades, including a designation by *Baseball America* in 1988 as the best spring training facility in the land. With its four practice fields arranged in a cloverleaf, the complex was something of a novelty back then. Today, all of the practice fields continue to have the same outfield dimensions as the main stadium as well as covered dugouts, but their presence abutting the main stadium is no longer novel. Two pitching centers provide ten mounds apiece as well, and a batting facility houses six cages. The 80-acre complex was originally built by the county at a cost of $5.5 million to lure the Astros from Cocoa Expo in Cocoa Beach.

After the Houston Colt .45s spent their first two springs at Geronimo Park in Apache Junction, Arizona, in 1962 and 1963, the team moved to Cocoa Beach to join the Grapefruit League in 1964. Houston built a large following on the Atlantic Coast in the two decades to follow, then Osceola County made it an offer it couldn't refuse. At a time when Cocoa Beach was playing hardball with the Astros, refusing to pay for a ballpark renovation the team had requested, Osceola County funded construction of the Kissimmee complex using tourist taxes provided by the Tourist Development Council.

Kissimmee's coup paved the way for the construction of a number of other new Grapefruit League yards and led to the relocation of several teams in the late 1980s. New complexes followed in Port Charlotte (Texas Rangers, 1987), Plant City (Cincinnati Reds, 1988), Davenport (Kansas City Royals, 1988), and Port St. Lucie (New York Mets, 1988), all of which lured teams from stadiums in other towns.

While the process through which upstart cities received teams seemed like a dirty business, it did result in the construction of more modern stadiums for the teams and players.

Today, Osceola County Stadium remains one of the least utilized spring parks. No minor league team uses Osceola County Stadium during the summer. For several years, the Osceola Astros—later known as the Kissimmee Cobras—of the Florida State League used the field, but the team rarely attracted large crowds and Houston eventually moved its Class-A affiliate to Lexington, Kentucky. From 1989 through 2012, the ballpark also served as the main training center for the Jim Evans Academy of Professional Umpiring. In February of 2012, however, Major League Baseball announced that it was ending its relationship with Mr. Evans and his school after several Academy employees displayed racist imagery and used racially incendiary language at a company social event.

Although Osceola County Stadium was heralded as the finest spring training facility in baseball when it debuted in 1985, today it is not even the best park in town. Just a short drive west, Champion Stadium provides a much more festive atmosphere, while accommodating nearly twice as many fans per game, offering great sight lines, and serving superior concessions. The newer parks like Champion provide fan amenities, quirky ballpark design features, and interesting seating locations—like berms and outfield pavilions. The older facilities like Joker Marchant Stadium and McKechnie Field have their own quirks and eccentricities. Osceola County Stadium falls into a gray era of Florida ballpark construction that occurred between when the old-timey and modern parks were built. While the Astros' stadium is functional, it falls short of being the magical place a baseball park can be. In the spring of 2012, there was a sense among Grapefruit League observers that if Osceola County wished to retain the Astros beyond 2016, it would have to build a

Osceola County Stadium seats fewer fans than any other spring training park.

new complex in a less congested part of town for the Astros and another big league team to share. Time will tell if that sentiment was right.

GETTING TO THE PARK. Osceola County Stadium is accessible from the Florida Turnpike. From the north, take Exit 244 and turn right onto Highway 192. Follow Highway 192 for one mile and then turn right on Bill Beck Boulevard, which leads to the park. From the south, take Exit 242 and follow Highway 192 for three miles before turning right onto Bill Beck Boulevard. For those traveling to Kissimmee from the Viera/Melbourne area, the best option is to follow Highway 192/Space Coast Parkway all the way to Kissimmee, and then take a left on Bill Beck Boulevard.

SEATING. After the ballpark underwent its renovation, attendance at Osceola County Stadium rose to its highest levels in years in 2003. Then, prior to the start of the 2004 Grapefruit League season, Houston signed free agent pitchers Andy Pettitte and Roger Clemens. The Astros set a new team record, drawing an average of 5,067 fans to their 12 games at Osceola County Stadium in 2004. Seven of the 12 games sold out. Since then, however, interest in the Astros has cooled considerably in Kissimmee. The Astros struggle to attract 4,000 fans per game, and typically finish last in the fifteen-team Grapefruit League in average attendance.

Osceola County Stadium offers Box and Reserved seats with the ticket prices varying according to the different sections' proximity to the infield. The Box sections are located below the mid-level walkway; the Reserved sections are above. The seats are all comfortable green plastic chairs with cup-holders. Each aisle seat sports the Osceola County seal, which depicts a farmhand rustling cattle.

Section 101 is in deep left field, while Section 110 is directly behind home plate, and Section 119 is in deep right field. There are eight rows of seats in most of the lower level, except for Sections 105–107 and 113–115 where there are three rows, marked 6–8, due to the space occupied by the dugouts.

Above the walkway, the Reserved sections are numbered similarly, with Section 201 in deep left field, Sections 210 and 211 behind the plate, and Section 220 in deep right field. Sections 201 and 220 offer eleven rows, marked 9–19, while all other sections offer rows marked 9–22. The roof covers Rows 16–22 in Sections 202–206 and 215–219. Sections 201 and 220 are not covered at all, nor are 207–214 — where the roof covers the press box but not the grandstand.

General Admission ticket holders are allowed to stand beyond the seating bowl in the outfield corners. Because these locations are not elevated or tiered, the view is poor. General Admission tickets are sold only after all of the seats have been purchased. If the Yankees or Phillies are in town, this may well be the case, but otherwise games don't sell out.

THE BALLPARK EXPERIENCE. A significant number of Texans makes the flight across the Gulf of Mexico each spring, and a fair number of Disney tourists

A screen rises behind the center field fence to serve as a "batter's eye" for hitters.

find their way to games as well. The ballpark is more of a tourist destination than a haven for retirees and local hardball aficionados as some Florida parks are.

During the seventh-inning-stretch, the ballpark P.A. plays "Deep in the Heart of Texas," in true Houston Astros tradition.

One interesting feature of the park is its white marble cornerstone, which can be found at ground-level in the food court inside Gate A. The stone is engraved: "1985 Osceola Stadium. This cornerstone laid by the most worshipful grand lodge of free and accepted Masons of Florida."

For autograph seekers, the patios down the left and right field lines are known as Autograph Alleys, owing to their proximity to the bullpens and to the players. Down the right field line, there is also a playground known as "Astroland."

The concession menu includes southern favorites like sweet tea and boiled peanuts. One stand serves many of the hot dog variations that fans find at the regular season stadiums. The Chicago Dog (Vienna Beef brand), Dodger Dog (Farmer John), Fenway Frank (Kayem), and Milwaukee Bratwurst (Klement's) are popular sellers.

ON THE TOWN. In addition to the Disney theme parks, there are dozens of other amusement centers in the Kissimmee area. The downside of this is hideous traffic. March is traditionally one of Disney's busiest months, and not one but two big league teams train in town. Fortunately, while the roads may get clogged, the area can otherwise handle the demands of so many people. There are seemingly unlimited dining options in Kissimmee, including all of the national chains and many local favorites. As fans approach Osceola County Stadium they are greeted by neon signs, announcing dinner specials and nightly buffets. Hotel accommodations are plentiful near the ballpark, and rooms can be secured at affordable rates. Although the demand is great, the supply is even greater. This is a welcomed relief for fans arriving from places like Fort Myers and Sarasota, where it can sometimes feel like a stroke of good fortune to find lodging — at any rate — without booking well in advance.

Perhaps more than any other Florida town, Kissimmee has embraced the alligator as its emblem. That means alligator chowder can be ordered at most restaurants in town, alligator jerky can be purchased at most convenience stores, and alligator boots, belts and hats can be bought at most boutiques. Miniature rubber alligators are also abundant on the shelves of tourist information centers. Naturally then, visitors desiring to see live alligators in Kissimmee can satisfy this urge. **The Gatorland Zoo**, a few miles north of Kissimmee on Highway 92, is a commercial alligator farm and research center. The complex includes a zip-line that enables tourists to ride right over scores of swarming gators. Scenes from *Indiana Jones and the Temple of Doom* were filmed on site using some of the 5,000 resident alligators.

For a more rustic view of the prehistoric reptiles, visitors head to **Jungle Land Zoo** four miles west of downtown Kissimmee on Highway 192. Here, a mile-long trail offers glimpses of alligators in their natural habitat. The theme park is difficult to miss, as a 126-foot-long alligator marks its entrance, situated parallel to the highway in the parking lot of the Gator Motel. This is the second-longest artificial alligator in the state of Florida, trumped only by the 200-foot colossus in Christmas, a few miles east of Orlando on Highway 50.

During his days as an Astros pitcher, broadcaster and manager, Larry Dierker was a frequent spring guest at Kissimmee's **Big Bamboo Lounge** (4849 West Irlo Bronson Memorial Highway), where he and other members of the Astros family would mingle with fans. Dierker liked the bar so much that when he retired as Astros manager, he opened "Larry's Big Bamboo" inside Minute Maid Park in Houston. Unfortunately, the original "Boo" was leveled by hurricanes in 2004, and never reopened. It still retains a cult-like following, if only in memory.

Jay Bergman Field on the campus of the University of Central Florida in Orlando provides even more baseball for fans who don't get their fill in Kissimmee. The Golden Knights, who play in the Atlantic Sun Conference, opened the stadium in 2001, and named it after the university's long-time baseball coach. Bergman Field seats 2,230 people amidst its grassy outfield berms and delightful palm trees. It's one of the finest fields in the college ranks and is well worth a visit.

Fans also enjoy professional basketball at nearby **Amway Arena** in Orlando, where the NBA Orlando Magic plays.

Champion Stadium

(LAKE BUENA VISTA/KISSIMMEE)
Atlanta Braves

Champion Stadium
ESPN Wide World of Sports Complex
700 Victory Way, Lake Buena Vista/Kissimmee
407–939–4263
http://espnwwos.disney.go.com/complex/champion-stadium/
http://atlanta.braves.mlb.com
Opened: 1998. Seating Capacity: 9,500
• 15 miles east to Kissimmee (Astros)
• 36 miles southwest to Lakeland (Tigers)
• 62 miles east to Viera (Nationals
• 72 miles to the southwest to Tampa (Yankees)

THE CENTERPIECE OF Wide World of Sports, Champion Stadium is one of the most architecturally ambitious ballparks in the Grapefruit League. It is also the tallest, cleanest and most extravagant park on the Florida circuit. With seating for 9,500, it ranks third in size behind only Tampa's Steinbrenner Field and Fort Myers' Jet Blue Park. Yet, Champion provides a more intimate setting for a game than either of those venues. Thanks to its double-deck design, the grandstand places 80 percent of fans between the first and third base bags. Another winning feature is the festive grass berm that begins just beyond third base, wraps around the left field foul pole, and continues to left-center field.

The complex sits within the Disney-operated "town" of Lake Buena Vista. The Disney complex is so sprawling that it merits its own postal code; thus, the company is free to call the area whatever it wants. But it's not really a community; it's a resort and entertainment destination. As a result of this name-play, though, fans will sometimes see Champion Stadium listed with an address in Kissimmee, and other times with an address in Lake Buena Vista. As for the Wide World of Sports complex itself, it was originally known as Disney's Wide World of Sports, but after Disney merged with ABC/ESPN it was renamed ESPN Wide World of Sports.

This sign welcomes fans to the ESPN Wide World of Sports Complex (courtesy The Gup Collection).

In addition to housing Champion Stadium, which opened as the Braves' spring home in 1998, the 220-acre complex includes facilities and fields for athletes who participate in more than two dozen other sports. The complex includes: four practice baseball fields that the Braves use during spring training; several golf courses, including one that hosts PGA Tour events; a 7,500-seat tennis complex; four softball diamonds; multipurpose fields for football, soccer, lacrosse, and field hockey; a 5,500-seat field house for indoor sports like basketball and volleyball; another field house for track and field events; a cross-country course; a sports bar; sports equipment and apparel shops; and a PlayStation Pavilion where visitors play the latest video games. In addition to hosting amateur and professional tournaments for the sports already mentioned, the complex also hosts national and international competitions for Grappling, Judo, Taekwondo, Karate, Rope Jumping, Paintball, Cricket, Rugby and other sports.

The $100 million complex — built on the site of former swampland — opened in March of 1997. The next spring the Braves moved in. While it might sound easy for a spring training ballpark to get lost amidst all of these fields and facilities, such is not the case. With its Spanish Mission towers, arching exterior walls, and gigantic faux pennants that double as advertisements, Champion Stadium stands out. The park features a tasteful yellow façade, green iron gates, and a green tile roof. The first concourse fans enter as they pass through the turnstiles runs behind the lower seating bowl and beneath the upper deck. As at the newer regular season yards, fans don't see the ugly concrete underside of the upper deck, but rather an attractive flat ceiling over the concourse. From this first concourse, fans follow tunnels to a second concourse that runs atop the last row of lower level seating. The upper deck hovers over this wide concourse, providing shade to those below on hot days. Here, fans can enjoy a full view of the game while buying concessions or trekking to the spotless restrooms. Stairways and elevators lead to the second deck. The covered concourse on the second level features the type of designer floor tiles one might find in a remodeled kitchen. The hallways are lit by fancy light sconces. Additional concession stands and bathrooms appear on this concourse, so that upper level fans don't have to leave the second deck once the game begins.

The seats on both levels are forest green and made of comfortable plastic, except for the last six sections in right field, where green metal bleachers with backs appear. As for the lawn seating — nowhere else in the Grapefruit League do fans enjoy as quality a view of the infield from a berm location. The view from the upper deck is also excellent, as the top shelf is much lower than the upper levels found in regular season parks. The second level is, in fact, more like one of the loge levels found at a big league park. Four luxury boxes and two open-air party suites flank the press box at the top of the upper level. The Braves' executive offices also overlook the field.

As for the playing field, it measures 335 feet to the foul poles, 385 feet to the power alleys and 400 feet to center. The outfield wall is dark green and largely free of advertising. The light poles are painted the same dark green. The Braves' bullpen is in right field, behind the outfield wall, while the visiting team's pen is in left field foul territory, parallel to the foul line. From the right field concourse, fans may peer down into the Atlanta bullpen to watch the relievers. From this location, fans are also able to see the Braves' parking lot where placards mark the spots reserved for head honchos like the team's manager and general manager.

Colorful replica pennants, huge and metallic, sprout from the left field berm, rising on high poles. These showcase the names of various companies — a rental car agency, a credit card company, a soft drink maker, a cell phone service provider, and so on — while also composing a visually appealing art-deco adornment to the park. Across the outfield, a large structure rises atop the outfield fence, spanning from left-center to right-center, to serve as the hitter's backdrop. This also hides from view the batting cages and practice fields beyond the stadium. The structure closes in the park nicely, creating a cozy environment, while also providing room for the scoreboards and video board. For several years two very large Cracker Jack boxes appeared on this outfield wall. That was back when the field was called Cracker Jack Stadium. The Walt Disney Company and Frito-Lay/Pepsi, which makes Cracker Jack, had a special naming-rights deal. It was not the traditional cash exchange, but rather in exchange for the naming rights to the ballpark, the company

From 1998 through 2006 the park was known as Cracker Jack Stadium and giant Cracker Jack boxes flanked the scoreboard.

sponsored a number of Disney theme park attractions. Upon the expiration of the ten-year deal, though, Frito-Lay opted not to renew the contract. That cleared the way for Disney to strike a new ten-year deal with Hanes Brands in 2007. As a result, the stadium is now named after the clothing manufacturer's popular Champion label.

Interestingly, the Tampa Bay Rays have played two regular season series at Champion Stadium. In May of 2007, they hosted the Texas Rangers for three games at Disney, and then in April of 2008, they hosted the Toronto Blue Jays for three games. Both times, the Rays swept the series. These cameos at the Wide World of Sports complex were the product of the Rays' stated desire to make Greater Orlando an extension of their home market. Both years, the team requested and received permission from MLB's central offices to play at Champion Stadium.

Prior to arriving in Disney, the Braves had trained at Municipal Stadium in West Palm Beach from 1963 to 1997. The 5,000-seat stadium was poetically located at 715 Hank Aaron Drive. It was surrounded by a six-field complex built for the Braves in 1962. The Montreal Expos shared the facilities with Atlanta from 1969 to 1972 and from 1981 to 1997. The stadium was demolished, though, when both teams departed before the spring of 1998.

Prior to their time in West Palm Beach, the Braves had made camp in Jacksonville (1906), Miami (1916–1918), St. Petersburg (1922–1937), Bradenton (1938–1940, 1948–1962), Sanford (1942), and Fort Lauderdale (1946–1947). As the Boston Braves, the team also spent several springs in such Georgia towns as Thomasville, Augusta, Athens, Macon and Columbus, establishing southern roots that preceded the team's relocation from Boston to Milwaukee and then on to Atlanta.

As for baseball's history in the Kissimmee area, Tinker Field was built in 1912 in downtown Orlando. The facility hosted a revolving lot of spring teams in its early years, before the Washington Senators arrived in Orlando in 1936. The Senators/Minnesota Twins trained at Tinker Field from 1936 to 1990, excluding the World War II years of 1943 to 1945 when teams didn't travel south. By the time the Senators arrived in 1936, the facility had been dedicated in honor of Orlando resident Joe Tinker, of "Tinker-to-Evers-to-Chance" fame.

When Tinker Field was rebuilt in 1963, it continued to be named after the famous Cubs shortstop. The renovation replaced the wooden grandstand with a concrete seating bowl. Ceiling fans were added to the underside of the grandstand roof to keep fans cool. And more than 500 of the 5,500 seats in the park were ones that had once resided at Washington's Griffith Stadium. The new Tinker Field also included a memorial to former Senators owner Clark Griffith. In later years, the massive Citrus Bowl would tower over the right field fence of Tinker Field, occupying nearly half the outfield skyline.

The Orlando Rays, a one-time AA affiliate of the Tampa Bay Rays, used Tinker Field from 1998 to 2000, as members of the Southern League, before moving to Champion Stadium. But the Baby Rays spent just three seasons at Disney before relocating to Montgomery, Alabama in 2004 to become the Montgomery Biscuits. Today, Disney attracts most of the high-profile high school and collegiate tournaments that take place in the Orlando area, but local youth teams continue to play at Tinker Field. The metal seats have begun to rust though, and the wooden bleachers have become warped. Either the ballpark will need to be renovated soon, or Tinker Field's long life may be nearing an end.

Another historically unique, although shorter-lived Grapefruit League facility existed just eight miles southwest of Champion Stadium's current location. Built on the site of Circus World, which had been developed in 1973 by Ringling Bros., the Boardwalk and Baseball theme park opened in 1987. It was located at the junction of Interstate 4 and Route 27, outside Haines City in the northeast corner of Polk County. Sponsored by Anheuser-Busch, the 366-acre park featured amusement rides, exhibits from the National Baseball Hall of Fame, and a turn-of-the-century replica boardwalk. The Kansas City Royals moved into the portion of the complex known as Baseball City at the start of the 1988 Grapefruit League season, making use of a brand new 8,000-seat stadium, five practice fields, administrative offices and player dorms. Baseball City Stadium also featured a restaurant that allowed fans to watch the game while enjoying a meal. The Hall of Fame attractions included memorabilia from such icons as Babe Ruth, Ted Williams, Willie Mays, Warren Spahn, Stan Musial, Al Kaline and Aaron. Among the items on display were a Size 46 Yankees jersey worn by Ruth, and a locker from the clubhouse at old Yankee Stadium.

The amusement park portion of Boardwalk and Baseball included 30 rides, a six-story-high movie screen, the boardwalk, a professional dance facility, and several restaurants. The Royals drew moderately well when the complex first opened, but after the theme park closed in the 1990s attendance plummeted. The Royals decided to head west for a new complex in Surprise, Arizona, in 2003. And Baseball City was demolished. Today, several big box stores sit on the site of the former baseball play land.

While the Baseball City complex will surely not be remembered historically as one of the more influential spring training facilities, at the very least it would seem to have provided Disney with a blueprint of how *not* to combine baseball and amusement attractions. Wide World of Sports complements its spring training park with facilities and attractions used by other athletes and fans of different sports. It doesn't simply cater to tourists looking to have a good time on vacation.

Perhaps the Walt Disney Co. should not get all of the credit for the vision behind its unique sports complex, however. Shortly after Wide World of Sports opened, Russell and Nicholas Stracick of All Pro Sports Camps brought a $1 billion lawsuit against the entertainment giant, claiming that they had met with Disney in the late 1980s to pitch a sports complex they called Sports Island. According to the plaintiffs, Disney passed on the project then a few years later unveiled plans for Wide World of Sports. In August of 2000, a jury awarded All Pro Sports Camps $240 million. Disney appealed the verdict and two years later, in September of 2002, the two sides reached on out-of-court settlement.

No matter whose brainchild Wide World of Sports was, it is a unique stop on the Grapefruit League tour, and will remain so. The Braves' lease with Disney runs through 2017, and it seems likely the relationship between the team and entertainment company will continue long beyond that time.

Advertisements for Champion brand apparel flank the batter's eye in center field (courtesy The Gup Collection).

GETTING TO THE PARK. From I-4, take Exit 65 and follow Osceola Parkway West. Turn left onto Victory Way. Parking is plentiful on site. Priority parking is close to the stadium on an asphalt lot, while general parking is offered free of charge on a large field behind the stadium.

SEATING. Champion Stadium offers four different seating options: Lower Reserved, Upper Reserved, Bleachers and Berm Admission. The stands are well designed, angling all sections toward the infield, while rising at an appropriate grade to keep fans close to the field and close to ground level. It's wise to order tickets in advance, as the Braves perennially finish near the top of the Grapefruit League in home attendance. Considering it's only a seven-hour drive from Atlanta to Orlando, and considering that many Disney tourists also visit this fine park, it's easy to understand why the Braves flirt with or surpass the 8,000 fans-per-game mark most springs. Ordering in advance also makes sense because the box office adds a day-of-game surcharge to all tickets bought at the stadium on game-day.

The Lower Reserved consists of Sections 107–117. Section 107 is even with first base, while Sections 112 and 113 are behind home plate, and Section 117 is even with third base. Located entirely below the first-level concourse, these sections provide great views from Rows A–U. The overhang of the upper deck covers Rows P–U. Here, the view of the game is not affected, while seat-holders are protected from sunrays and the occasional rain shower. The protrusion of the dugouts eliminates Rows A–B in Sections 107–110 and 116–117.

The Upper Reserved consists of Sections 207–220 in the second deck. Section 207 is even with first base, Section 214 is behind home plate, and Section 220 is even with third base. Most sections contain Rows A–T, except for Sections 210–218, which contain Rows A–N due to the protrusion of the press box. A trellised sunroof provides shade to those seated in the back rows.

The right field bleachers provide first level views of the field from Sections 101–106. Section 101 is in deep right near the foul pole, while Section 106 is just beyond the first base bag. These are comfortable bleachers with contoured back-rests.

The Lawn begins just past third base and continues across left field home run territory, finally ending near the hitter's backdrop in center. It is sloped perfectly for those wishing to enjoy a quality view of the game while stretched out on a beach blanket or towel. When the sun gets too warm, the first level concourse offers room for fans to stand in the shade for an inning or two.

THE BALLPARK EXPERIENCE. If Champion Stadium is guilty of anything, it is of trying too hard to provide the ultimate ballpark experience, rather than just letting the atmosphere develop organically. For example, midway through the day the public address announcer is apt to say, "Okay, fans. Let's see if we can get the wave going. Starting in right field ... one ... two ... three ... go!" And an artificially induced wave begins.

The advertising takes the form of giant faux pennants.

Still, the ballpark experience is unique. And it is refreshing to be greeted by smiling security guards and ushers dressed in referee uniforms, particularly for those visiting immediately after attending a game at Osceola County Stadium — Kissimmee's other spring training venue — where the ballpark staff is notorious for being less than welcoming.

After parking for free on one of the expansive grass fields near the stadium and then being literally "welcomed" to Champion Stadium by ushers at the turnstiles, fans encounter a four-piece brass band playing festive music on the concourse. As game-time approaches and the final notes of the National Anthem fade into the breeze, the scoreboard shoots colorful fireworks into the sky. The brass quartet performs three-minute sets on the Braves' dugout roof during the game, a roving emcee asks fans trivia questions and oversees other forms of between-inning field entertainment, fans sing "Take Me Out to the Ballgame" en masse in the middle of the seventh, and a traditional ballpark pipe organ plays throughout the game. After the last out, more fireworks fill the sky.

The stadium's sparkling cleanliness extends to the restrooms, which are immaculate. Family restrooms offers spots where mom or dad can attend to small children, while even the regular men's and women's rooms offer tiny toilets and miniature sinks for the kids.

Concession stands throughout the park offer a diverse array of treats at reasonable prices. Favorites include the Buffalo Chicken Sandwich, Chili Cheese Fries, Steak and Cheese, and Burger. Mickey Mouse Ice Cream Pops and Chocolate Milk are popular items for the younger demographic. As one might expect, Champion brand apparel is featured prominently at the souvenir stands.

ON THE TOWN. Wide World of Sports is located at the southern tip of Walt Disney World. Epcot Center is a mile north, while MGM Studios is just a bit to the northeast. The Typhoon Lagoon and Downtown Disney are northwest of the stadium.

For hackers, the golf courses at Disney include: **The Magnolia**, the longest; **The Palm**, the most challenging; **Osprey Ridge**, one of the finest courses in Florida; **Lake Buena Vista Course**, a wooded track that's fun to play; **Eagle Pines**, which has 16 water holes; and **Oak Trail**, a nine-hole walking course.

Tournaments related to any of a variety of different sports often take place at Wide World of Sports concurrent to Braves games. Fans are free to watch many of these competitions.

A popular pre- and post-game hangout is the **Wide World of Sports Grill** (700 Victory Way), directly across the street from the stadium. The multilevel sports bar is designed along the lines of an ESPN Zone. Inside the lobby, a glass display case houses an arrangement of bats signed by Braves hitters and balls signed by Braves pitchers. With a family atmosphere, plenty of games playing on the many TVs, and surprisingly reasonable prices, this is the best bet for those looking to have lunch in air-conditioned comfort before the game.

For those venturing into the great wide world beyond Disney, nearby Parkway Boulevard, Market Street, and West Irlo Bron Memorial Highway offer hotels and restaurants. One favorite spot that was created by the gentleman who also brought the world the Red Lobster chain, is **Charley's Steakhouse** (2901 Parkway Boulevard). All of Charley's prime beef is aged between four and six weeks, then it's seasoned for about a day and a half, and it's flame-grilled in a 1200-degree open pit, over a fire made of oak and citrus. The steaks are delicious!

Joker Marchant Stadium

(LAKELAND) Detroit Tigers

Joker Marchant Stadium
2125 North Lake Avenue, Lakeland
863–686–8075
http://www.milb.com/team1/page.jsp?ymd=20060222&content_id=4279
   4&vkey=team1_t570&fext=.jsp&sid=t570
http://detroit.tigers.mlb.com
Opened: 1967. Renovated: 2003. Seating Capacity: 8,500
• 33 miles northeast to Lake Buena Vista/Kissimmee (Braves)
• 40 miles west to Tampa (Yankees)
• 49 miles northeast to Kissimmee (Astros)
• 53 miles west to Clearwater (Phillies)

LAKELAND HAS BEEN the spring home of the Detroit Tigers since 1934, excepting the war years of 1943 to 1945 when the Tigers trained in Evansville, Indiana. No other major league team enjoys as long a relationship with its spring city. The Philadelphia Phillies and Clearwater have the second longest affiliation, dating to 1947. The history shared by the Tigers and Lakeland is well represented by two ballparks in the city: Joker Marchant Stadium — where the team has played since 1966 — and Henley Field — Detroit's previous Lakeland home, which today functions as a college stadium.

A visit to Tiger Town offers the pleasures of watching spring ball in an environment untainted by the cluttered highways and crowded tourist attractions that can make attending spring games elsewhere in the Sunshine State more complicated than desirable. Nestled in the heart of citrus country, the Tigers' complex occupies a 78-acre parcel north of downtown Lakeland. The complex is just half a mile from the shores of glistening Lake Parker. In addition to Joker Marchant, the Tigers have at their disposal six practice fields, eight batting cages, and indoor workout facilities.

Thanks to an $11 million renovation prior to the 2003 spring season, Joker Marchant is more modern and fan-friendly than most stadiums its age. Right from

Two exterior towers were built in 2002.

the start, it makes a nice impression, presenting ballpark pilgrims with one of the Grapefruit League's most attractive exterior facades. The Mediterranean design features ornate towers and arches that rise like those of a fortress. The highlight is a tower outside the home plate gate adorned with a tall color mural of a prowling tiger. Above this majestic beast, appear the words "Florida Home of the Detroit Tigers" in blue and orange script. On the plaza nearby, the Detroit team's classy Old-English "D" is emblazoned in a patch of concrete and surrounded by bricks. The bricks are stamped with messages from Tiger loyalists. For example, one reads, "Detroit Tigers, Thanks for the great memories since 1955," and another reads, "Always a loyal Detroit Tigers fan. Always."

After taking a moment to appreciate these nice tributes to the team's identity and culture, fans pass through the yellow stucco arches that lead to the wide concourse that runs at ground level beneath the grandstand. Not only does the concourse offers a diverse array of ballpark treats, and picnic tables where fans find shelter from the sun or rain, but it also includes a trio of classy bronze busts. The first of these honors the Lakeland recreation director after whom the stadium is named. The second pays tribute to Tigers icon Al Kaline. The third remembers the 1968 Tigers, who came from behind three games to one to vanquish the Cardinals in an epic World Series that prompted the Detroit Free Press to declare "We Win." The palm trees that grow inside the ballpark gates, where the grandstand ends and roof disappears, add another delightfully Floridian touch to the park.

Runways lead from this first concourse to an interior walkway that bisects the seating bowl, running between the Box and Reserved seats. This pedestrian path is quite close to the field. There are only eight rows of seats in front of it. It's also very narrow. As for the seats, the ones in the grandstand are forest green. The press box, which is the same pale yellow that appears on the face of the stadium outside, is flanked by two luxury boxes on the first base side and four on the third base side. All of the luxury boxes have adjoining opera-house-style balconies where fans can sit outside if they desire.

The main seating bowl is low to the field, intimate, and cohesively reflective of the Mediterranean design. However, two other design features play prominent roles in defining the ballpark landscape, and leave decidedly different impressions on fans. The first of these is a grass berm in left field home run territory that enhances the stadium's aesthetic charm. The second is a massive bank of bleachers in left field foul territory that detracts from the quaint and homey atmosphere the stadium otherwise maintains.

The berm extends from the left field foul pole to the center field batter's eye, offering sun worshippers about fifty feet of sloped lawn upon which to spread blankets and beach towels. On the crest of this well-manicured hillside, a row of palms makes for a scenic outfield view. Beside the berm, in deep left field foul territory, a small Wiffle ball field provides a place for the kiddos to run off some steam.

The bank of bleachers on the third base side represents the highest freestanding seating location in the Grapefruit League outside of Fort Myers, where the Green

Monster seats at Jet Blue Park hover in the clouds. From the top rows of Lakeland's concrete staircase, fans have their pick of watching the game far below, the motor boats that trace ripples on the surface of Lake Parker beyond the outfield fence, or the ospreys that circle around their nests in the ballpark light towers. Fans can also look down from this vantage point onto the top of the sunroof that shelters the grandstand. For those sitting elsewhere in the stadium, the monstrosity in left field is hard to ignore, as its silver benches shimmer in the sun when unoccupied. A more modest structure — separate from the main grandstand — along the right field foul line, houses comfortable seats and provides a nice vantage point from which to watch the game, without offending sensibilities.

The green outfield fence yields to allow for a stretch of see-through mesh in deep right so fans can peer into the home and visiting bullpens which run parallel to one another, but perpendicular to the outfield fence. A modern scoreboard rises behind the fence in right, along with a video board. A pitch-speed-tracker appears independently of the other board, in right-center. And a very basic scoreboard appears atop the wall in left. Several leafy trees rise along the back of the outfield fence, giving the ballpark a cozy enclosed feel, even though a cloverleaf of practice fields can be found not far beyond its outfield. Joker Marchant's outfield is one of the largest in the Grapefruit League, measuring 420 feet to center, and 340 feet down the lines. The home dugout is on the first base side. Both teams use a clubhouse facility in deep right.

Joker Marchant Stadium was originally designed and built by the city of Lakeland at a cost of $360,000. Lakeland made this investment upon realizing Henley Field was no longer equipped to accommodate the flocks of snowbirds descending on Lakeland each spring. The increased interest in the team was spurred by Detroit's highly successful 1960s decade. Lakeland recreation director Marcus Thigpen Marchant was one of the main proponents of building the new yard, and hence it was named in his honor. The ballpark and other Tiger Town facilities were built on the site of an old World War II flight school that had been known as the Lodwick School of Aeronautics. For years afterward, an asphalt flight-strip ran behind Joker Marchant's outfield wall, and Tiger players often made use of the former hangers for indoor workouts. The Tigers' minor leaguers had actually been working out at the old airport since 1953, while Detroit's major leaguers had been using Henley Field.

At the time of its opening, Joker Marchant seated 4,200 fans. Several renovations through the years have enlarged and improved it. In 1972, the Tigers played their first night game in Lakeland thanks to a new set of lights. The left field bleachers were added after Detroit's American League East championship in 1987, expanding capacity to 7,027. Then, the most comprehensive renovation yet took place between the 2002 and 2003 spring seasons. Dallas-based architectural firm HKS, which had previously helped design the Braves' Champion Stadium, drew up the blue prints. The lion's share of funding for the $11 million project came from the state of Florida, which had committed $7 million to the proposed project in 2001, contingent on Lakeland and the Tigers agreeing on a long-term lease extension.

Joker Marchant Stadium has undergone several renovations through the years to account for its current form (courtesy The Gup Collection).

Prior to Florida's pledge it had been rumored that several Arizona communities were courting the Tigers. After the pledge, the two sides quickly reached a 15-year agreement to keep the Tigers in Lakeland through 2016.

The work at Joker Marchant increased its capacity to 8,500, adding nearly 1,000 seats and the left field berm which can accommodate another 500 people. The bank of seating was added down the right field line, and three new rows of Field Box seats were installed in front of the pre-existing seats behind home plate. The new field level seats brought the first row 15 feet closer to home plate, positioning some fans closer to the batter's box than the pitcher. To complete the new-look seating bowl, the old orange and blue seats were removed and replaced with green seats.

A second level was added to the structure behind home plate, enlarging the press box to include additional broadcast booths for TV and radio, and adding the six luxury boxes. The boxes are named after Tiger legends Ty Cobb, Charlie Gehringer, Hank Greenberg, Willie Horton, Hal Newhouser, and Kaline. The protective screen that rose behind home plate and ran at an angle up to the press box was replaced by a much smaller screen that rises straight up and stops, allowing foul balls to fall into the stands where they become souvenirs.

As for the stadium exterior, two distinctive towers were built — one that houses an elevator shaft, and one that houses a stairway — to provide access to the press box and luxury suites. The concourses were expanded to provide more space for concessions and restrooms. The home and visiting clubhouses were doubled in size. Previously the visiting clubhouse, which measured just 16 feet by 32 feet, had been cited by opposing teams as a reason why they preferred not to schedule games at Joker Marchant. A new practice field was also added behind the left field berm. And the covered batting cages beyond the stadium's right field fence were expanded to include eight tunnels.

While this work was taking place at Tiger Town during the summer of 2002, Lakeland's Florida State League team — then known as the Lakeland Tigers and now known as the Lakeland Flying Tigers — used Henley Field. The spring home of the Tigers from 1934 through 1965 was actually constructed in 1923 to house the springtime Cleveland Indians. The Clevelanders made Lakeland their March home through 1927. After departing, the Indians did not return to Polk County until 1993 when they moved into Chain of Lakes Park in Winter Haven, ten miles southeast of Lakeland. The second time around, the Indians stayed in Polk County for fifteen years, before bolting Winter Haven for a new home in Goodyear, Arizona, in 2009.

As for the Tigers, prior to arriving in Lakeland, they had trained in just one other Florida city — Tampa in 1930. Otherwise, the Tigers had spent their springs mainly in Georgia, Louisiana, and Texas, never staying in one town for more than a few years. The team trained in San Antonio in the spring of 1933, immediately before setting up in Lakeland.

In recent years, the Tigers and Lakeland have made it known that they would like to find a mutually-agreeable corporate sponsor after whom to name Joker Marchant Stadium. This pursuit has been ongoing for a while, and whether or not it will eventually prove fruitful, remains to be seen.

GETTING TO THE PARK. Tiger Town is two and a half miles south of I-4. From I-4, take Exit 33 and follow Route 33 South directly to the complex. First-time visitors usually park on the first base side of the stadium on the large field that charges $7 or more. Savvy fans, on the other hand, give a small donation to the church across the street from the complex and spend the money they saved on an extra concession treat or two.

SEATING. The Tigers consistently draw crowds in the 7,000 range. And each March presents several games for which the seats in the grandstand and bleachers sell out. Fans that prefer not to sit on the berm would be wise to order tickets in advance. The largest crowd in recent memory was a March 2011 game against the Red Sox that reportedly drew more than 10,000 people, many of whom stood shoulder to shoulder atop the berm. Detroit starter Justin Verlander didn't disappoint; he allowed just one run over 5⅓ innings. The crowd also saw Tiger slugger Miguel

A massive bank of bleachers along the left field line is the only thing discordant at this otherwise delightful park (courtesy The Gup Collection).

Cabrera hit a long home run. But in the end the Red Sox prevailed 2–1 in ten innings.

Joker Marchant offers six different ticket options: Field Box, Box, Reserved, Left Field Reserved, Bleachers and Outfield Berm. The Field Boxes consist of the first three rows (AA–CC) in Sections 105–108, behind home plate. These are the new rows that were added in 2003. The fans in these seats are closer to home plate than the players are in the dugouts. The Box Seats consist of Sections 100–112, excluding the three rows of Field Boxes. Section 100 is located just past the end of the infield dirt on the first base line. The seating bowl does not extend quite so far on the third base side, where Section 112 is even with the third base bag. Sections 100 and 101 in shallow right field do angle nicely toward the infield. In fact, the seating bowl curves back toward the field at such an appreciable angle in right that a large screen — similar to the one behind home plate — stands in front of Sections 100 and 101 to protect fans from line drives. There are eight rows of seats in most Box sections, except for Sections 103, 104, 109 and 110, where the protrusion of the dugouts allows room for only three rows, marked FF–HH.

The Reserved seats are located above the low interior walkway. Section 200 is in shallow right field, while Sections 206 and 207 are behind home plate, and Section

210 is midway between third base and home plate. Beneath the press box, Sections 205–208 offer Rows A–Q, while the base line sections (200–204, 209, 210) contain Rows A–W. The sunroof covers Rows K and higher in Sections 202–210, and provides shade to the entirety of these sections. The roof does not cover Sections 200 and 201.

The Left Field Reserved consists of ten rows of field-level bleachers that begin where the infield dirt meets the outfield grass, and continue to medium-depth left field. Section 301 is closest to the infield, while Section 304 is closest to the outfield fence. Unlike the newer sections in right field, these seats point toward the outfield, forcing fans to look over their right shoulders to see the home plate area. And because the metal backs on these bleachers form a near right angle with the benches, many fans find the Bleachers—which are just plain benches without backs—more comfortable.

The Bleachers represent the 24 rows of metal benches above the Left Field Reserved. Section 401 is closest to the infield, followed by 402 and 403. From the upper rows, Lake Parker is visible beyond the fence in right-center.

The left field berm offers a great place to shag home run balls during batting practice, a peaceful place to get a tan, and room for families with children to spread

Fans spread blankets on the left field lawn (courtesy The Gup Collection).

out their toys. From the footpath that runs along the top of the berm, fans can look out the back of the stadium to see minor leaguers working on Kaline Field. The berm is accessible from the main concourse, which allows ticket holders easy access to the rest of the stadium for concessions or seat hopping.

THE BALLPARK EXPERIENCE. On the way into the game, arriving fans should take care to observe the street names within the complex. That's because the streets are named after former Tigers, just like the parking aisles outside Hammond Stadium in Fort Myers are named after famous Minnesota Twins. There's something that just feels right about walking down Kaline Drive or Horton Way as you head to a baseball game.

Joker Marchant provides a festive atmosphere and Tigers fans enjoy their day at the park without putting too much emphasis on the game's outcome. The ballpark has a decidedly minor league flavor, perpetuated by the old-style pipe organ that plays the traditional favorites. The third-inning announcement of "Dog Row" brings smiles to many faces, as one lucky row of ticket holders receives free hot dogs courtesy of a local sponsor.

For years, Tigers fans delighted in hearing affable P.A. announcer Sandy Shaw announce this and other promotions at the park, but Mr. Shaw passed away in 2011. Many of the traditions he started from the press box live on, however.

The ballpark concession items include Little Caesar's Pizza, which should come as no surprise, seeing as Tigers owner Mike Ilitch made his fortune with the pizza chain. Little Caesar's is also sold at Comerica Park in Detroit. Joker Marchant also features delicious Pulled Pork Sandwiches, Barbecue Pork Nachos, and a grill that serves Burgers, Turkey Burgers, and Italian Sausages. The Foot-Long Chili-Cheese Hot Dog is also popular.

Because the bullpens are located in right field home run territory where fans can't access them, Joker Marchant is not a very good ballpark for autograph collectors. After all, who has more time to sign autographs than those bored relievers, who often seem grateful for the opportunity to interact with fans during the early innings? The best bet for those looking to collect signatures is to head for the box seats on the first base side, before or after the game, when the players transition between the dugouts and the clubhouse building in right field.

ON THE TOWN. Lakeland may no longer be the sleepy little town it once was, but it still represents a marked contrast to the several bustling cities that house other Grapefruit League stadiums. Visitors enjoy quaint streets named after different citrus fruits, eleven lakes, a bird sanctuary, an art museum, a symphony hall, lakeside golf courses and Florida Southern College — the campus of which was designed by Frank Lloyd Wright.

With a small seating bowl located entirely between the dugouts, **Henley Field** (Florida Avenue) continues to serve as the home ballpark of the Florida Southern Moccasins and the Lakeland High School Dreadnoughts. Just a mile south of Joker

The Tigers' former Lakeland home, Henley Field, has stood since 1923.

Marchant, the Tigers' previous ballpark provides an intimate setting for a game. It seats 1,000 on metal bleachers that are entirely covered by a roof. Florida Southern may be more famous for its golf alumni (Rocco Mediate, Lee Janzen) but its baseball team is a perennial Division II contender too. Each March, the Moccasins play an exhibition game against the Tigers at Joker Marchant, then return to Henley Field where spring fans visit to watch them play. In 2012, the team also played an end-of-March exhibition against the Baltimore Orioles at Ed Smith Stadium in Sarasota. In total that spring, the Mocs were outscored 25–2 against the big leaguers—11–1 against the Tigers, and 14–1 against the Orioles.

Another nearby baseball attraction for traveling fans is **Chain of Lakes Park** (500 Cletus Allen Drive, Winter Haven). Built on the shores of Lake Lulu in 1966, the hillside ballpark served as a March hardball hub for more than half a century. The Red Sox were its big league tenant, before the Indians. The Boston team used the park from 1966 to 1992, then moved to Fort Myers. Although Grapefruit League ball has not been played at Chain of Lakes since the Indians departed for the Cactus League, it was still standing in the spring of 2012. Plans were afoot though, to soon demolish it to make way for a new retail and dining complex. Presumably Winter Haven will install some sort of historical marker or display to remember the city's baseball history.

II.

ARIZONA'S CACTUS LEAGUE

Scottsdale Stadium

(SCOTTSDALE) San Francisco Giants

Scottsdale Stadium
7408 East Osborn Road, Scottsdale
480–312–2580
http://www.scottsdaleaz.gov/stadium/
http://sanfrancisco.giants.mlb.com
Opened: 1992. Renovated: 2006. Seating Capacity: 10,500
• 5 miles south to Phoenix (A's)
• 6 miles east to Salt River Fields (Diamondbacks & Rockies)
• 10 miles south to Tempe (Angels)
• 11 miles south to Mesa (Cubs)

THE SAN FRANCISCO GIANTS' roots in Arizona extend back to when they were still playing their regular season games in New York. It is quite fitting, therefore, that they play at one of the circuit's most historic sites. The Giants haven't always trained in Scottsdale, but they have been nestled in this hip western city just east of Phoenix since 1984. Thus, the Giants' relationship with their spring city is the second lengthiest in the Cactus League, predated only by the marriage of the Cubs and Mesa, which began in 1979.

When the New York Giants first arrived in Arizona, they played in Phoenix. That was back in 1947, a full decade before the team would head a bit farther west to stake out new regular season turf in San Francisco in 1958. That first season, the Giants were joined in the Grand Canyon State by just one other team: Bill Veeck's Cleveland Indians, who arrived in Tucson the same year. Together, the two clubs formed what is widely recognized as the first modern Cactus League, even though it was only a league of two. After the Indians beat the Giants 3–1 at Tucson's Randolph Park (later known as Hi Corbett Field) on March 8, 1947, the teams met six more times in Tucson and eight more times in Phoenix. The Cactus League gained another regular member in 1952 when the Chicago Cubs, who had previously held their spring camps at isolated Santa Catalina Island off the coast of California, moved their camp east to Mesa, where they would remain until 1965 before heading back to California for a year.

Cacti grow on the right field concourse.

The several expansions of the Major Leagues proved instrumental in boosting Cactus League membership. New editions to the big leagues that possessed regular season homes in the western part of the country tended to choose the Cactus League over the Grapefruit League. The Los Angeles Angels of Anaheim, San Diego Padres, Seattle Mariners, Milwaukee Brewers, Arizona Diamondbacks and Colorado Rockies are all examples of teams that chose the thin dry air of Arizona over the humidity of Florida upon joining MLB.

As for the Giants, they've been one of the Cactus League's constants or near-constants through the years. They trained in Phoenix from 1947 to 1983, except for 1951. That year, the Giants swapped training sites with the New York Yankees and trained in St. Petersburg, in order that Yankees owner Del Webb could showcase his team to his friends in Phoenix. Before agreeing to the deal, Giants owner Horace Stoneham made it perfectly clear that he and the Giants would be returning to Phoenix Valley in 1952. On March 12, 1951, the Yankees made their Arizona debut playing before 7,398 fans at old Phoenix Municipal Stadium. A 19-year-old rookie named Mickey Mantle went hitless in one at bat against the Indians that day, but went on to finish the spring with a .402 batting average, 9 home runs and 31 runs batted in, counting spring exhibitions played in other cities as the Yankees made their way back east. In the nine games Mantle played in Phoenix and Tucson he batted .469 (15–32). The 1951 spring season was also the last one that Joe DiMaggio would spend with the Yankees. The story that DiMaggio planned to retire broke in Phoenix when the Yankee Clipper told reporters on March 3, that he hoped to play one more solid season and then retire.

The Giants returned to Phoenix as promised in 1952 and remained at Phoenix Municipal Stadium until the spring of 1984 when they moved to nearby Scottsdale. Although the Scottsdale Stadium site dates to 1956, when the first incarnation of the park opened as a Baltimore Orioles spring roost, the ballpark the Giants now call "home" has stood since only 1992. Today's Scottsdale Stadium is certainly a more modern park than the one the Giants found when they first arrived, but the field is the same as ever: spacious and surrounded by scenic vistas. Just a few blocks away, historic Old Town Scottsdale offers sidewalks lined with hitching posts, saloons, and grain stores. Thanks to this melding of modernity with western nostalgia, and its festive urban location, Scottsdale Stadium perennially attracts more than 10,000 Giants rooters per game. For years the Giants competed with the Cubs, who play in Mesa, for bragging rights in the Cactus League attendance race, but in recent years the Diamondbacks and Rockies, both of whom play at Salt River Fields at Talking Stick just east of Scottsdale, have drawn more fans per game than the two stalwarts.

Prior to the arrival of the Giants in 1984, the original Scottsdale Stadium had served as spring home to the Orioles, Red Sox, Cubs and Athletics. The old ballpark featured a charming redwood façade, a prickly exterior cactus garden, and a hand-operated scoreboard. The field measured 430 feet from home plate to the center field fence, but the seating bowl was cozy, seating fewer than 5,000 fans. Today, "new" Scottsdale Stadium offers the same great views of the Camelback Mountains the old park did, while accommodating twice as many fans. The park has 8,200 fixed seats and room for nearly 4,000 people on its outfield lawns. While there isn't much shade to be found in the grandstand, and while the upper seats take the form of less-than-entirely-comfortable metal bleachers, the spacious left field berm is one of the largest and nicest in the Cactus League. And the trees on the berm create some nice swaths of shade for fans that have gotten their fill of sunshine for the day. Even the folks watching the game from the sunny stands around the infield get a chance to cool off, thanks to the ballpark misters. No, we're not talking about misters as in gentlemen, but rather misters as in little nozzles mounted on the underside of the sunroof that periodically emit cool bursts of water that waft down onto the fans in the form of mist.

The field, as mentioned, is rather large. It measures 360 feet to the left field foul pole, 330 feet to the right field foul pole, 390 feet to the power-alleys and 430 feet to center. Of course that didn't stop Barry Bonds from swatting more than his share of long balls at this yard during his tumultuous tenure with the Giants. In 2003, Bonds took a mighty rip at a pitch from the Mariners' Freddy Garcia and sent the ball clear over a 100-foot high light tower in right-center field. The base of the pole is planted 370 feet from home plate, and the ball was reportedly still rising when it went over the light-bank at the top.

The Camelback Mountains loom behind the stadium.

In that controversial slugger's later years, Scottsdale Stadium became the site of an annual press conference Bonds would inevitably hold to address his pursuit of Hank Aaron's all-time home run record and whatever the latest allegations were concerning his suspected use of performance enhancing drugs. Eventually, Scottsdale also played a role in the Bonds steroid saga when Scottsdale resident Kimberly Bell added her voice to the chorus of those accusing Bonds. Bonds' longtime mistress levied some of the most damning charges against Bonds in court and in the court of public opinion, including ones related to changes in his body parts and their various sizes and appearances.

A year before Bonds ever arrived in Scottsdale (via Pittsburgh) for his first Giants camp, Giants fans enjoyed the team's first season in a rebuilt spring yard. The 1992 reconstruction of Scottsdale Stadium was financed with $7 million in general obligation bonds. The blueprints were drawn by HOK Sport, the same firm that designed Oriole Park at Camden Yards in Baltimore. The Orioles' new park opened less than a month after the rebuilt Scottsdale Stadium, thus beginning the retro trend that swept across the major leagues. Like Oriole Park, Scottsdale Stadium features a number of design elements that are throwbacks to the classical ballpark era, as well as design elements that pay tribute to the region's history and its cultural identity. The old-time features at Scottsdale Stadium include antique light sconces inside and outside the park, red brick concourses, and framed articles of primitive baseball equipment that decorate the concourse. A sense of unity with the Old West neighborhood is attained through the generous placement of cacti, desert flowers, and Jacaranda, Paloverde, Shamel, Red Gum Eucalyptus and Chinese Elm trees on the 11-acre site. The plants and trees appear inside the ballpark gates, along the sidewalks outside, and on the grounds surrounding the practice facilities beyond the outfield fence.

At street level outside, red brick pillars support green iron gates that separate the sidewalk from the concourse behind the seating bowl. Another ring of pillars supports the stadium grandstand, the underside of which is visible above the concourse. A green metal sunroof matches the gates on the concourse to cap the structure. Inside, field level seats appear along both base lines and extend all the way out to the foul poles. Meanwhile, grass berms offer outfield seating in home run territory. A black screen rises above the green patch of outfield fence in center to complete the hitters' backdrop. The San Francisco bullpen is in right field home run territory behind the outfield fence, while the visiting pen occupies the same space in left field. To allow the relievers a view of the game, the bottom half of the outfield fence consists of chain-link.

The ballpark and the grounds surrounding it were the beneficiary of another renovation in 2006. The project, which cost $23.1 million, was jointly funded by the Arizona Sports and Tourism Authority, Maricopa County, and the City of Scottsdale. It added a concourse connecting the expansive left field seating berm and the smaller right field berm, and added a party deck on the right field berm. It also added a full practice field and a practice infield beyond the right field fence, and enlarged the Giants' clubhouse. The work also made field and facility improvements to the Giants' minor league complex that sits a few miles away. The result of this significant capital investment was the Giants extending their lease with Scottsdale for another twenty years. The team will play at Scottsdale Stadium through at least the 2025 season.

The ballpark really does present a gorgeous view. The seats on the right field side treat visitors to the looming backdrop of the four Camelback Mountain peaks. They begin behind the stadium on the third base side and continue toward the outfield, running seemingly parallel to the left field line. The ballpark also offers the chance for visitors to enhance their knowledge of the region's sporting history by visiting the Scottsdale Hall of Fame and the Arizona Fall League Hall of Fame, both of which reside on the concourse behind home plate.

The Scottsdale Scorpions utilize Scottsdale Stadium during the Arizona Fall League (AFL). The AFL was formed by Major League Baseball in 1992 as a developmental league for top prospects. It plays from early October through mid–November, providing the big league teams the chance to closely monitor the progress of their prospects, something not always possible with players who participate in the Caribbean Winter Leagues. Each AFL team is affiliated with five Major League feeder organizations that contribute six players apiece to their AFL team each fall. The Scorpions are affiliated with the Los Angeles Angels of Anaheim, Washington Nationals, Boston Red Sox, Philadelphia Phillies, and the Giants.

Aside from serving as spring home to the Giants and fall home to the Scorpions, Scottsdale Stadium houses the Scottsdale Giants of the short-season Arizona League. The 16-team rookie circuit, which dates to 1988, typically begins play in the third week of June and finishes in the last week of August. It is primarily intended for recently drafted high school and college players.

In March of 2006, Scottsdale Stadium was one of the sites utilized for the World Baseball Classic. Three different teams trounced a hapless South African team at the Scottsdale yard in Pool Play that spring, including the United States by a score of 17–0.

From 1992 through 1997, the Giants' Triple A affiliate in the Pacific Coast League played at Scottsdale Stadium. But the Phoenix Firebirds were forced to relocate when the Arizona Diamondbacks entered the National League as an expansion team. The Giants' PCL affiliate now plays in Fresno, California.

Before the Giants arrived in Phoenix in 1947 the team had trained in several different states, including California, Florida, Georgia, Louisiana, Tennessee and Texas. The team's Florida roots include spring stints in Sarasota (1924–1927), Pensacola (1936), Winter Haven (1940), Miami (1934–1935, 1941–1942, 1946) and St. Petersburg (1951). In 1937, the team trained in Havana, Cuba.

Fans find some shade beneath the trees on the outfield berm.

Concurrent with much of their time in Phoenix, the Giants also utilized a practice facility in Casa Grande, Arizona, about 40 minutes southeast of Phoenix and roughly half-way to Tucson. Mr. Stoneham developed the Francisco Grande complex in 1961 as his answer to Walt O'Malley's Dodgertown in Vero Beach, Florida. The Giants' complex featured four baseball fields, including one that hosted preseason games. The complex also included a luxurious golf course, an in-ground swimming pool shaped like a baseball bat, a parking lot shaped like a baseball diamond, flower beds shaped to resemble bats and balls, and the Francisco Grande Hotel, where the players stayed. After the new Phoenix Municipal Stadium was built, the Giants continued to use the complex as their minor league headquarters, and players continued to stay at the hotel during spring training. After the team moved to Scottsdale in 1984, the United States Football League's Arizona Wranglers and Denver Golds used the complex as their respective training bases. Today, the golf course, hotel and even the baseball-bat-shaped swimming pool remain at the Francisco Grande Hotel and Golf Resort.

GETTING TO THE PARK. Scottsdale Stadium is located two blocks east of North Scottsdale Road at the intersection of Osborn Road and Civic Center Drive. From the 101 Loop, take the Indian School Road Exit. Follow Indian School Road West to Drinkwater Boulevard and turn left. The ballpark is on the left, near the Civic Center, Court House and Scottsdale Hospital. Parking is free in the municipal garage adjacent to the ballpark on Drinkwater, even though signs read, "Three Hour Parking." Free street parking can also be found on East Second Street. For later arriving fans, there is a pay lot beyond the ballpark's right field side on 75th Street.

SEATING. Scottsdale Stadium offers seven different ticket categories: Lower Box, Upper Box, Outfield Box, Line Box, Reserved Grandstand, Reserved Bleachers, and Lawn. The even numbered sections appear on the right field side and the odd numbered sections appear on the left field side. Each aisle seat bears the Scottsdale seal — a cowboy riding a bucking stallion. Ticket prices vary by game as the Giants' pricing system sets a price for each seat based on current demand. The best bet for thrifty spring travelers is to target weekday games against lesser opponents.

The Lower Boxes (101–122) consist of Rows A–H, except behind the dugouts in Sections 107–116, where they consist of Rows C–H. Section 101 is directly behind home plate. Sections 121 and 122 are located where the infield dirt meets the outfield grass. The Upper Boxes (200–216) are located behind a mid-level walkway in Rows J–O. Section 200 is behind the plate, while Sections 215 and 216 are just beyond the corner bases. The Reserved Grandstand (300–316) is located directly above the Upper Boxes, taking the form of metal bleachers with backs. There are ten rows, except in Sections 300–304 where there are only six rows due to the press box. The sunroof covers the entire 300 level.

The Line Boxes (123–126) are located in shallow right and left field, while the

Outfield Boxes (127–130) are closer to the foul poles. All of these sections contain Rows A–H.

The Reserved Bleachers reside on the 200 level, beginning where the main seating bowl ends just past the corner bases, and continuing nearly to the foul poles. Sections A–D sit along the right field line—with Section A closest to the infield. Sections E–H sit along the left field line—with Section E closest to the infield. These sections offer 15 rows of benches without backs.

The Lawn seating areas in left and right field home run territory are far from home plate due to the field's gargantuan proportions but the view of the game is unobstructed. The walkway connecting the left and right field berms is unique in that it runs behind the slope of the lawn and offers no view of the field.

THE BALLPARK EXPERIENCE. For 1:00 P.M. starts, the Giants take batting practice before the stadium gates open. Back when Barry Bonds was king of the baseball world, fans would congregate on 75th Street beyond the right field foul pole and wait for balls to carry over the bullpen, over the outfield Lawn, and into the street. Today's fans stake out the players' parking lot on 75th Street, which is enclosed only by temporary iron fences, in pursuit of autographs.

The concession stands are located on the brick concourse that runs beneath the seating bowl. A few private vendors set up on the concourse, offering Kettle Corn, fresh Strawberries with Whipped Cream, and Barbecued Pork. The Salty Senorita serves spicy Mexican treats. The favorite ballgame concession of any true Giants fan though, is an order of Gordon Biersch Garlic Fries.

On the concourse behind the home plate grandstand, a circle of raised bricks forms a pitcher's mound. A bronze strip inlaid between the bricks leads to a batter's circle surrounded by palm trees. The metal path is inscribed with the words, "The distance to home plate from the pitcher's rubber is sixty feet, six inches. The ball travels approximately 55 feet after the pitcher releases the ball. Therefore if the pitcher throws a 95 M.P.H. fastball, the batter has approximately ¼ of a second decision whether or not to commit to swing and approximately ½ of a second to attempt to make contact with the ball."

Fans looking to bone up on their knowledge of Scottsdale baseball history should pick the brain of the cowboy-hat-clad volunteers manning the turnstiles and seating areas. These gentlemen represent the Charros, a civic organization that has supported spring training in Scottsdale since the 1960s.

Another way to gain a fuller grasp of the game's ties to this old western town is to simply walk the ballpark concourse. The Arizona Fall League Hall of Fame honors its inductees with bronze plaques that display each member's name, year in the league, and team. Through 2011, the Hall included 23 men, including managers Terry Francona, Jerry Manuel and Mike Scioscia, pitchers Roy Halladay, Chris Carpenter and Troy Percival, and hitters Albert Pujols, Ryan Howard and Derek Jeter.

Also appearing on the wall are the names of the Joe Black Most Valuable Player

The Arizona Fall League Hall of Fame resides on the concourse.

Award winners. Founded in 2002, the award recognizes the AFL's top player each year. The award is named in honor of the first African American pitcher to win a World Series game. Black accomplished the feat as a member of the Brooklyn Dodgers after a stellar 15–4 campaign that earned him the 1952 National League Rookie of the Year Award. After his playing career, Black served Major League Baseball as a front office executive and Negro Leagues advocate. A 31-year resident of Phoenix, Black was a vocal proponent of the Arizona Fall League and its mission. Among the more recognizable winners of the Joe Black Award is Dustin Ackley. The Seattle Mariners farmhand won the award in November of 2010, and then claimed a starting spot with the Mariners the very next season.

Sadly, one final plaque on this wall memorializes Cincinnati Reds outfielder Dernell Stenson, who was murdered in a carjacking incident in November of 2003, while a member of the Scorpions. The AFL's annual good sportsmanship award is named in honor of Stenson.

Also on the concourse, the Scottsdale Sports Hall of Fame offers photographs and text pertaining to the greatest athletes in the city's history. Each athlete's plaque lists his or her high school or college affiliation and provides a paragraph summarizing his or her accomplishments. Most of the honorees played for Arizona State University, Scottsdale High School, Coronado High School, Arcadia High School, or Saguaro High School. The most famous member of this group is Jim Palmer whose plaque reads, "Scottsdale High School, 1963. First-team All-State in football, baseball and basketball. Caught 54 passes in 1962, twice hauling in four touchdown passes in one game. Became an eight-time 20-game winner for the Baltimore Orioles."

ON THE TOWN. Aside from offering a Western atmosphere, Old Town Scottsdale houses a number of trendy clubs, boutiques, leather goods stores, and art galleries just a few blocks from the ballpark. The heart of the neighborhood is located at the intersection of Main Street and Scottsdale Road. **The Salty Senorita** and **Hacienda de Mexico** are popular post-game restaurants, but no establishment in town is as synonymous with "spring training" as **The Pink Pony Steakhouse** (3831 North Scottsdale Road). The Pink Pony opened in 1949 and became an immediate favorite of Dizzy Dean who was spending the winter in Phoenix. Dean took to talking baseball with owner Charlie Briley, and soon became one of Briley's regular hunting companions. During the ensuing decades scores of famous baseball players, managers and front office staffers made the upscale restaurant their Greater Phoenix hangout. Today, the pink stucco building at the corner of Old Scottsdale

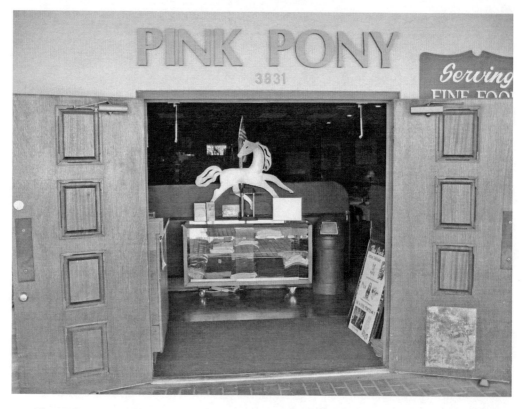

The Pink Pony Steakhouse was a frequent hangout of Dizzy Dean, among other stars of the game's earlier era.

Road and Main Street stands like a monument to the legends of the game that passed through the Old West in the early days of the Cactus League. The walls are covered with autographed photos and jerseys from players like Willie Mays, Ferguson Jenkins, Reggie Jackson, Willie McCovey, Bob Uecker and countless others.

The other famous baseball hangout in Scottsdale is **Don and Charlie's** (7501 East Camelback Road), which is usually packed with fans during the month of March. Big league manager Dusty Baker is a frequent dinner guest with his family, and several players visit as well. The walls are covered with funky memorabilia like old ticket stubs, jerseys and player caricatures. The menu features slathered ribs, hickory burgers and prime steaks. And the chatter revolves around one thing: baseball!

Scottsdale is also home to baseball commissioner Bud Selig, and to the **Alcor Life Extension Foundation**, the cryonics lab where the head and body of Ted Williams have been frozen since the time of his death in 2002.

Salt River Fields
at Talking Stick

(SCOTTSDALE) Arizona Diamondbacks
and Colorado Rockies

Salt River Fields at Talking Stick
7555 North Pima Road, Scottsdale
480–270–5000
http://www.saltriverfields.com/
http://arizona.diamondbacks.mlb.com;
http://colorado.rockies.mlb.com
Opened: 2011. Seating Capacity: 11,000
• 6 miles southwest to Scottsdale (Giants)
• 13 miles southeast to Mesa (Cubs)
• 14 miles south to Phoenix (A's)
• 16 miles south to Tempe (Angels)

THE RELOCATION OF the Diamondbacks and Rockies from separate ballparks in Tucson to Salt River Fields at Talking Stick in 2011 cemented the Cactus League's province as one existing exclusively within the Phoenix Valley. The arrival of the last two Tucson holdouts ensured that neither fans nor players would face so much as an hour's ride to traverse the short distances between the Arizona spring circuit's parks. More than just consolidating the physical footprint of the Cactus League, though, Salt River Fields was groundbreaking in another way. At the time of its debut, it was immediately lauded as the most thoughtfully designed spring complex yet built. From a fan's perspective, the ballpark and surrounding practice facilities are an absolute delight. Unlike at Arizona's other two-team complexes, the main stadium sits in the very middle of the two resident organizations' twelve practice fields, four practice infields, batting cages, practice mounds, and other workout facilities. Fans are encouraged to arrive early and stay late, and to roam the beautifully landscaped footpaths that wend from practice field to practice field, before crossing a bridge that spans a manmade lake to access the stadium.

Cactus Gardens adorn the outfield concourses (courtesy Jim Tootle).

The lake is just one of many features that helped Salt River Fields meet the standards required to earn LEED Gold Certification for New Construction set by the U.S. Green Building Council. It was the first professional baseball park to earn that coveted distinction, achieving the honor a year before Marlins Park in Miami would. The lake, which is stocked with fish to keep it algae free, provides water to irrigate all of the fields on the 140-acre complex. Other environmentally friendly features of the complex include the main stadium's thoughtful positioning, innovative grandstand roof, and terracotta shade screens that combine to minimize the amount of solar heat to which the park is exposed. Other features that contribute to Salt River Fields' environmentally friendly credentials are its 85 salvaged trees and cacti, which were uprooted from other locations and replanted on the grounds, and 2,400 new trees that provide a habitat to area critters. The complex's water and energy supplies also draw heavily from renewable sources.

From the very start, ballpark pilgrims have fawned over Salt River Fields at Talking Stick. Not only is the fan access to player workouts unparalleled, but the stadium provides its own delights. The grandstand, for example, treats fans to much more shade than is typical of Cactus League facilities. Other selling points include the larger than usual outfield berm, plentiful standing room, unique party areas, and a top-notch menu. After the Diamondbacks and Rockies combined to draw nearly 360,000 fans to 33 games in the park's inaugural year, *Ballpark Digest* named Salt River Fields at Talking Stick its "2011 Ballpark of the Year."

Further distinguishing Salt River Fields from its Cactus League brethren is its celebration of the Salt River Pima-Maricopa Indian Community (SRPMIC), which funded the entirety of the $100 million project. Unlike the other spring training fields in use today, no public financing contributed to the development and construction of Salt River Fields at Talking Stick. Built on Native American land that also houses a sprawling resort casino, a championship golf course, and other entertainment venues, the baseball complex may be the Native American community's first foray into the wonderful world of MLB stadium construction, but the people of this community were proud to cite a long and rich sporting history as they embarked on the spring training project. In fact, proponents of the ballpark adopted the slogan "Bringing Baseball Home," as the SRPMIC unveiled the Pima-Maricopa vision to build a baseball paradise on its reservation just east of Scottsdale.

As early as 2,000 years ago, ball games were taking place in the Americas. Centuries before Abner Doubleday, Alexander Cartwright or any of the other supposed "creators" of baseball would hold a bat or ball there were more than 200 ball courts in Arizona. Many of these have been unearthed by archaeologists. The Pima and Huhugam people, in particular, were ardent game players. They partook mainly in two games—a men's contest that resembled basketball and a women's sport that resembled field hockey. These, they staged on sunken courts, surrounded by walls and positioned so that crowds of people could watch. The games sometimes utilized hollow balls and sometimes solid ones that were made of rubber from the latex trees that grew in abundance in Mexico. The women's game utilized a stick that was made of a local wood like mesquite. The designers of Salt River Fields actually toured some of these ancient courts, including one within Casa Grande Ruins National Monument in nearby Coolidge, Arizona, to gain better perspective on how to incorporate Native American design features into their baseball grounds.

The plot of land upon which Salt River Fields at Talking Stick would come to reside had been home to a golf course. The course was leveled to make way for the baseball fields after the SRPMIC worked closely with the architectural firm HKS to draw up the ballpark blueprints. The grandstand's unique layered roof, in particular, is said to reflect the architecture once prevalent among the region's Native American people, who valued greatly whatever shaded spaces they could create. The jagged grandstand roof is probably the ballpark's trademark feature. It is actually composed of three different panels, each of which is sloped at a distinct angle from the others. This is so the structure, as a whole, will cast the maximum possible amount of shade on the seats below. Indeed, about three-quarters of the grandstand are shaded by the time the typical afternoon game reaches the middle innings.

In 2009, the Diamondbacks and Rockies both reached agreements with the SRPMIC to move their respective camps to the community grounds as soon as the facility could be built. Both clubs signed 20-year lease agreements that should keep them at Salt River Fields through at least 2030. Construction began in November of 2009, and by the spring of 2011 the complex was ready for play. On February 26, 2011, the Diamondbacks—occupying the third base dugout, and the Rockies—occupying the first base dugout, kicked off the Cactus League season. The Rockies won 8–7 before an overflow crowd of 12,514 cheering fans. Since then, over-capacity crowds have been the norm at this park that seats 7,000 in the comfortable green chairs of its grandstand and offers room for 4,000 more on its perfectly sloped outfield berm. The wide concourses and large standing areas in the outfield corners allow for the park to be full without feeling too crowded. Fans seated around the infield—particularly those in the unique Pepsi Patio high above the main seating area—enjoy sweeping views of Red Mountain, the Four Peaks and the Superstition Mountains beyond the outfield walls.

As for the name of the complex, the "Salt River" portion is easy enough to deduce; after all, the stadium and other fields sit within the Salt River Pima-Maricopa Indian Community. The "Talking Stick" part, though, needs a bit more explanation. For centuries a "Talking Stick" has been used by the Native American people as a way to record historical events and milestones. In the days before paper, the stick was especially important, serving as a sort of journal that could be passed down from one generation to the next. What exactly that has to do with baseball, may remain a bit of a mystery, but the idea of a Talking Stick invokes the image of an autographed or annotated baseball bat, which is something to which today's fans can surely relate.

Fans on the outfield lawn soak up the sun (courtesy Jim Tootle).

The official logo of the complex, which appears on area signage and is painted on the grass behind home plate, also has a rustic Native American appearance. At the same time, it reflects the identities of the two home teams. The outline framing the logo is a box. Inside the box, a jagged line rises from the lower left corner, as if to depict a desert mountain range. But then, as the "range" ends at the far right of the graphic, the line depicts a diamondback-shaped snake head. Thus, the logo offers nods to the mountain landscape familiar to Rockies fans, as well as to the rattlesnake familiar to Diamondbacks rooters. This ingenious design was crafted by a gentleman named Royce Manuel. The Pima artist currently maintains the SRPMIC's talking stick.

Further fusing the Native American reverence for the natural world with the identities of the Rockies and Diamondbacks are the practice field throughout the complex. The Rockies' fields are on the right or "Mountain" side of the grounds. These fields have names like Adobe, Wild Horse, and Red Clay. The Diamondbacks' fields are on the left or "Desert" side of the grounds. They sport names like Devil's Claw, Whirlwind, and Mesquite. Each team also enjoys the luxury of an 85,000-square-foot clubhouse. As for the ballpark gates, the most commonly used entrances are the ones in center, left and right field, while the entrance behind home plate is the most scenic — with its manmade lake and water display — but is not as close to the main parking lots as the other gates are.

Even those who are unable to attend Salt River Fields at Talking Stick during the spring might pay the park a visit during a stay at the adjoining Talking Stick Resort Casino. The ballpark is utilized throughout the calendar year for concerts and festivals, such as a popular Independence Day Music Festival. The Arizona Rookie League Diamondbacks and Rockies also use the field during the months of June throughout August. In the fall, the Salt River Rafters of the Arizona Fall League use the park.

Prior to arriving at the SRPMIC grounds, both the Diamondbacks and Rockies had spent the entirety of their relatively short spring histories in Tucson. Upon joining the National League as an expansion team in 1993, the Rockies moved into historic Hi Corbett Field. The Diamondbacks, who joined the Senior Circuit in 1998, spent their springs at Tucson Electric Park (later renamed: Kino Veterans Memorial Stadium). They shared the park with the White Sox until the Chicagoans departed for the Phoenix Valley in 2008. From 2011 through 2013, Kino Veterans Memorial Stadium housed the Triple-A Tucson Padres of the Pacific Coast League, while a new park was being considered for them in Escondido, California. Before that, the Tucson Sidewinders, a Diamondbacks affiliate in the Pacific Coast League, had used the park from 1998 through 2008.

Hi Corbett Field's history is far richer than Kino Veterans Memorial Stadium's, and its absence from the Cactus League has been more sorely felt. The ballpark was the spring home of the Cleveland Indians from 1947 through 1992. The park actually debuted as a professional facility in 1928, though, when the Arizona State League (ASL) was formed. The Tucson Cowboys joined the Bisbee Bees, Miami Miners

Tucson's Hi Corbett Field was a Cactus League mainstay from 1947 until 2010.

and Phoenix Senators to compose the first Arizona alliance recognized by the National Association of Baseball Leagues. In those early days Tucson's Randolph Municipal Baseball Park, as Hi Corbett was then known, was the finest diamond in Arizona. It was the only field that offered a grass infield, as the other clubs played on "scratch" diamonds consisting of gravel and hard-packed sand. After just three seasons, the ASL merged with the Texas League to form the Arizona-Texas League (also known as the Border Conference). Tucson placed a team in the new alliance throughout the next three decades. Meanwhile, Major League Baseball arrived in Tucson in 1947 when Indians owner Bill Veeck and New York Giants owner Horace Stoneham brought their teams to Arizona. Bob Feller was a member of the Indians at the time. As the team prepared to head west for the first time, he was one of several players to voice his excitement, stating that he "looked forward to training among the cowboys and the cactus." Feller later summed up the experience of training in Arizona in less enthusiastic terms, saying Tucson was "nothing but cottontails and rattlesnakes." Nonetheless, led by Feller and player-manager Mel Ott, the Indians won their first spring game in Arizona, beating the Giants 3–1 before 4,934 fans at Randolph Park on March 8, 1947. In total the Indians attracted 15,600 fans to seven games that spring. The Indians returned to Tucson for spring training every year afterward, until 1993 when they moved to Winter Haven, Florida.

Although the Indians didn't bring any African Americans to Arizona in 1947, historians often cite Veeck's desire to integrate his team as a factor in his decision to take his club west. The Southwest was considered a more tolerant racial environment than Florida's Deep South. Larry Doby joined the Indians during the 1947 regular season and Satchel Paige followed in 1948, and while they were later treated better in Arizona than they would have been in Florida, they still were not treated as equals among their white teammates. Each spring Doby and Paige found lodging with host families in Tucson's African American community, while their teammates stayed at the Santa Rita Hotel.

In 1951 Randolph Park was renamed Hi Corbett Field in honor of a ninth-generation Tucsonan named Hiram Steven Corbett (1886–1967). Corbett, who served five terms in the Arizona State Senate, was an avid sportsman who did much to promote the state's athletic interests.

In its later years as a Cactus League outpost, Hi Corbett Field was characterized by its distinctive Southwestern façade, the beige stucco of which was complemented by a clock tower above the ticket office. Inside, the patchwork seating bowl placed nearly all of the seats above the interior concourse. The majority of these were found around the infield in high-rising bleachers. Only the seats directly behind home plate were shaded by the small sunroof atop the press box. The stadium

The Camelback and McDowell Mountains rise in the distance to create a gorgeous backdrop for a game (courtesy Jim Tootle).

configuration looked very much like the type one would expect to find at a facility that had been enlarged gradually over a period of decades. Since 2012, Hi Corbett Field has served the University of Arizona Wildcats baseball team. The Pac-12 Conference school spent more than $200,000 to upgrade the field before moving into the city-owned stadium three miles south of its campus. The Wildcats capped their very first season at Hi Corbett by winning the 2012 College Baseball World Series.

Surely, today's Cactus League fans expect more modern amenities than clunky old Hi Corbett Field provided at the end of its long run. Likewise, fans of the spring game relish the convenience of having so many ballparks within close proximity of one another in the Phoenix Valley. As for those old-timers and traditionalists who lament the loss of Tucson from the Cactus League, there is at least some consolation to be had in the acknowledgement that it took a park as fine as Salt River Fields at Talking Stick to supplant the game's longtime home in Tucson.

GETTING TO THE PARK. Salt River Fields at Talking Stick is located just east of Scottsdale in Phoenix's East Valley. From North Phoenix, take I-17 South to 101 North. From Sky Harbor International Airport, take 202 East to 101 North. Then, take the Via De Ventura exit off the 101 and turn right. Turn left on Pima Road and the entrance to the Talking Stick Resort will soon appear. Another option is to take the 101 to the Indian Bend Road exit, and follow Indian Bend west to Pima Road. The stadium is visible from the 101, and the complex signage is plentiful, so it's pretty difficult to get lost. Parking on the paved lots and grass fields of the baseball complex costs $5.

SEATING. The Diamondbacks and Rockies draw more fans to Salt River Fields at Talking Stick than any other stadium-sharing duo draws during the Cactus League season. Although, the official capacity of the ballpark is 11,000, crowds typically approach 12,000 when the Diamondbacks are playing. The home-state favorites sold out 14 of their 16 home dates in 2012. The Rockies don't draw quite as well, but still manage to finish among the top handful of teams in the Cactus League in annual attendance. Through 2012, the largest crowd in Salt River Fields at Talking Stick history turned out on March 16, 2012 when 12,599 fans watched the Diamondbacks beat the White Sox, 4–2.

The ballpark offers five ticket categories in the lower bowl, and three different types of "party zone" seating on the press box level. Down in the main bowl, there are two tiers of seating, separated by a midlevel walkway. At field level, Section 101 is in right field foul territory, Section 112 is behind the plate, and Section 123 is in left field foul territory. Sections 109 through 115, between the dugouts, sell as Dugout Boxes, while the seats immediately behind the dugouts—Sections 104–108 on the first base line, and 116–120 on the third base line — sell as Dugout Reserve. There are 12 rows in the Infield Box sections, but due to the protrusion of the large dugouts, the Dugout Reserve sections offer just eight rows, beginning with Row 5.

Further down the lines, in shallow outfield foul territory, fans find the Baseline

The large roof over the grandstand makes Salt River Fields one of the friendliest parks in the Cactus League for those seeking shade (courtesy Jim Tootle).

Reserve (Sections 101–103 and 121–123). At many spring parks this is the place where the stadium designers and financiers opt to provide metal bleachers instead of seats. But at this park fans find the same comfortable green stadium chairs as in the rest of the grandstand.

The second tier of seating in the lower bowl is raised so that the traffic on the midlevel walkway does not interfere with views. There are 16 rows in this level, which includes sections that don't extend quite as far into the outfield as do the ones on the level below. All of the seats on this level sell as Infield Reserved, whether they're in shallow right field at Section 203, behind the plate in Section 212, or in shallow left field at Section 221.

Upstairs, the Pepsi Patio is located atop the press box. The Coors Light Zone (first base line) and Miller Light Zone (third base line) appear on either side of the press box. Only the pavilion-style seats of the Pepsi Patio are available to individual ticket buyers, while the other party zones are reserved for group functions.

The Berm seating area spans the outfield except in dead center, offering room for 4,000. Many fans planning to sit in this part of the park bring blankets. Courteously, stadium management provides fans with SPF-30 sunscreen via dispensers located atop the Berm.

THE BALLPARK EXPERIENCE. Unlike many Cactus League facilities, Salt River Fields at Talking Stick encourages fans to arrive early and stay late. The ballpark gates open two hours before game-time so that fans can watch the home team finish taking batting practice, then watch the visitors take their swats if they so choose. The players of both home teams sign autographs at field level before and after games, but the Diamondbacks go one step further when they're the home team, offering a daily pregame autograph session on the left field concourse. Typically two players sign, beginning an hour and fifteen minutes before the first pitch.

The ballpark caters to families with young children, offering a Wiffle ball field and other attractions on the right field concourse. The typical spring also sees some older kids visit Salt River Fields at Talking Stick en masse as well. Several Denver-area high school baseball teams visit the complex to play early season games and watch the big leaguers. On game-day, they usually sit on the Berm, wearing their uniform jerseys. In 2012 the Ponderosa Mustangs of Parker, Colorado were one such team to visit; they cheered wildly when Todd Helton hit not one, but two home runs in a game against the Reds.

Another highlight of the 2012 spring season was the presence of the ageless Jamie Moyer in Rockies camp. The 49-year-old lefty made the Colorado roster and won two games to become the oldest pitcher to ever win a regular season game, before he was released in May.

The highlights of the Salt River Fields concession menu include a specialty hot dog stand behind Section 213 that has seven types of hot dog with all different toppings. The Chicago Dog is a favorite, as is the Arizona Dog, which is actually a bison wiener, topped by green chili peppers and chopped onions. Fans also enjoy a gourmet pizza courtesy of Crust, a popular local chain. Also popular is the Mexican food from Salty Senorita, the Sausage and Meatball Sandwiches from Hungry Hill (just like they have at Chase Field in Phoenix), the Sweet Potato Fries, Italian Ice, Chocolate Coated Berry Skewers, Kettle Corn and Cold Stone Ice Cream. The Chocolate Chip Cookies doled out by a colorful vendor who roams the grandstand are also excellent. Dos Equis and Devil's Ale highlight the beer list.

ON THE TOWN. The **Talking Stick Resort** offers a casino, golf course and various other entertainment venues and restaurants that many fans visit during their tours of the Cactus League. Room rates at the resort are surprisingly affordable. Guests enjoy access to a free trolley that shuttles them to and from the ballpark on game-day. For gamblers, the Casino has Poker, Keno, Slot Machines and the full array of Table Games. For those interested in learning more about the local Native American heritage, the lobby of the Talking Stick Resort doubles as a **Cultural Center**, showcasing pottery, tapestries, and other artwork made by the Pima-Maricopa people. Talking Stick also offers a wealth of old Arizona photos and artwork throughout the resort. The restaurant options range from fine-dining at the

Orange Sky, to twenty-four-hour casual at the **Blue Coyote,** to club scene at **Degree 270.**

Fans looking to enjoy the nearby **Salt River** will find a number of river rafting companies ready to assist. The river has its rapid areas and also its calmer stretches as it cuts through the Sonoran Desert.

Tempe Diablo Stadium

(Tempe) Los Angeles Angels of Anaheim

Tempe Diablo Stadium
2200 West Alameda Drive, Tempe
480–858–7500
http://www.tempe.gov/index.aspx?page=573&recordid=267
http://losangeles.angels.mlb.com
Opened: 1968. Renovated: 2005. Seating Capacity: 9,558
• 7 miles north to Phoenix (A's)
• 10 miles north to Scottsdale (Giants)
• 12 miles east to Mesa (Cubs)
• 15 miles west to Maryvale (Brewers)

Tempe Diablo Stadium once seemed destined to go the way of most other early-generation Cactus League facilities. Surely, it was supposed by some spring observers, it would fade into obscurity as the big league game passed it by in favor of more modern facilities. But a timely renovation in 2005 staved off the park's extinction. The $20 million project updated the stadium to meet the expectations of today's fan, while vastly expanding the surrounding practice complex. Concurrent with this work, the Angels, who have played at Tempe Diablo Stadium since 1993, signed a new lease extension that will keep them in town through at least 2025. Thus, one of the Arizona Circuit's most inviting and intimate ballparks was preserved for another generation of snowbirds to enjoy.

Just as has been the case been since the park hosted its first spring team — the Seattle Pilots— in 1969, the rustic desert rock formations known as the "Tempe Buttes" form the perfect backdrop for a game. One of the buttes towers behind the third base grandstand, another rises behind the left field foul pole, while still another sits beyond left-center field. An American flag flies atop the dome-shaped butte behind the foul pole, and usually fans turn to face it during the pre-game singing of the National Anthem, rather than the much lower flag on the pole in center field. The ritzy Marriott Buttes Resort—visible high above the field in left-center—is

Tempe Diablo Stadium originally opened as home to the Seattle Pilots in 1969 (courtesy Tempe Diablo Stadium).

built into the side of one of the buttes, and is visible from the ballpark seats. Other than at Phoenix Municipal Stadium, there isn't a more scenic backdrop for a game in the Grand Canyon State. Nor is there a more fitting one; the buttes represent Arizona's image as a brambles-and-rock desert state quite well. Sure, the Camelback Mountain peaks visible from the seats at Scottsdale Stadium are impressive too, but those are off in the distance. As is also the case at "Phoenix Muni," at Tempe Diablo the rocky landscape is up-close and encompassing, thus making it all the more breathtaking.

The Angels, of course, should feel right at home playing in a park where rock formations adorn the outfield. After all, the team's regular season home, Angels Stadium of Anaheim, features a fake rock formation known as the "California Spectacular" beyond the fence in left-center. That rocky landscape was erected inside the ballpark back when the Walt Disney Company owned the Angels in the 1990s. In Tempe, the buttes—which are actually volcanic rock formations—are natural, making them far more amazing.

Another aspect of the Tempe experience that should remind road-trippers of Anaheim is the horrendous traffic fans face on game-day. The roads that access Tempe Diablo Stadium become quite congested before and after games. Further evoking a game in California's Orange County, just as Anaheim fans can see the local freeway running beyond the outfield fence, fans in Tempe watch cars pass on

I-10, otherwise known as the Maricopa Freeway, beyond Tempe Diablo Stadium's right field fence.

As for the ballpark itself, Tempe Diablo Stadium is quite handsome. It has a dark red brick façade, which is complemented by green trim and beige stucco. A product of the most recent renovation, the façade also sports a gigantic halo-encircled "A" atop the main entrance. This design element is reminiscent, of course, of the "Big A" that stands outside Angels Stadium of Anaheim. While in Anaheim the "Big A" is the highest object to be found in the parking lot, in Tempe the stadium itself towers over the small lot behind the grandstand. Fans traverse a wide stairway to reach the ballpark and pass through its gates. The stairs actually take the form of three staircases set side-by-side and these are lined with large flower beds that sprout an assortment of red flowers on each landing.

The Arizona Sports and Tourism Authority funded the majority of the 2005 renovation, contributing $12 million to the project. Most importantly from the Angels' point of view, the work outfitted the 75-acre complex behind the stadium with four new practice fields. Previous to the opening of the quartet of diamonds, which are arranged in a cloverleaf pattern, the Angels' big leaguers had practiced on the two pre-existing fields near the parking lot, while their minor leaguers had trained at a completely separate facility in Mesa. Since the debut of the renovated complex in January of 2006, however, the entire Angels organization has enjoyed a spring home in Tempe.

Even after the renovation, the stadium looks newer on the outside than within. As part of the renovation, much of the park was reseated in 2005. Not only were new seats added at field level between the dugouts, but comfortable green stadium seats were installed in the infield sections, to replace the old aluminum seats and aluminum bleachers that had previously appeared. Even after the work, though, the park still sports bleacher benches with backs in the sections past the first and third base bags. A grass seating berm begins in shallow left field foul territory and wraps around the foul pole to continue nearly all the way into center.

Excepting the luxury boxes above the concourse on the first base side, all of the seats at Tempe Diablo are located below the concourse. This makes for some great sight lines. The concourse is covered by a trellised green sunroof. The walkway is narrow and usually crowded, especially when fans seeking sun-relief leave their seats for the shady area where standing is allowed at the back of the path. There is a white line painted onto the concourse that demarcates where standing is allowed and where the concourse should be left clear for pedestrians.

The outfield fence measures 367 feet from home plate down the right field line, 340 feet down the left field line, 400 feet in the power-alleys, and 420 feet in dead-center. It's nice that the field is smallest in left, since that allows fans seated on the berm a closer view of the infield than they'd enjoy otherwise. The Angels use the first base dugout and their bullpen sits largely out-of-sight behind the fence in right. The visitors use the third base dugout, and their bullpen is in left field foul territory, leaving room for fans to enjoy the area behind the fence in left on the berm. These design choices make the berm a great place to watch the game, even if it positions fans looking toward the midday sun, and even if it doesn't provide the view of the buttes that the infield seating areas do.

Like the low seating bowl and low press box, the light poles and foul poles contribute to the park's delightful old-timey atmosphere. Silver metal poles rise to support tiny light banks that offer just three rows of bulbs. As for the yellow foul poles, they measure only about three inches in diameter and rise only about 15 feet, well below regular season standards. The scoreboard/video screen can be found above the fence in right-center. Several skinny palms flank the board, but fail to block the view of traffic on I-10. The protective screen behind home plate is of the modern variety that rises straight and does not continue back to the press box; thus foul pops fall into the stands for fans to claim.

Tempe Diablo Stadium debuted as the spring home of the expansion Seattle Pilots on March 7, 1969. The Pilots beat the Cleveland Indians 19–3 that day before a crowd of barely 1,000 fans. Although the Pilots moved to Milwaukee and became the Brewers at the conclusion of the following spring, they first spent one final March in Tempe as the Pilots. The franchise then continued training in Tempe in 1971 and 1972, before moving to Sun City, Arizona. When Seattle was awarded a

Rocky buttes rise along the left side of the stadium (courtesy Tempe Diablo Stadium).

second expansion team in 1977, the Mariners made Tempe their preseason home. The Seattleites stayed through the 1992 spring, before moving to a brand new complex in Peoria. Even today, a contingent of Mariners fans remains in Tempe, and turns out to support the Seattle club whenever it visits.

The Angels' arrival in Tempe coincided with the completion of a $5.8 million renovation to Tempe Diablo Stadium, two-thirds of which was funded by Maricopa County. The rest was paid for by the city of Tempe. Groundbreaking for the remade park took place on April 22, 1992. The following spring the former "Tempe Stadium" was dedicated to the Diablos, a local civic organization that staffs the park with friendly ushers and raises money for and rallies interest in the spring game. That first renovation enlarged the concourse and added the sunroof over the concourse. The work also expanded the concession and bathroom areas, remodeled the ballpark exterior, added a new home clubhouse in right field, and installed the infield seats that were replaced by the more recent renovation.

In March of 1995, Tempe Diablo Stadium made national news when the very first "replacement players" of the Major League Baseball work-stoppage appeared in an exhibition game between the Angels and Arizona State University. In 1999, the stadium was the scene of a freak injury when Angels shortstop Gary DiSarcina suffered a broken arm when he was accidentally struck by a bat swung by an Angels coach. In 2002, the Angels and San Diego Padres found themselves embroiled in a bench-clearing brawl at the park. Not only were several Angels suspended as a result of the fracas, but pitcher Dennis Cook opened the season on the disabled list due to a rib injury suffered during the incident. In 2012, Tempe saw larger and more enthusiastic crowds than usual, as the fervor surrounding Angels' free-agent acquisitions Albert Pujols and C.J. Wilson was the talk of the Cactus League.

Before training in Tempe, the Angels kept one of the more unusual spring schedules. Dating back to the organization's inception in 1961, the team had played its spring games in Palm Springs at a park known as Angels Stadium (later named the Polo Grounds). The Angels would spend the majority of the spring in the Los Angeles suburb, but would follow I-10 east into Arizona for a prolonged road-trip each March. Toward the end of their years in Palm Springs, the Angels would play road games in Arizona for the first two weeks of spring training, and then return to Palm Springs where each Cactus League team would visit them for a two-game series. The team's park in Palm Springs was a small stadium with an open wooden press box behind home plate. The outfield was ringed by palms and offered views of the San Jacinto Mountains. Because the stands were so close to home plate, a protective screen spanned nearly the entire infield and gradually sloped back to the press box, forcing fans to watch the game from inside a chicken-wire cage.

From 1966 to 1979, the Angels split each spring between Palm Springs and Holtville, California, where they utilized a four-diamond complex. Holtville was not far from where the Padres trained in Yuma, Arizona, making for plenty of exhibitions between the two teams.

In 1982 and 1983, the Angels spent half the spring in Palm Springs and half in

Fans watch the game from luxury boxes on the first base side of the press box, 1969 (courtesy Tempe Diablo Stadium).

Casa Grande, Arizona, making use of a baseball complex originally developed by San Francisco Giants owner Horace Stoneham in the 1950s. From 1984 to 1992, the Angels split time between Palm Springs and Gene Autry Park in Mesa. The team finally cut ties with Palm Springs in 1993, choosing to operate its big league camp in Tempe and its minor league camp in Mesa.

Today, the Angels' big leaguers and minor leaguers alike enjoy a modern spring training workout complex in Tempe. At the same time, visiting fans enjoy a stadium that provides a quaint and intimate ballpark experience. Fans looking to enjoy a taste of spring ball as it existed in Arizona in an earlier era would be wise to set their sights on Tempe Diablo Stadium.

GETTING TO THE PARK. From I-10, take the Broadway exit and follow Broadway West, then turn south on 48th Street. The complex is at the intersection of 48th Street and Alameda Drive. Early arrivals find street parking in the industrial park across Alameda Drive from the stadium. Lot parking is available behind the home plate grandstand and beyond the right field fence. Those who park on the street are able to avoid some of the post-game traffic.

Another option is to take advantage of the Angels Spring Training Trolley.

The city of Tempe provides free parking and free ride passes to baseball fans. The trolley picks up fans at the corner of Mill Avenue and 5th Street and drops them off at the corner of 52nd Street and Campus Drive. The free parking is available at City Hall Garage (117 East 5th Street), Centerpoint Parking Garage (730 South Ash Avenue) and Hayden Station Garage (3rd Street & Ash). To avoid a charge, fans must present a valid current-day ticket stub to Tempe Diablo Stadium upon departing the garage.

SEATING. Tempe Diablo Stadium offers a low seating bowl containing 26 rows. The rows are marked A through Z, beginning with A at field level. Capacity is listed at just 9,558, making this one of only two ballparks in the Cactus League to hold fewer than 10,000 fans; the other is Phoenix Municipal Stadium, which has a capacity of 8,500. In Tempe, the majority of the seats offer great views. Unfortunately, the seats are not very well shaded though, and more than half of them take the form of less-than-entirely-comfortable metal bleachers. These are basically benches with back supports. Only about 3,200 of the "seats" take the form of the comfortable stadium chairs installed in 2005. Another 3,500 "seats" exist as bleachers. The rest of the fans use the left field seating berm. It could be worse, though,

Fans enjoy the game from the outfield berm.

and prior to the 2005 renovation it was. Until that time, even the stadium chairs were made of uncomfortable metal instead of molded plastic. The ushers are friendly older folks who represent the Diablos quite well in making fans feel welcome.

Section 12 is directly behind home plate, while Section 1—which abuts the seating berm in left — is located just a bit past third base. In right field foul territory, meanwhile, the bleachers continue much farther down the line, before ending with Section 24 near the foul pole.

Games against the Cubs and Giants usually sell out, while the Mariners also draw well as prodigal sons come home to visit their former home in Tempe. Ticket scalpers congregate on 48th Street, Broadway and Alameda Drive, usually asking not much more than face value.

The seats in Sections 5–17 are actual seats, and sell as Homeplate MVP seats or Field MVP seats, depending upon their proximity to home plate and to the front of the section. Sections 5 and 6 are behind the visitors' dugout on the third base side, while Sections 16 and 17 are behind the Angels' dugout. The rest of the seats take the form of aluminum bleachers. The generously-named Field Box seats, are located in shallow left (Sections 1–4) and shallow right (Sections 18–22). The Grandstand seats, meanwhile, appear even farther down the line in right (Sections 23 and 24). The Lawn begins in medium-depth left field foul territory and wraps around the foul pole, continuing into left-center.

A picnic area behind the lawn seating along the left field line offers tables with umbrellas that are available on a first-come, first-served basis.

THE BALLPARK EXPERIENCE. The asphalt parking lot behind the main stadium provides a place where fans can fire up hibachis, crack open cold beverages, and toss around the old pigskin or horsehide, even if signs installed in the lot say tailgating is prohibited. Some people sit in lawn chairs facing the Angels' practice fields while eating burgers and soaking up the sun. Others sit by their cars. It's not hard to pick out the road-trippers from California; besides having California license plates, their cars often have Rally Monkeys or Angels banners affixed to the antennas.

Fans are allowed to stand right next to the chain-link fence that surrounds the practice fields and outdoor batting cages where players prepare for the game. Most fans in search of a souvenir wait for batting practice homers to fly over the fence into the parking lot. Others wait on Alameda Drive. Fans also wait for pre-game autographs or photo opportunities along the temporary metal fence that bisects the parking lot to form a pathway through which Angels players and coaches walk when transitioning from the practice area to the stadium.

Once inside, fans may pay homage to the late Gene Autry by visiting the bust of the former Angels owner on the first base side of the concourse. The sculpture depicts Autry wearing his trademark cowboy hat and neckerchief. A plaque below reads: "Gene Autry's career has spanned more than 60 years in the entertainment

Fans line up to greet Angels' manager Mike Scioscia as he walks from a practice field to the stadium.

industry, a career that has encompassed every facet of the business from radio and recording artist to motion picture star, television star, broadcast executive and Major League Baseball owner. His great love for baseball prompted him to acquire the expansion Los Angeles Angels in 1960."

Speaking of the "Singing Cowboy," Autry's hit song "Back in the Saddle Again" plays through the stadium public address system after every Angels' win.

There is a plaque on the concourse behind home plate, which reads: "Tempe Diablos. In honor of their silver anniversary and in deep appreciation for the 25 years of dedicated support for Cactus League Baseball in Tempe, the city of Tempe salutes the Tempe Diablos. In recognition of their outstanding contributions and countless hours of voluntary service as well as financial support, this stadium facility has been designated Tempe Diablo Stadium. February 27, 1993. By Mayor Harry E. Mitchell."

As for ballpark treats, the prices are a bit high, but the quality is good. Best of all, the fare is grilled right on site. Highlights include the Bigger Better Burger, which is a half-pound bacon cheeseburger, and the Blazin' Burger, which comes topped with jalapenos and Monterey Jack cheese. Either fistful of beef can be combined with Garlic Fries and a drink via the stadium combo deal. Vegetarians will appreciate the Mushroom Sandwich, while carnivores will likely respond with a disgruntled, "yuck!" The Gelato makes for a nice dessert or palate-cleanser between burgers. As for the beer selection, discriminating fans will find Full Sail, Red Hook and Fat Tire on tap.

ON THE TOWN. Tempe is a college town that offers visiting fans a full complement of pubs and southwest style restaurants. Unfortunately none of these are located in the neighborhood surrounding the baseball park. The landscape near Tempe Diablo Stadium projects more of an office park meets freeway vibe. Perhaps this is why Tempe Diablo Stadium enjoys one of the more active tailgating traditions in the Cactus League. Those wishing to check out the **Arizona State University** campus will find its main drag just a mile or so northeast of Tempe Diablo Stadium. Follow Alameda Drive East and take a left on Mill Avenue and that will take you into the heart of the university district. Favorite university district watering holes include **Tavern on Mill** (404 S. Mill Avenue), **Devil's Advocate Bar and Grill** (955 E. University Drive), and **Four Peaks Brewery** (1340 E. 8th Street) but there are literally dozens of bars and restaurants in the area from which visiting fans may choose.

HoHoKam Stadium

(Mesa) Chicago Cubs

HoHoKam Stadium
1235 North Center Street, Mesa
480–964–4467
http://hohokamstadium.com/
http://chicago.cubs.mlb.com
Opened: 1977. Rebuilt: 1997. Seating Capacity: 12,632
• 10 miles west to Phoenix (A's)
• 11 miles north to Scottsdale (Giants)
• 12 miles east to Tempe (Angels)
• 13 miles north to Salt River Fields (Diamondbacks and Rockies)

THE CUBS, WHO have played at HoHoKam Stadium since 1979, are due to open a new $99 million spring training complex five miles west of their present home in 2014, barring any construction delays. Shortly after the Cubs move to their new Mesa home, it seems likely that another team will move into spacious and pleasantly located HoHoKam Stadium. After being completely rebuilt prior to the spring of 1997, the park surely has some life remaining as a Cactus League facility. As of this book's publication date, though, it was unclear exactly who would move into the park, which sits beside a cemetery in a residential neighborhood. The Oakland A's were one team rumored to be mulling a move to HoHoKam, though the City of Phoenix was blocking Mesa's efforts to secure an $8 million grant from the Arizona Sports and Tourism Authority that would be used to eliminate several of the bleacher sections down the park's right and left field lines and replace them with festive party decks, and to otherwise update the park in advance of the A's proposed arrival in 2015. Phoenix wished to extend its own lease with the A's, which was set to expire after the spring of 2014.

Such games of musical chairs have been common to the spring game since its earliest days, of course. One city tries to lure a team away from another, while neither the prospective city nor the soon-to-be-abandoned one ever quite knows whether the baseball team in question wants to relocate or is just trying to shake

From the street, HoHoKam Stadium resembles a scaled down version of a regular season park.

as many facility-upgrades as possible out of its current landlord before re-upping its lease. In any case, HoHoKam Stadium will almost certainly remain a Cactus League outpost after the Cubs depart. Thus, it receives full treatment in this book. For Cubs fans, this chapter also provides a forward-looking description of the new Mesa ballpark the Cubs will soon inhabit.

It is somewhat ironic that the Cubs, who have historically played at one of the smallest regular season ballparks on the North Side of Chicago, have played for years at one of the largest spring training venues in Mesa. The new park that Mesa is building for the Cubs is even bigger ... and for good reason: the Cubs led all major league teams in spring training attendance every season between 1985 and 2002. After the Giants outdrew them by just 26 fans in 2003, the Cubs reclaimed the spring attendance title in 2004, attracting 189,692 fans to 16 games (11,855 per game) to set a new spring training record. That mark was narrowly broken by the Cubs and their fans the very next spring, before the Cubs and their fans set the bar still higher, when the Cubs drew 203,105 fans to 19 home dates in 2009. By the end of the 2012 spring season, however, the Cubs had slipped to fourth in the Cactus League, drawing a respectable 9,580 fans per game. Apparently many Chicagoans, who had visited HoHoKam in the past, had decided to save their travel kitty for the spring of 2014 when the new Mesa ballpark opens.

Those who continue to turn out at HoHoKam in the Cubs' final years at the park find a festive game-day atmosphere offering more than just a few touches and flavors of the Wrigley experience. Even before arriving at HoHoKam, fans are reminded of the game-day atmosphere in Chicago. Just like in Wrigleyville, the parking facilities in Mesa are too few, and fans must venture into the nearby neighborhoods in search of a place to leave their road-trip cars. Street signs make it clear that visitors who parallel park on the residential streets surrounding the park will be towed or ticketed, although parking on the lawns of area homes is perfectly acceptable ... for a fee, of course. Because sell-outs are common, ticket scalpers do a lucrative business in the streets near the stadium too.

HoHoKam Stadium is more impressive inside than it is outside. It is surrounded by an asphalt parking lot on one side, and grass soccer fields that double as game-day parking areas on the other. Although the structure is quite large, its façade was not designed to inspire awe. The exterior is composed of tan stucco that rises to meet a brown metal roof. Right angles dominate the utilitarian design, eschewing the arches and fancy brickwork that adorn some of the newer spring stadiums. Likewise, the ballpark grounds are neither impressive nor offensive. They're pleasant, if a tad crowded.

After passing through the gates, fans encounter a fully covered concourse that is more similar to the type found at old-time major league stadiums like Wrigley Field or Fenway Park than at spring training parks. HoHoKam honors great players that have played on its grounds, with banners that hang above this concourse. There are also banners recognizing each of the current Cactus League teams. Each league member's name appears on a banner that reflects its team uniform — green for the Oakland A's, orange for the San Francisco Giants, black for the Chicago White Sox, and so on.

Although the concourse is wide, it tends to clog with fans just before the game begins. The clubhouse shops, behind third base and home plate, are also crowded with fans. People arrive at the ballpark in a happy mood, and tend to have fun. As at Wrigley, it is a tradition at HoHoKam for fans to put their all into the nightly singing of "Take Me Out to the Ballgame." The Mesa rendition is led each day by one lucky fan who finds the microphone thrust upon him, regardless of whether he can carry a tune or not.

The one-level press box and six accompanying luxury boxes are located above the home plate grandstand. The press box is composed of tan bricks, while its windows are surrounded by dark brown metal trim. The same tan bricks line the interior walkway that bisects the seating bowl. The infield seats take the form of green stadium chairs on both the first level and second level. Past the corner bags, though, the seats take the form of bleachers with backs on both levels. In home-run territory, fans find inviting outfield seating lawns. Beyond these berms, off in the distance, mountains rise to create a lovely backdrop for a game.

As for the field, it measures 350 feet to the foul pole in right, 410 feet to straight-away center, and 340 feet to the pole in left. The outfield gaps measure 390 feet from the plate. On the left field berm fans find a digital scoreboard that features a large video screen. In center field, a home-plate-shaped building forms the batter's eye. The longest side of the building is painted green to provide an ideal backdrop for hitting, while the sides and point of the pentagon protrude back into the outfield seating area to offer bathrooms and concession counters.

The bullpens appear in right field home run territory, tiered so that they run parallel to the outfield fence. The home team's pen is closest to the field of play, while the visitors' is raised about three feet above it. Thanks to a stretch of chain-link fence that interrupts the green padding that otherwise encircles the field, fans in the grandstand enjoy a clear view of both pens. The home dugout is on the first base line.

HoHoKam Stadium, in its present form, opened in 1997.

Beyond the park in center field, sits a practice field. In right, meanwhile, there resides a practice infield, a batting cage, and a 14,000-square-foot clubhouse. The Cubs also have a larger main practice complex a mile south of the stadium. The team's Fitch Park has four full practice diamonds, a practice infield, and a clubhouse that accommodates up to 200 players. The satellite campus was constructed following the spring of 1996 at the same time HoHoKam Stadium was being rebuilt.

The new HoHoKam opened in 1997. Immediately after the 1996 Cactus League season had ended, the old HoHoKam had been leveled, and the new stadium — designed by the acclaimed ballpark architects at HOK Sport — was built in its footprint. In addition to the Cactus League Cubs, the new HoHoKam has served as home to the Mesa Cubs of the Arizona Rookie League, and to the Mesa Solar Sox of the Arizona Fall League. In 2002 the Arizona State University Sun Devils played their home games at HoHoKam, while Packard Stadium underwent a renovation. HoHoKam is also the annual site of the Western Athletic Conference (WAC) baseball tournament each May. The double-elimination tourney determines which WAC team will receive an automatic bid to the NCAA Division 1 Baseball Tournament.

The original HoHoKam Park had opened in 1977 to replace Rendezvous Park as spring home of the Oakland A's, who had arrived in Mesa in 1969. The Cubs had played in Mesa from 1952 to 1965, before departing to spend the 1966 season in Long Beach, California. Then, they moved to Scottsdale in 1967. They remained in Scottsdale through the 1978 Cactus League season, before swapping sites with the A's in 1979. During the Cubs' second stint in Mesa, old HoHoKam Park was expanded often, as the city tried to accommodate the ever-growing horde of visitors. Finally the park could be renovated no longer, and so, the new one was built at a cost of $18 million.

As for old Rendezvous Park, it originally opened in 1920. The grounds surrounding it included a swimming pool and facilities for the Mesa parks department. Its 3,000 seats took the form of wooden plank bleachers in the grandstand and folding chairs in the box sections. The park was razed following the 1976 spring season.

The Cubs were originally lured to Mesa by Dwight W. Patterson, a Mesa rancher who served as Chief Big Ho of the Mesa HoHoKams. The civic organization originated in 1951 under Patterson's leadership, naming itself after the agriculturally-based tribe of Native Americans that inhabited the Salt River Valley from around the time of the birth of Christ until the 15th century AD, at which time records of its existence abruptly disappear. In the language of the Pima tribe, the words Ho Ho Kam roughly translate to "those who vanished." For more than 60 years however, the Mesa HoHoKams have refused to vanish or waiver in their support of Major League Baseball.

Before Patterson and the 35 other original HoHoKams convinced Cubs owner Philip K. Wrigley to bring his club to Mesa in 1952, the Oakland Oaks of the Pacific Coast League had trained in Mesa. The Cubs actually had visited Mesa in 1950 to play an exhibition series against the Oaks at Rendezvous Park.

Today, the HoHoKam group continues to exist as a highly successful volunteer organization that staffs the ballpark's parking, concession, and seating areas. HoHoKam volunteers are friendly and helpful. The playing field in Mesa is named "Dwight W. Patterson Field."

Prior to joining the Giants and Indians in the fledgling Cactus League in 1952, the Cubs had spent the majority of their spring history secluded on a Pacific island. From 1921 to 1951, the Chicago team trained on 76-square-mile Santa Catalina Island, except for the World War II years when the Cubs trained in French Lick, Indiana. William Wrigley, Jr. acquired majority interest in the largely undeveloped terrain off the coast of Los Angeles in 1919, hoping to turn it into a resort. Wrigley installed streetlights and sewers, and constructed hotels, dance halls and casinos. But the onset of the Great Depression doomed the island's prospects as a tourist destination. Santa Catalina did, however, provide the Cubs with one of the most unique spring camps the game has ever known. The island featured a practice field — named Wrigley Field — that matched the exact field dimensions of Chicago's Wrigley Field. Even the famous Waveland Avenue rooftop viewing decks were replicated by patios built into a mountainside overlooking the field. Each spring Cubs players ran along trails that had been made by wild goats, then soothed their feet with fresh Eucalyptus, which grew on the island. A few weeks before the regular season, the Cubs would return to the mainland to play major league teams in California's Orange League and minor league teams that trained out west. Today, the Wrigley Mausoleum is on Santa Catalina Island. And in recent years the island has become the tourist hotbed the chewing gum magnate once envisioned.

In 1937, a radio station in Des Moines, Iowa sent a young reporter named Ronald Reagan out west with the Cubs to cover the team's camp on the island. After covering the workouts, Reagan accompanied the team to Los Angeles where the Cubs played several exhibition games. It was during that trip to LA that Reagan first auditioned for Hollywood. Shortly thereafter, he gave up sports broadcasting and became an actor.

In their long history, the Cubs have only spent one four-year stint in Florida. They played in Tampa from 1913 to 1916. They also trained in New Orleans (1907, 1911–1912), Vicksburg (1908), Hot Springs (1909–1910) and Pasadena (1917–1921).

If all goes according to plan, in 2014 the Cubs will move into a new park in Mesa. A groundbreaking ceremony for the stadium-to-be-named-later took place in July 2012, in hopes that that the field would be ready by January 2014. Located on the former site of the Riverview Golf Course, within Mesa's Riverview Park, the new complex carries an estimated construction cost of $84 million. The project is

From the 200-level seats, fans enjoy sweeping views of the Superstition Mountains.

being funded almost entirely by the City of Mesa, which in 2010 passed a city proposition to provide up to $99 million for the park and its surrounding infrastructure. The baseball grounds will be accessible from Mesa's Eighth Street, and will span from roughly Dobson Road to the Loop 101 area. The new ballpark was designed by Populous—formerly HOK Sport—and will seat between 15,000 and 16,000 people. It will likely also serve the Arizona State University Sun Devils baseball team in some capacity although the details of a proposed partnership between the Cubs and Sun Devils were still being negotiated at the time of this edition's publication.

According to the lease agreement the Cubs signed as part of the ballpark construction plan, they will continue to play in Mesa through at least 2043. Their lease also offers options that could extend their stay for another 20 years. As part of the agreement, Mesa has committed to periodically make capital improvements to the stadium and surrounding facilities to meet the ever-changing demands of players and fans.

The seating bowl at the new park will offer comfortable green stadium chairs for about 12,000 fans, while the outfield berm and luxury boxes will seat another 3,000. The seating bowl will be below a wide concourse that encircles the field and offers views of the game. The press/luxury level will hover over the back rows of seats and front of the concourse, and will be accessible from stairways on the concourse. Not only will the complex include seven and a half practice fields on the third-base side, but plans were being developed to build a 6-acre dining and shopping district immediately outside the stadium's first-base side, to be known as "Wrigleyville West." Additionally, a 25-acre plot that abuts the baseball complex was being considered by Cubs ownership for the development of a posh resort that would cater to visiting fans and convention-goers.

The Cubs have been one of the top draws in the Cactus League throughout their time at HoHoKam Stadium. And no doubt they will continue to pack fans into the seats once they move to their new park. Here's betting they will break their own all-time Cactus League attendance record—and by a hefty margin—during their first season at the Riverview Park grounds.

Getting to the Park. HoHoKam Stadium is located a mile and a half north of Mesa's Main Street. From I-10, follow Route 60/Superstition Freeway to Route 87/Country Club Drive North, then turn right on Brown Road, and then turn left on North Center Street. The stadium is right beside the City of Mesa Cemetery. The paved parking lot is usually reserved for season-ticket holders. Earlier arriving fans also find spots on the stadium's grass fields. Many visitors also park in privately-owned driveways and front yards on East 14th Street, Center Street, and Brown Street. Those who park at these satellite lots may make use of bicycle taxis that patrol the streets before and after games. Young entrepreneurs tow two-person carts with ten-speeds, helping less energetic fans to the stadium. For those staying in Mesa, Routes 104 and 120 of the Valley Metro Bus system provide service to the ballpark.

Fans wishing to visit the new Mesa ballpark should head to Riverview Park (2100 West 8th Street) in the city's northwest quadrant. The park is conveniently located near the convergence of the 101 and 202 freeways.

SEATING. HoHoKam Stadium offers 8,000 fixed seats, and bleacher and lawn space for about 4,500 people. There are also six luxury boxes. During the first decade of the 21st Century, when Cubs' fervor was running high, only Lawn and Standing Room tickets were available at the box office on game day, but more recently fans have found a limited number of seats on sale as well. The ticket scalpers are easy to identify, as they hold signs that read, "I Need Tickets," or "Box Seats for Sale."

Sections 100 and 200 are directly behind home plate in their respective levels with odd numbered sections continuing down the right field line and even numbered sections continuing down the left field line. The aisle seat of each row is embossed with a picture of a white baseball set against a blue sky with a brown mountain range rising in the background. The placards that display the number of each section also offer raised dots to convey the same information in Braille.

The Field Boxes (Sections 100–116) are at field level on the infield. Most of these sections offer Rows A–N, but the ones behind the dugouts begin with Row C. The shadow of the press box provides afternoon shade to those in Sections 100–106.

The Terrace Boxes (Sections 200–212) are located above the midlevel walkway. Section 211 is midway down the first base line, while Section 212 is midway down the third base line. The trellised roof shades Rows AA–RR in all of these sections.

The Terrace seats are aluminum bleachers with backs. They are around the infield on the 200-level (Sections 213–218), and in outfield foul territory on the 100-level (Sections 117–124). The 200-level seats are covered by the roof.

The Patio Bleachers are on the 200-level in either outfield corner. These structures are separate from the main seating bowl. Sections 219–227 appear in deep right field, and Sections 220–228 appear in deep left, offering Rows AA–RR.

The Grandstand Bleachers (309–317) were added prior to the 2009 season in an area that previously served as standing room. They can be found above the 200-Level on the first base side, offering three rows (A–C) per section. Section 309 is even with the Cubs' on-deck circle, while Section 317 is aligned with the spot where the infield dirt meets the outfield grass, just past first base.

General Admission ticket holders sit on the outfield Lawn. The left field berm is sloped at a more dramatic pitch than the right field lawn. When the Lawn gates open, fans usually rush to claim the spots in front of the left field scoreboard. The right field lawn is much larger, with room for seating below the concrete walkway and on the gradually sloping hill behind it.

THE BALLPARK EXPERIENCE. Fans who park in Lot E exit their cars in plain view of the Cubs taking batting practice on the practice field outside the stadium.

The high chain-link fence prevents most balls from smashing down on windshields in the parking lot, but some blasts carry over and fans scramble to collect these and/or to locate their car insurance paperwork.

Autograph seekers congregate outside the stadium's right field corner and wait for the visiting team's bus to arrive. Once the bus parks, the players walk down a runway to enter the field through a gate near the right field foul pole.

To prevent fans from accidentally being hurt while scrambling for balls on the outfield lawns, for several years the gates to HoHoKam did not open until the visiting team's batting practice session had finished. However, in recent years the park has opened midway through batting practice, with only the outfield lawn remaining closed until BP finishes.

The Cubs Walk of Fame is located on the concourse beneath the grandstand; it takes the form of large banners that show photographs of past and current stars. Images of the old-timers appear in black and white, while more recent players are depicted in color. In addition to the players' names, each banner lists the years of each legend's service with the Cubs. These include: Ernie Banks (1953–1971); Billy Williams (1959–1974); Ferguson Jenkins (1966–1973, 1982–1983); Ryne Sandberg (1982–1994, 1996–97); Ron Santo 1960–1973; Harry Caray (WGN-TV 1982–1997); Jack Brickhouse (WGN TV/Radio 1940–1944, 1947–1981); Rogers Hornsby (1929–1932); Hack Wilson (1926–1931); Andre Dawson (1987–1992); and Rick Sutcliffe (1984–1991).

The general concession stands offer a Chicago Dog that comes topped with mustard, onions, pickles and tomatoes, and a Mesa Dog, that comes topped with chili, cheese, corn chips, and jalapenos. Some stands also serve a Hebrew National dog. The Pulled Pork and Breaded Pork Tenderloins are also Mesa favorites. As for the ballpark brew of choice, just like at Wrigley, it's Old Style.

While Wrigley Field tradition is honored in the boisterous singing of "Take Me Out to the Ballgame" midway through the seventh inning, the constant barrage of advertising spewed by the video-board and public address system can be a bit overbearing. When the game is in progress, the message board continuously scrolls the names of companies that have paid to advertise at the park. In between half innings the P.A. announcer reads commercial messages under the guise of naming the lucky "X Company" fan-of-the-game, who has just won a $25 gift certificate to "X," or a free car wash, or a free side order of fries on his next fast-food run.

It is worth noting that even when the Cubs have an away game, they use HoHoKam Stadium or the adjacent field for batting practice. Fans are permitted to enter the stadium about three hours before first-pitch to watch. Then they pile into their cars and follow the team bus to the game.

ON THE TOWN. Mesa is Arizona's third largest city, after Phoenix and Tucson. It sits about 20 miles east of Phoenix.

Visitors from Chicago find plenty of chain type restaurants and pre-game drinking establishments on Country Club Drive. The most popular Cubs hangout in town is **Diamond Sports Grille** (161 N. Centennial Way), which was previously called Sluggo's, and before that, Harry & Steve's. Legendary Cubs announcer Harry Caray and Cubs pitcher Steve Stone were the original owners of the joint, which is located right beside the Mesa Marriott Hotel. On game-day, the Diamond offers patrons a free shuttle service to and from HoHoKam Stadium. This is one of those classic spring training hangouts that every fan — whether they root for the Cubs or not — should make a point to visit at least once.

Another attraction that traveling fans will surely enjoy is the "**Play Ball: Cactus League Experience**" (51 East Main Street). The exhibit in Mesa illuminates the history of spring training in Arizona, with a particular focus on the game's presence in Mesa. Old photographs, uniforms, game programs, bats, balls and other pieces of memorabilia combine to tell the story. The Play Ball exhibit is a multi-site museum that has also set up displays at the Scottsdale Center for the Performing Arts, Goodyear Ballpark, the State Capitol, and Papago Park. It seems likely that this wonderful collection will ultimately find a permanent consolidated home in one of those locations, or perhaps someplace else. A permanent home for Play Ball within the Cubs' new Wrigleyville West complex has been floated as one possibility that would seem to make a lot of sense. Here's hoping that Mesa and the Cubs find a way to make that happen. Such a home base for the museum would allow a great many fans to access it during March, and would also serve as a draw for local fans and tourists alike during the other eleven months of the year.

Phoenix Municipal Stadium

(PHOENIX) Oakland A's

Phoenix Municipal Stadium
5999 East Van Buren Street, Phoenix
602–392–0074
http://phoenix.gov/parks/sports/phxmuni.html
http://oakland.athletics.mlb.com
Opened: 1964. Renovated: 2004. Seating Capacity: 8,500
• 5 miles north to Scottsdale (Giants)
• 7 miles south to Tempe (Angels)
• 10 miles east to Mesa (Cubs)
• 15 miles west to Maryvale (Brewers)

DESPITE A MAJOR RENOVATION prior to the start of the 2004 spring season, Phoenix Municipal Stadium continues to provide Cactus League fans with an old-time ballpark experience. And it's a good thing it does, because it's the last park of its kind. Hi Corbett Field in Tucson, the last contemporary of Phoenix Municipal Stadium, closed its gates to the spring game after the spring of 2010 when the Rockies relocated to Salt River Fields. Today, the park Phoenicians lovingly call "Phoenix Muni" or just "the Muni," is the oldest Cactus League yard, the smallest, and the only one without a trendy grass seating berm in its outfield. What it does offer, though, is the most amazing outfield view in all of the Cactus League. The red rock formations of Papago Park loom over left and center field, creating a breathtaking backdrop. The stadium itself is utilitarian, but quaint and charming. The façade is understated, and the seating bowl is composed disproportionately of bleachers. But it presents the sort of intimacy and simplicity that the new parks lack.

After visiting the newer, larger parks in Arizona — which sparkle in their own way — spending a day at the Muni seems like a step back in time. Obviously the park can't remain viable forever, not with so many spacious, gleaming monuments to the game attracting hordes of fans elsewhere in the Phoenix Valley, but fans should cherish the chance to enjoy the spring game in the up-close and personal environs of Phoenix Muni as long as it lasts. The Oakland A's hold a lease to play

Decorative sunscreens line the top of the exterior façade.

at the park through 2014. At the time of this book's writing, the A's were reportedly pursuing a deal with the City of Mesa to relocate to HoHoKam Stadium in 2015. The deal hinged on whether Mesa could secure an $8 million grant from the Arizona Sports and Tourism Authority to make upgrades to HoHoKam the A's had requested. What would happen to Phoenix Muni should that come to pass is anyone's guess. It seems unlikely, though, that the old park would attract another team without first undergoing another round of renovations. Barring the addition of a grass seating berm (perhaps in right field home run territory), a spacious food court (perhaps behind the home plate grandstand), and some new luxury box seating, it seems unlikely this classic Phoenix yard will endure.

Hopefully, Phoenix will find a way to keep the Muni alive, with or without the A's. More than just welcoming fans to the ballgame each March, the old park doubles as a history book, offering 16 markers on its concourse that chronicle Phoenix's baseball past. The timeline illustrates how no city has been more important to the Cactus League than Phoenix. Such was the case in the earliest days of the game' migration west and such is the case today when half of MLB's teams train in the Valley.

In March of 1929, the Detroit Tigers hosted the first spring exhibitions between big league teams in the Grand Canyon State, welcoming the Pittsburgh Pirates and

Chicago Cubs to Phoenix's Riverside Park. On March 29, the Tigers beat the Pirates 7–4 before a crowd of 2,000. The next day, they downed the Cubs 11–10 before a crowd of 3,500. The games were part of a spring tour that included stops for the Tigers in Los Angeles, El Paso, Houston, Beaumont, Fort Worth and Shreveport. Previously, the Chicago White Sox had played an exhibition game against a local team in Yuma in 1909, and the White Sox had played the New York Giants in Bisbee, as part of a barnstorming tour in November of 1913.

In 1947 the New York Giants and Cleveland Indians became the first major league teams to establish permanent spring bases in Arizona. Giants owner Horace Stoneham brought his club to south Phoenix, while Indians owner Bill Veeck brought his team to Tucson. The Giants played at the original Phoenix Municipal Stadium at the corner of Central Avenue and Mohave Street. The Indians played at Randolph Field (later renamed Hi Corbett Field). On March 8, 1947, the two teams met in Tucson for their first Arizona game, with Cleveland prevailing 3–1 before 4,934 fans. In the early years, the two clubs played against one another quite a bit. They also hosted visitors who usually trained in California such as the Cubs, White Sox, Pirates and Browns. Exhibitions against local minor league teams were also common.

After drawing 15,600 fans to seven games in 1947, the Indians return to Arizona every year until 1993 when they moved to Winter Haven, Florida to join the Grapefruit League. The Giants drew 23,000 fans to eight games in their inaugural Arizona campaign, and have returned to Greater Phoenix every spring since, except for one. In 1951 they swapped sites with the New York Yankees and trained in St. Petersburg, Florida.

Most historians point to 1954 as the year when the Cactus League officially formed. That was the first year four teams trained in Arizona. In addition to the Giants and Indians, the Cubs had arrived in Mesa in 1952, and the Orioles set up camp in Yuma in 1954. A number of occurrences contributed to the formation of that first league of four. First, the conclusion of World War II signaled an end of the wartime travel restrictions that had confined spring training to the cooler climes from 1943 to 1945. Having not traveled south for three years, several teams who had been less than fully enchanted with their previous spring camps used the layoff as an opportunity to reevaluate their spring regimen and establish a new tradition elsewhere. Second, baseball's unofficial policy barring African American players was in the process of dissolving. As teams became more interested in fielding integrated squads, the thought of training in the Deep South was less appealing. By 1953, five of the seven teams with blacks on their rosters trained out west. Another factor was the disbanding in the early 1950s of the Orange League, which had welcomed major league teams to California to train for more than two decades. This was the result of an agreement between Major League Baseball and the Pacific Coast League prohibiting spring games from taking place in PCL cities. Teams that had traditionally trained in California sought another warm dry region to set up camp.

Throughout the latter half of the 1950s and early 1960s, the Cactus League was a four-team circuit. After spending 1954 in Yuma, the Orioles played at the original Scottsdale Stadium from 1956 to 1958. The Red Sox played in Scottsdale from 1959 to 1965. The expansion Houston Colt .45's played at Geronimo Park in Apache Junction in 1962 and 1963. In 1964 the Giants opened a new incarnation of Phoenix Municipal Stadium, which had been built by Phoenix at a cost of $890,000.

After the spring of 1965, both the Red Sox and Cubs left Arizona, the Cubs heading to California and the Red Sox to Florida. This left the Cactus League with only its original two teams—the Giants and Indians. But the Cubs returned in 1967, moving to Scottsdale, and the expansion of 1969 brought the San Diego Padres to Yuma, and the Seattle Pilots to Tempe.

After Charlie O. Finley moved his Athletics from Kansas City to Oakland in 1968, he moved the team's training camp from Bradenton, Florida to Mesa. The expansion of 1977 added another team to the Cactus League fray: the Seattle Mariners, who moved into Tempe. That gave the Cactus League an eight-team circuit if the Angels, who trained in Palm Springs, California, were included.

Since the formation of this league of eight, only one team — the Indians—has left Arizona to establish a spring camp in Florida. And the Indians returned in 2009. Meanwhile, another seven teams have arrived in Arizona, either via the Grapefruit League or as expansion teams new to MLB.

And yet, despite all of this change and evolution, one aspect of the spring game has remained more or less constant: Phoenix Municipal Stadium. As always, the physical face of the park makes a scant impression on the South Phoenix landscape. But inside the park, the action between the lines is a delight. After parking in the stadium lot, fans approach the stadium via a spiraling pedestrian bridge that crosses the driveway and funnels fans toward the main entrance, which sits behind third base. The stadium hardly rises above street level. Canvas sunscreens decorated with photographs of gigantic baseballs form a paper-thin structure around the sta-

The light towers at "the Muni" once stood at New York's Polo Grounds.

dium's interior. Once inside, visitors notice that Phoenix Muni is actually much larger than it appears from the street. This is because most of the seating is set below street level.

The park's most distinguishing features are its wavy concrete roof, which resembles the one that covers the outfield pavilions at Dodger Stadium, its grandstand composed of large stones pressed into concrete, and its steel press box. Immediately behind the fence in left, cacti grow on a sandy embankment. Further away, but still looming dramatically over the field, the red rocks of Papago Park fill the view. These iron-rich sedimentary rocks formed up to 15 million years ago. One is particularly distinctive due to the circular hole in its center, earning it the name "Hole in the Rock." The hole has eroded over the course of millennia as the result of rainwater and wind. The HoHoKam tribe that once inhabited the Phoenix Valley used the ray of sunlight that shines through the hole to track the seasonal movements of the earth and to mark the summer and winter solstices.

As for the field, it measures 345 feet down the lines, 390 feet to the power-alleys, and 410 feet to center. The outfield wall is dark green. The majority of the ballpark's signage is located on billboards behind the outfield wall. Beyond the right field fence, a practice diamond features two infields—one in the traditional location and one carved into the other diamond's right field corner so as to allow two infield practices to occur at once. The A's use this two-headed diamond before games, but their main practice complex (four fields, batting cages, clubhouse) is located two miles away at Papago Park.

In center field, the hitter's backdrop takes the form of a wooden structure that matches the color of the outfield wall. This was a well-done variant to the black screens that more typically appear in the Grapefruit and Cactus League until Phoenix installed a large horizontal advertising banner across the top. In any case, the American flag still flies on the left field side of the structure, and the Arizona state flag still flies on the right side. The modest scoreboard in right is topped by a face clock. The bullpens are in outfield foul territory, parallel to the foul lines. The A's pen, like their dugout, is on the right side.

The concourse behind the seating bowl is quite wide. It runs behind the grandstand on the infield and then opens up down the lines, offering concession stands, rest rooms, benches, and the aforementioned timeline, which appears on concrete panels spread evenly throughout the stadium. At the two ends of the concourse in the outfield corners, elevated grass areas offer picnic tables beneath palm trees. Dirt squares on the concourse allow paloverde trees to grow. With their green bark and yellow flowers, these ornamental trees showcase the Oakland team colors.

All of the seating is below street level except for the small grandstand behind home plate. This raised area extends from the inside corner of the first base dugout to the inside corner of the third base dugout, housing 11 rows of seats in front of a one-level press box. Rather than utilizing plain concrete, the sides of this small grandstand have been inlaid with flat stones that add a touch of character.

When the current Phoenix Municipal Stadium replaced the original Phoenix

Municipal Stadium in 1964, the same light towers that had previously illuminated the sky above the Giants' Polo Grounds were installed in Phoenix. Twenty years later, after the Giants had departed for Scottsdale, the A's moved in. In addition to the Oakland team, the Phoenix Desert Dogs of the Arizona Fall League also use the park.

The 2004 renovation to the stadium cost $8 million, more than two-thirds of which was funded by a grant from the Arizona Sports and Tourism Authority. At that time, new dugouts were added, the administrative buildings were remodeled, and the press box was expanded from an 800-square-foot outdoor facility to a 3,000-square-foot air-conditioned facility. A new, less obtrusive protective screen was installed behind home plate. The ticket office, team shop and concourses were enlarged. Sunscreens were added above the concourse, and new entrance gates were added in left field and behind home plate. About 150 premium seats were added at field level behind home plate, too, but the seating bowl remained otherwise unchanged. In order to secure the state funding, the A's and Phoenix agreed to a ten-year lease at the time.

After spending the 1969–1978 pre-seasons in Mesa, first at Rendezvous Park and later at HoHoKam Stadium, the A's moved to Scottsdale Stadium in 1979 and then five years later moved to Phoenix. Prior to training in Arizona, the A's trained in such Grapefruit League bastions as Bradenton (1963–1968), West Palm Beach (1946–1962) and Fort Myers (1925–1936). The team was also a member of the Orange League, training in Anaheim from 1940 to 1942.

Aside from having served as the spring home of the Giants and A's, the Muni also served as a temporary home to the Los Angeles Dodgers during a portion of the spring of 2008. After departing their legendary Dodgertown camp in Vero Beach midway through that year's Grapefruit League season, the Dodgers played five Cactus League games before they headed to Los Angeles for the regular season. At the time the A's were in Japan, playing two exhibitions and two regular season games against the Boston Red Sox. With the A's overseas, the Dodgers moved into Phoenix Municipal Stadium. They hosted the White Sox at the Muni on March 20, and the Angels on March 22. The Dodgers won the first game 8–2, behind six shutout innings from Brad Penny, and then lost the second by a score of 4–2. The next spring, they moved into brand new Camelback Ranch.

Whether the A's will follow in the footsteps of most other Cactus League teams and move to a more modern facility themselves is anyone's guess. It does, however, seem likely that they eventually will. Ideally, from the perspective of those old-timers and purists who love the Muni, the park will be remodeled one more time and the A's will sign on for another decade or so of play. Failing that, there is also the possibility that the A's will pass on the opportunity to move to HoHoKam Stadium in 2015, in hopes that some other city in the Valley will eventually build them a brand new training complex. Given the typical funding and construction bureaucracy endemic to such a process, the latter scenario would keep the A's at the Muni through at least 2018. For the sake of those who appreciate the game's traditions and history, here's hoping this iconic spring park survives a bit longer.

GETTING TO THE PARK. The Muni is located in southeast Phoenix, a few miles east of Sky Harbor Airport. Tempe is just a stone's throw south of the park, while Scottsdale and Mesa are just east. From downtown Phoenix, the Muni is accessible by taking I-10 East to Highway 202 to the Priest Drive Exit. Follow Priest North and the park entrance appears after about a mile. From the airport, follow Van Buren Street directly to the park. The lot is large enough to accommodate a sold-out house, although its most distant reaches present a lengthy hike to reach the ballpark. Another option is to take the Valley Metro's Light Rail to the game. The Priest Drive/Washington Street station is just a block and a half from the park.

SEATING. Phoenix Municipal Stadium offers chair and bleacher seating for about 8,000 fans. In addition, the outer portions of the concourse accommodate 500 people as Standing Room ticket holders. On most days, though, the park welcomes small crowds by today's Cactus League standards. The average game draws about 5,800. When the Cubs or Giants come to Phoenix that number swells. The Angels draw well as the visitors too. Odd numbered sections appear on the first base side while even ones appear on the third base side. Section 1 is directly behind home plate. It's advisable to sit on the first base side since the seats there position fans toward the beautiful rock formations of Papago Park.

Two rows of folding chairs on the infield (Sections 1–20) are labeled Field Box and sell for a few dollars more than the rest of the seats in their corresponding sections. They're definitely worth the extra expenditure for those who liked to be as close to the action as possible.

The Lower Boxes are in Sections 1–19, spanning from behind one dugout to behind the other.

The Upper Boxes are the only seats above the mid-level walkway. They appear between the dugouts in the covered grandstand. Section A is behind the Oakland dugout on the first base side, while Section M is behind the visiting dugout on the third base side. Section F is directly behind home plate. The sunroof shades all eleven rows. The first row or two should be avoided, if possible, to eliminate the distraction of the walkway traffic.

The Outfield Reserved seats are metal bleachers with backs. Section 21 is located in shallow right field while Section 22 is in shallow left. Section 33 is out near the right field foul pole while Section 32 is near the left field pole. There are 18 rows of bleachers. The wide concourse behind the last row allows for plenty of standing room.

THE BALLPARK EXPERIENCE. The game-day experience at Phoenix Muni offers entertaining minor league caliber stunts and promotions that keep fans engaged. There is a daily race around the bases between two tikes. And once a game, a young fan is picked out of the crowd and presented a microphone to read the weather reports for cold cities around the country. Each time the child mentions snow, sleet or freezing rain, the sun-soaked fans in attendance cheer. Fans also

The red rocks of Papago Park form a delightfully Arizonan setting for a game.

sometimes compete in peanut tossing contests on top of the dugout roofs. Midway through the game, young ladies run onto the field to present the umpires with cold bottles of cold water. While the umps drink, the ladies dutifully cool them off with hand-fans.

Many fans bring their own fans, sun umbrellas or spray bottles to the game, and there is usually at least one usher or vendor patrolling the stands with a large spray-bottle looking for kids to soak. Adults and children alike make use of giant misting stations on the left and right field concourses.

The left field concourse houses a picnic area and barbecue station. The ballpark menu, on the whole, is rather basic. The Chili Cheese Fries and Cold Stone Creamery ice cream are the highlights.

It is much easier for fans to review the Cactus League timeline during batting practice, rather than once the game begins and people start walking and loitering there. The 16 cement markers read:

1. March 26, 1929: The first spring training game in Phoenix, Arizona was hosted by the Detroit Tigers. Immediately after the Ty Cobb era, the Tigers looked for inspiration and change for rebuilding, so therefore chose Phoenix for a portion of their spring training schedule. The Tigers hosted the Pittsburgh Pirates on an ideal Arizona baseball afternoon.

2. 1930s and World War II: During the 1930s spring training was played in California and Florida. At the onset of World War II, Commissioner Kenesaw Mountain Landis, in cooperation with the Department of Defense, barred teams from traveling west of the Mississippi and south of the Potomac in order to save the railway lines for troops and supplies. These four years of cold springs created a desire to reestablish spring training in warmer climates.

3. 1946: A league of two is formed when the Cleveland Indians persuaded the New York Giants to join them in Arizona for spring training. The Giants chose Phoenix to train for the spring, while the Indians adopted Tucson.

4. Spring of 1948: The relaxed sociopolitical climate of Arizona helped to further the integration of African Americans into the major leagues after Jackie Robinson broke the color barrier playing for the Brooklyn Dodgers. The Giants and Indians each acquired two African American players to their rosters.

5. Spring 1951: New York Yankees co-owner and Phoenix resident/developer Del Webb trades spring training sites with the New York Giants in order to show off his talented team to Phoenix family and friends. This brought the Yankees to Phoenix for one year with a talented 19-year-old rookie named Mickey Mantle.

6. Spring of 1952: New York Yankees owner and Phoenix resident/developer Del Webb convinced the Chicago Cubs to make the "Valley of the Sun" home for spring training. They ultimately settled in Mesa, Arizona.

7. 1954: The "Cactus League" officially began, comprised of four teams, after the arrival of the Baltimore Orioles and the Chicago Cubs to the state. Both teams joined the New York Giants in the Phoenix Valley, playing at Scottsdale and Mesa, while the Cleveland Indians remained in Tucson.

8. 1964: Phoenix Municipal Stadium, often referred to as "Muni," opened for its first spring training season as the home of the Giants who brought with them the lights from the Polo Grounds which illuminated the night skies of New York until September 18, 1963.

9. March 8, 1964: Willie Mays hit the first home run at Phoenix Municipal Stadium, 420 feet to left-center field, in the stadium's inaugural game. The Giants defeated the Cleveland Indians 6–2 in front of an opening crowd of 8,502 people.

10. Spring of 1972: The Oakland A's return to spring training as the defending World Series champions and the first Cactus League team to bring a World Series championship to the Valley.

11. Spring of 1984: The Oakland A's make Phoenix Municipal Stadium their home.

12. 1986: A study deemed Phoenix Muni as a viable temporary solution in

attracting a MLB team to the Valley. The plans included expanding the stadium by more than four times its original size. This plan was not implemented, as instead Bank One Ballpark was constructed prior to the Diamondbacks' first season in 1998.

13. Fall of 1989: As a result of the devastating earthquake in the San Francisco/Oakland Bay area during the World Series, the A's returned to Phoenix Municipal Stadium for practice. Before resuming the series, the A's played against their minor league players in an exhibition game at Phoenix Muni, with all proceeds going to the earthquake relief fund.

14. 1994: The Oakland A's make Phoenix their home for all operations with renovations at Phoenix Municipal Stadium and construction of a training complex atop a former World War II German prisoner of war camp in Papago Park.

15. Summer of 1996: The Arizona Diamondbacks called Phoenix Muni home with their first ever professional team which competed in the Arizona Rookie League. The Rookie League is a player development league, which plays in June through August of each year.

16. 2004: The Cactus League celebrates its 50th year and new Phoenix Municipal Stadium renovations are completed.

The wavy roof above the grandstand bears a slight resemblance to the one at Dodger Stadium.

ON THE TOWN. **Papago Park** provides more than just fabulous sight lines for fans sitting on the first base side of Phoenix Municipal Stadium. It also offers a wealth of recreational activities for Phoenix Valley residents and tourists. The 1,200-acre park houses the A's practice complex, a four-field softball complex, an archery range, fishing lagoons, the Hall of Flame Museum of Fire Fighting, the Papago Municipal Golf Course, the Phoenix Zoo, the Desert Botanical Garden, walking trails, biking trails and more. All of these attractions are open to the public during spring training. The park was formed in 1879 when it was designated an Indian reservation for the Maricopa and Pima tribes. During World War II, from 1943 to 1946, Papago Park was used as a German prisoner of war camp. After the war, the camp was modified to serve as a veteran's administration hospital and as district headquarters for the largest Army Reserve unit in Arizona. The park was officially purchased by the city of Phoenix in 1959.

The retractable-roof home of the Diamondbacks, **Chase Field,** is on display for fans during spring training. The Diamondbacks offer daily tours of the stadium on Monday through Saturday, starting at 9:30 A.M., 11:00 A.M., and 12:30 P.M. The tours last approximately 75 minutes, taking visitors onto the field, into the club-houses and dugouts, up to the press box, and into the team store.

For nightlife, baseball wanderers usually congregate in Phoenix's festive **Copper Square**. Favorite Diamondbacks haunts that double as A's hangouts during spring training include: **Majerle's Sports Grill** (24 North 2nd Street), **Coach and Willie's** (412 South 3rd Street), and **Jackson's on Third** (245 East Jackson Street).

Maryvale Baseball Park

(MARYVALE) Milwaukee Brewers

Maryvale Baseball Park
3600 North 51st Avenue, Maryvale/Phoenix
623–245–5500
http://milwaukee.brewers.mlb.com
Opened: 1998. Seating Capacity: 10,000
• 8 miles west to Glendale (Dodgers/White Sox)
• 12 miles north to Peoria (Mariners/Padres)
• 15 miles east to Phoenix (A's)
• 17 miles west to Surprise (Royals/Rangers)

THE MILWAUKEE BREWERS play at one of the Cactus League's most charming parks, even if it's usually only about half full. Maryvale Baseball Park is a creatively designed, intimate place to watch a game. Its seats all offer unobstructed views of the field. Its outfield berm is perfectly sloped and even offers some shade. Its surrounding practice complex allows for access to player workouts. And some uniquely Milwaukeean traditions make a visit to the park festive and fun. Maybe someday the Brewers will win their first World Series and interest in their spring games will spike. Or maybe a vibrant entertainment district will spring up around Maryvale Baseball Park, to lure fans into what is now an economically depressed corner of Phoenix. Until some sort of phenomenon along those lines gives fans reason to take a second look at Maryvale Baseball Park, it will remain one of the best-kept secrets in the Cactus League.

Rumors circulated midway through the 2012 spring season that the Brewers might abandon Maryvale in the near future. Some observers speculated that the club would move to Phoenix Municipal Stadium in the event that the A's move to Mesa's HoHoKam Stadium, after the Cubs open their new Mesa park in 2014. Others wondered if the Brewers would ponder a move to the Grapefruit League. Even the Brewers eventually admitted that a stadium change might be in the cards. They said they were happy with the ballpark in Maryvale, but dissatisfied with the clubhouse and workout facilities. In the end, Phoenix persuaded the Milwaukee

A distinctive sign welcomes fans to Maryvale.

team to extend its lease by agreeing to implement $1.5 in upgrades to the Maryvale Complex in time for spring training 2013. The work, which was approved by the Phoenix City Council in April 2012, added 2,000 square feet of space to what was previously a 22,000-square-foot big league clubhouse and another 2,000 square feet to the previously 17,000-square-foot minor league clubhouse. It also upgraded the complex's weight room. In exchange for this work, the Brewers agreed to remain in Maryvale through at least 2014. And they agreed to a series of eight one-year options to follow that initial term, which could keep them in Maryvale through 2022. All indications are that if the City of Phoenix continues to make incremental improvements to the complex, the Brewers will stay.

A modern art sensibility prevails in Maryvale, where fans encounter a towering sign that welcomes them to the ballpark. The sign sits high atop white staging that is nearly as tall as the light towers inside. At the very top of the structure, a cursive purple "M" appears, with "Maryvale Baseball Park" written below in smaller font. The letters are formed by pieces of wrought iron. Like the sign, the ballpark projects a funky modern personality. To start, the park possesses no exterior façade. Iron gates and several small concession stands line the back of the concourse. The field and seating bowl are set entirely below street level. The stadium's trademark feature is its press box. The large blue structure hovers above the field, supported by thick white pillars that rise on the front of the concourse. Accessible only by narrow metal staircases, the structure's floor is 20 feet above the concourse. The raised level is quite long, wrapping around the foul territory behind home plate to cast a tremendous amount of shade on the concourse and seats below. The box is no mere rectangular structure. Rather, its front face is much higher on the two ends than in the middle directly behind home plate. As a result, the roof of the box slopes from each high corner down to a gully in the center, before beginning its ascent to the other corner. Above the windows through which media members watch the game, horizontal slats of white steel form a trellised visor, while also endowing the façade with an even more distinctive look. On either side of the box, a white trellised roof extends toward the nearest foul pole, 20 feet above the concourse. Triangular white support cables rise atop this roof. The cables are similar to the type found above suspension bridges. Beneath this post-modern edifice lies an absolutely beautiful green field.

The field is small by major league standards, and its asymmetrical dimensions add to its charm. The left field foul pole is 350 feet from home plate. From the pole, the left field fence juts out toward the left field berm to form a triangular parcel 355 feet from the plate. The blue fence then continues to the left-center field gap, which measures 374 feet. Behind the 400-foot deep fence in center, a blue metal wall serves as the hitter's backdrop, while providing a small window for a center field cameraman. The fence measures 378 feet in right-center and 340 feet down the right field line.

The wide concourse behind the last row of seats allows fans to walk laps, if they choose, around the entire field. The concourse also offers shaded standing

Paloverde trees line the top of the outfield berm.

room beneath the trellised roof, and picnic tables where fans can sit and eat. The seating bowl is the smallest in the Cactus League, offering just 7,000 chairs, while there is lawn space for 3,000 more. Around the infield, the seats take the form of comfortable blue stadium chairs. Past the corner bases, relatively comfortable metal bleachers with backs appear. Where these bleachers end, the lawn begins in outfield foul territory. After the bullpens, the much larger outfield lawn spans the entirety of home run territory, interrupted only by the hitter's backdrop in center. The immaculately kept Maryvale berm is steep, allowing fans to easily see over the heads of those sitting or standing in front of them.

Rather than existing on the field in foul territory, the bullpens are actual pens, fenced off from the field of play. They begin where the seats end and run parallel to the foul lines out toward the poles. A low chain-link fence separates each one from the fans on the berm above. The Brewers' pen, like their dugout, is on the first base side. The Milwaukee relievers enjoy the shade cast by a cloth roof covering their bench, while the visiting relievers enjoy no such luxury.

Unlike at practically every other Arizona park, there's no mountain view in Maryvale. Above the outfield berm runs a walkway that connects to the concourse at either end. Above the walkway, rises another sloped hillside that offers a row of ornamental paloverdes. Some fans enjoy a distant but shaded view of the game from beneath these yellow and green trees. For those seated on the infield, the pretty paloverdes seal in the field from the outside world and give the park a cozy feel. In left-center a small scoreboard stands between two of these trees, informing fans of the line-score, number of outs, count, and batter's name. The board is basic, but just right.

In addition to the main stadium, the 56-acre complex houses five full practice fields, two practice infields, eight practice pitching mounds, eight covered batting cages, and the aforementioned major and minor league clubhouses. Originally the site was envisioned as a two-team complex, as the White Sox nearly committed to join the Brewers at Maryvale. But the Chicago team decided to train at Tucson Electric Park with the Diamondbacks instead. Of course both of those teams would leave Tucson before long, moving to Camelback Ranch and Salt River Fields, respectively. And the Brewers have remained the lone tenant at Maryvale Baseball Complex, where the practice fields are named after great players in Brewers history, like Rollie Fingers, Paul Molitor, Robin Yount, Cecil Cooper, and Don Sutton. A cloverleaf of fields is located behind the home plate and first base sides of the main stadium, while another field and practice infield lie beyond right field home run territory. Rolling green hillsides and attractive rock and flower gardens lie between the fields, while an observation tower rises in the middle of the complex, allowing coaches to monitor the entire camp from one location.

The Phoenix neighborhood of Maryvale stretches from 39th Avenue to 83rd Avenue between McDowell Road and Maryland Avenue. This western part of Phoenix could use some economic development and revitalizing. But the area has served the Milwaukee club well. At the time of the Brewers' arrival, they were already a team in transition. That off-season, it had been decided that the Brewers would move from the American League to the National League. This was done ostensibly, so there would be an even number of teams in each league after recent expansions had added three teams to the National League (Marlins, Rockies, Diamondbacks) but just one to the American League (Rays). Having an even number of teams—14 in the American League and 16 in the National League — ensured that no team would have to sit idle for the lack of an opponent to play. Later, with the move of the Astros to the American League in 2013, baseball would unbalance the leagues and create the need for at least one inter-league series at all times.

Groundbreaking on the Maryvale complex occurred in April of 1997 on land donated by Phoenix developer John F. Long. Long also loaned Maricopa County more than $10 million toward the project's $23 million price. The county continued to pay back the loan until 2015, using the proceeds from a $2.50 surcharge on rental-car contracts. Including the interest repaid to Long, the county's contribution totaled $17 million. The city of Phoenix — which owns and operates the stadium — picked up the remaining balance.

The opportunity to bring the Brewers to west Phoenix arose when the city of Chandler refused to upgrade Compadre Stadium, where Milwaukee had trained from 1986 to 1997. Compadre Stadium was located in a rural area 30 miles southwest of Phoenix, next to the fairways of Ocotillo Country Club. Its seating bowl was carved into rocky desert terrain, forming a basin that was well below grade. The stands held 5,000 fans, while room existed for several thousand more on the left field hillside.

Compadre Stadium's construction was funded by the Compadres, a Chandler-based civic organization. With their resources waning in 1993, the Compadres sold the stadium to the Maricopa County Stadium District. The Compadres, Maricopa County, and the Brewers all wanted to keep the Brewers in Chandler and recognized that certain improvements needed to be made to Compadre Stadium. In 1993, the city of Chandler asked the Compadres to negotiate a renovation plan with the Brewers. After two years of negotiations, the Compadres completed this assignment, only to see the Chandler City Council and Mayor nix the deal. The Brewers had no choice but to look elsewhere, and Phoenix, led by Long, seized the opportunity. As construction began on the land Long had donated, the Brewers signed a 15-year lease with the city of Phoenix to play at Maryvale through 2012.

The Brewers drew large crowds in Chandler, even if their tenure in the city was not enduring. Compadre Stadium's inaugural game on March 7, 1986, attracted a crowd of 6,075 fans that turned out to watch the Brewers play the Cubs. On March 26, 1988, 9,812 fans, a Cactus League record at the time, watched the Brewers and Cubs play. In 1989, Milwaukee topped the 100,000 mark in spring training attendance for the first time, welcoming 102,814 fans to Compadre Stadium.

By comparison, the Brewers drew only 3,102 fans to their inaugural game at Maryvale Baseball Park in 1998, an 8–4 loss to the Padres. And they have finished ahead of only the Reds and Indians in recent years in spring attendance. The Brewers typically attract only about 80,000 fans to their 15 or 16 home games. But the crowds are friendly ... usually. During the spring of 2012 the spring slate got off to a bit of a rough start, though, when reigning National League MVP Ryan Braun was booed and heckled in front of his home fans after failing a urine test for performance enhancing drugs during the off season. Braun's defense was that the sample collector did not follow the proper procedures, and eventually he was pardoned on this technicality. But the general public still viewed him as a cheater. Upon stepping into the batter's box at Maryvale Baseball Park for his first spring at-bat of 2012, Braun received a partial standing ovation. But the cheers were soon drowned out by a chant of "Ur-ine, Sam-ple! Ur-ine, Sam-ple!" Amidst the cacophony of jeers, Braun struck out against the Giants' Madison Bumgarner. The next time he came to bat, Braun face a chant of "Cheater, Cheater, Cheater," and struck out again. By the next game, though, the Maryvale fans had forgiven the slight and returned to their usually friendly ways.

Prior to training in Chandler, the Brewers had made their spring home in Sun City from 1973 to 1985. A retirement community designed by former Yankees owner Del Webb, Sun City Stadium featured concourses that accommodated golf carts, so senior citizens could park behind the last row of seats and watch the game in comfort. Because there was such little foul territory, a protective screen rose in front of the first row of seats all the way around the small seating bowl.

The franchise originally played its spring games at Tempe Diablo Stadium. After debuting in 1969, the expansion Seattle Pilots returned to Tempe in the spring of 1970 and one month later departed to become the Milwaukee Brewers. The bizarre saga unfolded after the Pilots had declared bankruptcy after drawing just 677,944 fans to Sicks' Stadium in Seattle in 1969. Major League Baseball offered $650,000 to subsidize the team's spring training costs in 1970 while an ongoing search for a long-term solution continued. One week before the start of the 1970

The press box is designed to cast as much shade as possible on the seats.

regular season, Milwaukee car dealer Bud Selig bought the team for $10.8 million. Just two weeks later, Milwaukee's County Stadium, which had been vacated by the Braves five years earlier, opened as home to the Brewers.

Today, Maryvale Baseball Park provides the Brewers with one of the finest spring venues in Arizona. The Phoenix Brewers of the Arizona Rookie League also use the Maryvale complex, playing their games at Paul Molitor Field.

GETTING TO THE PARK. The Maryvale complex is located on 51st Avenue between Thomas Road and Indian School Road. From downtown Phoenix, follow I-10 west to 51st Avenue North. The ballpark is on the left. Because the neighborhood surrounding the complex is not welcoming to street parking tourists, and because pre-game tailgating is an important part of Milwaukee baseball tradition, most fans arrive early and park in the stadium lot. When the Cubs or Giants are visiting, the crowds tend to be large, sometimes prompting the Maryvale parking attendants to direct cars to a nearby Wal-Mart, which has ample room for the overflow.

SEATING. Following a rare playoff appearance in 2011, the Brewers averaged larger-than-usual crowds of about 5,600 fans per game during the spring of 2012. But good seats were still available on game-day for every Brewers home date.

All of the seats are below the concourse, contributing to sight lines that are unobstructed by pedestrian traffic. The 26-row seating bowl extends just a short distance past the corner bases on either side of the diamond. The elevated press box is shaped and positioned to provide the maximum amount of shade. Thanks to the box and the sunroof above the concourse, the back six rows are shaded as 1:00 P.M. games begin. The first base side enjoys increasing shade with each passing minute, and by mid-afternoon practically all of the seats are in the shade, as well as the lawn seating area in right field. Because the Brewers rarely attract large crowds, the friendly ushers allow fans to freely seek upgraded seats by the time the third inning arrives.

There are four seating options: Field Box, Infield Reserved, Outfield Reserved, and Lawn. Section 100 is behind home plate. The odd numbered sections continue down the right field line and the even numbered sections continue down the left field line.

The Field Boxes occupy Rows 1–26 of the best 11 sections in the stadium: Sections 100–110. Not only do these infield sections provide the best view, but the most comfortable seats, offering actual chairs, as compared to the bleachers with backs in the rest of the bowl. Section 109 is at the mid-point of the Brewers dugout on the first base line, Section 100 is behind the plate, and Section 110 is at the midpoint of the visiting dugout. These sections offer Rows A–Z, except for the dugout sections (107–110) which offer F–Z.

The Infield Reserved consists of the first two sections of bleachers on either side of the infield. Sections 111 and 113 are located at first base, while Sections 112 and 114 are at third. Sections 111 and 112 begin with Row F, due to the presence of the dugouts in front of them, while Sections 113 and 114 begin with Row A.

The Outfield Reserved consists of the final two sections of bleachers on either side of the diamond. These are located where the infield dirt meets the outfield grass. Sections 115 and 117 are in shallow right field, while Sections 116 and 118 are in shallow left.

The Lawn begins in shallow left and right, where the seating sections end. It runs above the bullpens in foul territory, and then continues around the foul poles and across the outfield. As mentioned earlier, it's a great berm from which to watch a game.

THE BALLPARK EXPERIENCE. Tailgaters usually park in Lot B where there is room to set up a hibachi while enjoying an outfield view of minor league workouts. Those who don't find the thought of flying to Arizona with a grill from home and lugging it around in a rental car appealing, but who still wish to partake, can stop into the nearby Wal-Mart and buy a cheap hibachi and some coals before the game. Then they can use the set for a few more games before disposing of it before flying home.

After eating their bratwurst, Maryvale fans walk through the practice complex, where players are taking batting practice, working on practice mounds, or receiving hitting instruction from coaches in the batting cages. Some fans stand in the outfield corners of the fields where batting practice is in progress. The gates around these fields are often left open, allowing young fans to run out onto the warning track to scarf up balls. Temporary bleachers near each field's home plate area provide a place for older fans to watch the action.

Inside the main stadium, fans looking for autographs assemble on the right field concourse before the game. The home and visitor locker rooms are located beyond the concourse here, separated from the stadium by an iron gate. The Brewers big leaguers take batting practice at the field beyond the main stadium in right field and visible through the chain-link fence at the back of the right field lawn. The visitors, meanwhile, sometimes take their practice swings inside the stadium, making the grassy embankment in the outfield a good spot for ball hounds. A recent trend, however, has seen visiting teams take their practice swings at their own complexes before arriving in Maryvale. This has become almost standard practice across the Cactus League since the consolidation of teams in Phoenix Valley facilitated by the closure of the camps in Tucson.

The sausage race —famous in Milwaukee — is no mere Wisconsin phenomenon, as the very same mascots that appear at Miller Park — Hot Dog, Bratwurst, Italian Sausage, Chorizo and Polish Sausage — are at Maryvale Baseball Park during spring training. The race takes place in the middle of the sixth inning. The mascots start out by the right field foul pole and race down the right field line toward home plate. After their exploits on the field, the tall sausages pose for pictures and sign autographs on the right field concourse.

Just as the ticket prices to Maryvale Baseball Park are cheaper than at many points elsewhere in the Cactus League, the food and beverage offerings are more affordably priced. The Brats and Polish Sausage are Klement's brand, just like in Milwaukee. They are cooked over hot coals on the concourse and are delicious. Fans also find 16-ounce jars of Milwaukee's famous Secret Stadium Sauce on sale in the Fan Zone on the right field concourse. Kettle Corn is another popular concession that goes quite nicely with a frozen Margarita or Daiquiri. Miller products make up most of the beer selection, while discriminating fans seek out the stands that sell Leinenkugel's Sunset Wheat.

A Milwaukee tradition that prevails in Maryvale is the daily rendition of "Beer Barrel Polka" during the seventh-inning stretch. Some of the ushers really get into the spirit. And the fans sing along.

Sausage mascots race on the field in the middle of the sixth inning then pose for pictures with young fans.

ON THE TOWN. As is the case in Milwaukee, the Maryvale baseball experience is confined to the ballpark complex, eschewing the pre-game watering holes and sports bars that are common destinations for fans whose teams play in other major league cities. Brewers fans are content to bring their own beer, prepare their own treats, and entertain themselves in any parking lot that offers enough room for a game of catch. This is just as well in Milwaukee, where Miller Park is located amidst the junction of overlapping highways. And it is just as well in Maryvale, a Phoenix neighborhood that is not particularly inviting to tourists.

Those who don't have the time or inclination to cook their own food at the stadium may, however, may visit the **Sizzler** (5060 W. Indian School Road) or **Peter Piper Pizza** (4105 N. 51st Street) before arriving at the baseball complex.

Fans looking to connect with Brewers' history can visit **Compadre Stadium** (1425 W. Ocotillo Road, Chandler). The stadium is part of the former Chandler Sports Complex, which was renamed the **Snedigar Sports Complex** in 1999, in honor of James Snedigar, a Chandler police officer who died in the line of duty. Today, the baseball field hosts low-level college baseball tournaments and youth baseball camps, while the surrounding grounds are used for community recreation. The facilities include Little League fields, softball fields, soccer fields, a skate park and a cricket pitch that opened in 2008. The grass is a bit on the burned-out side by late spring, but the complex is impressive nonetheless.

Peoria Stadium

(PEORIA) Seattle Mariners *and* San Diego Padres

Peoria Stadium
16101 North 83rd Avenue, Peoria
623–773–8700
http://peoriasportscomplex.com/
http://seattle.mariners.mlb.com; http://sandiego.padres.mlb.com
Opened: 1994. Seating Capacity: 11,333
• 6 miles southwest to Glendale (Dodgers/White Sox)
• 11 miles west to Surprise (Royals/Rangers)
• 14 miles east to Maryvale (Brewers)
• 15 miles east to Phoenix (A's)

AT THE TIME OF ITS OPENING, Peoria Sports Complex set a new standard for Arizona spring training facilities. As the first camp designed for two major league tenants and their accompanying minor leaguers, the Peoria facility provided a blueprint for other Arizona cities to follow as they developed their own fields of dreams in the ensuing years. The majority of the Cactus League complexes built since Peoria's opened in 1993, have been designed to house two home teams. These include Surprise Stadium (Rangers/Royals), Camelback Ranch (Dodgers/White Sox), Goodyear Ballpark (Indians/Reds), Salt River Fields at Talking Stick (Diamondbacks/Rockies), and the since abandoned Tucson Electric Park, which at one time housed the Diamondbacks and White Sox. The single-team complexes that have opened since Peoria's debut, meanwhile, have been limited to Maryvale Baseball Park, whose developers had originally hoped to attract a second team besides the Brewers, and the Cubs' new ballpark in Mesa scheduled to open in 2014.

Peoria Sports Complex arrived at a time when the spring game was just starting to draw larger and larger crowds. The designers at HOK Sport were perhaps a bit too optimistic, in designing the main stadium to seat more than 11,000, considering that the Mariners and Padres have never drawn especially large March followings. The park tends to feel a bit sterile on days when a fair number of the seats are

The back of the scoreboard doubles as a billboard to welcome fans.

empty. Nonetheless, it remains a modern facility that wisely provides seating all around the field, wide concourses, ample restroom space, and the best menu in the Cactus League.

The complex was built at a time when city officials were beginning to grasp the economic impact a Cactus League team, or better yet — two, could have on a community. And in that regard, Peoria Sports Complex has succeeded. A lively entertainment district thrives in the streets nearby the complex. The City of Peoria acknowledged the impact its two home teams have had on its economy when it extended its lease agreements with both the Mariners and Padres in 2012. Both teams use the complex not only during spring training but as a year-round player development center. Injured players and new draft picks use the complex during the summer, as well as two Arizona Rookie League teams. After the regular season, the complex is home to the Peoria Javelinas of the Arizona Fall League.

In March of 2012, both teams reached an agreement with Peoria to extend their lease by twenty years. In return to committing to Peoria through the 2034 season, the teams will benefit from $48 million in renovations to the complex that the city will fund. Between the spring trainings of 2013 and 2014, the city will install new state-of-the-art clubhouses for both teams at a cost of $15 million each. The work will expand each team's indoor space from 39,000 square feet to 58,000 square feet. Another $12 will be spent on playing field improvements, seating improvements, lighting enhancements, façade adornment, and the installation of a party deck on the outfield berm.

In addition to the main stadium, the Peoria Sports Complex includes 12 full practice fields, four practice infields, 20 batting cages, 30 practice pitching areas, and the two clubhouse buildings. The Mariners' fields and facilities are located behind the grandstand of the main stadium, while the Padres' fields and facilities are behind the first base and right field side of the main stadium. The 145-acre complex, located just a few miles northwest of Phoenix, was built at a total cost of $32 million. The main stadium cost $7.7 million. The Maricopa County Stadium District funded $21.5 million of the project, with the rest coming from the City of Peoria and the two home teams. The Mariners actually arrived in 1993 when the complex was still under construction, and the Padres arrived the following spring. The main stadium officially opened in 1994 after the complex's soft opening in 1993.

Although the playing field inside the main stadium is below street level, it is not sunken to the extent that many of the more recently constructed Cactus League fields are. As a result, the exterior façade of the stadium rises higher than at most of the other new Cactus League parks, and the concession concourse runs behind the seating bowl at ground level, rather than above the seating bowl as at most modern spring parks. The exterior façade reflects the earth tones of classic southwestern architecture. It consists of large beige and red sandstone bricks at ground level, and then beige stucco that rises to meet a blue trellised sunroof. Inside the stadium, this color scheme continues, as dark blue seats appear amidst a grandstand composed of the same large sandstone bricks.

Both home teams enjoy equal representation inside the park. The Mariners and Padres logos appear on the face of the beige stucco press box. Each team's championship seasons (since they began training in Peoria) are also commemorated on the façade. The press box also displays diamond-shaped placards honoring the Padres or Mariners rookie who had the best spring camp each year. In 2012, Mariners infielder Alex Liddi won the award. The roof of the first base dugout reads, "San Diego Padres," while the roof of the third base dugout reads, "Seattle Mariners." Both team logos appear on the outfield wall near the hitter's backdrop. The logos also appear on the bottom of the left field scoreboard. On the concourse beneath the grandstand, each team has its own separate clubhouse shop.

The outfield fence is the same dark blue as the plastic stadium chairs and metal trellised roof. While much of the fence is covered by advertising, its top two feet consist of chain-link to allow fans on the outfield lawn a clear view of the field. The very top of this chain-link rim is lined with a yellow ribbon for the benefit of umpires who must determine whether deep fly balls leave the yard. The fence in front of the bullpens—in home run territory in right (Padres) and left (Mariners)— consists entirely of chain-link, so that fans can see the relievers warming up.

At first glance, the field appears fairly generic, its dimensions measuring a symmetrical 340 feet to the foul poles, 385 feet to the outfield gaps and 410 feet to center. A closer inspection however, reveals that the lawn is actually rather quirky, owing to the fact that the hitter's backdrop is not behind the outfield fence but attached to it. The 39-foot-high "Blue Monster" in center field is in play. Balls must clear the brick wall to leave the stadium. Balls that hit the wall bounce back toward the center fielder and wind up as doubles or long singles. Not only is center the deepest part of the ballpark, but the fence there is four times higher than in the rest of the outfield.

While the outfield view at Peoria Stadium is not as spectacular as at some other Cactus League parks where rocky buttes and towering mountains loom over the field, the seemingly ubiquitous Sun Valley peaks rise far off in the distance. These are particularly impressive in the early innings of night games when the sun continues to shine on them long after the ballpark has been enveloped in darkness.

The Mariners and Padres usually play 14 home games apiece at Peoria Stadium. They also play three "road" games against one another, bringing the total number of games each team has at the park to about 17. Prior to moving to Peoria, the Padres and Mariners had both trained at just one spring training camp apiece. The Padres joined the Cactus League in 1969, the same year they joined the National League as an expansion franchise. For more than two decades, San Diego played at Desert Sun Stadium in Yuma, Arizona, one of the most remote outposts of the Cactus League. The 6,700-seat stadium was part of a complex that also included four practice fields arranged in a cloverleaf pattern. The site eventually came to be known as the Ray A. Kroc Baseball Complex, in honor of the San Diego businessman who bought the Padres in 1974 and thwarted a plan to relocate the team to Washington, D.C. In addition to serving the Padres, the Yakult Swallows of the Japanese Baseball League used the Kroc Complex throughout the 1980s, spending January and February in Yuma. The best thing about the Yuma complex as far as many Padres fans were concerned, was that it was located just 190 miles from San Diego. Visiting fans would span that distance in three hours by car. In 1989, a long-distance runner and Padres fanatic named Anna Teter took six days to complete the journey on foot. She ran from the parking lot of San Diego's Jack Murphy Stadium to the parking lot of Yuma's stadium.

Another bit of unusual Cactus League lore was born a decade later when singer/songwriter Garth Brooks spent the entire spring with the Padres as a non-roster invitee. By participating in a full slate of workouts and games in Peoria in 1999, the country music star attracted tens of thousands of additional fans to the Cactus League. The Padres donated $200,000 to the Touch 'Em All Foundation, a children's charity, in recognition of Brooks' contribution to the same organization. Brooks wasn't in Peoria just to raise money for a good cause, though. He was there to play ball. The 36-year-old was so serious about his game that he skipped the 1999 Grammy Awards, where he was nominated for three awards, so that he could continue workouts in Peoria. Although the hopeful second baseman batted just .045 for the Padres (1–22), he never let his struggles affect his temperament, finding

The scoreboard rises on the left field berm.

plenty of time to sign autographs. On several occasions he delighted the crowd by singing a song or two after the game.

Prior to their arrival at Peoria Stadium, the Mariners had spent the whole of their spring history in Tempe. The expansion Mariners played their first game at Tempe Diablo Stadium in 1977 and stayed through the 1992 season. Previously, another expansion team from Seattle, the Seattle Pilots, had spent the 1969 and 1970 spring seasons in Tempe before moving to Milwaukee and becoming the Brewers at the start of the 1970 regular season.

Since moving to Peoria, the Mariners have drawn better than the Padres. They typically draw about 120,000 fans to their spring slate, while the Padres draw about 85,000 to their games. The most memorable Mariners camp occurred in 2001 when Ichiro-mania first gripped Peoria. With the arrival of Japanese sensation Ichiro Suzuki, who had signed a free agent contract with the Mariners, thousands of Japanese fans and nearly as many media members flocked to Peoria. Despite getting off to a slow start in Cactus League competition, Ichiro won the 2001 Rookie of the Year and American League Most Valuable Player awards.

When the Padres opened Petco Park in San Diego in 2004, they gave the Mariners the honor of christening the stadium with them. San Diego and Seattle departed the Peoria Sports Complex a few days early that year to play their final two exhibition games against one another in San Diego. Both games were played before sold out crowds.

Considering neither the Mariners nor the Padres have a history of changing spring sites frequently, and that both have signed on the dotted line to remain in Peoria through 2034, it would appear that this fine facility will continue to serve both teams for a good long time.

GETTING TO THE PARK. Peoria is located just outside Phoenix's northwest quadrant. From I-17 take the Bell Road exit and follow Bell Road to 83rd Avenue. Turn left on 83rd and follow it for half a mile. The complex is on the left. Most fans park in the complex lot. Savvy fans stay at the nearby La Quinta Hotel (16321 N. 83rd Avenue) and walk to the stadium. The large west lot behind the grandstand provides closer access to the Mariners' fields and facilities, while the east lot, beyond the outfield seating berm, is closer to the Padres' portion of camp.

SEATING. There are six different ticket options at Peoria Stadium: Club, Infield Box, Outfield Box, Upper Box, Bleachers and Lawn. The Mariners typically attract about 7,500 fans per game, while the Padres draw about 5,500. Apparently the prospect of escaping the chilly northwest is more alluring to Mariners fans than the prospect of a lateral move —from San Diego to Arizona — is for Padres fans.

Most of the ushers are volunteers who belong to the Peoria Diamond Club. These friendly people seem content to look the other way when fans leave their $5 lawn seats to seek out $18 Infield Boxes. It is not possible, however, to seat-hop into the Club seating areas which are up above the main seating bowl on the same level as the press box.

The seating bowl is fairly steep and every aisle seat bears the Peoria emblem, which depicts the sun, a cactus, a mountain peak, and a lake. The 100-Level seats are below the mid-level walkway, while the 200-Level seats are above it. Sections 100 and 200 are behind home plate, while even numbered sections continue down the right field line and odd numbered sections continue down the left field line.

The Club sections are located on either side of the press box. Sections 300 and 302 are on the first base side while Sections 301 and 303 are on the third base side. There are four rows in each section. These are the farthest seats from the field and highest above it.

The Infield Boxes provide great views. They consist of Sections 100–114. Section 114 is the last section behind the first base dugout, while Section 113 is the last Section behind the third base dugout. Sections 100–104 are behind home plate and offer Rows A–M, while Sections 105–114 are behind the dugouts and offer Rows E–M. The screen behind home plate rises straight up, allowing foul pops to fall into the crowd.

The Outfield Boxes begin immediately after the dugouts and extend almost all the way to the foul poles. Sections 116–122 follow the right field line, and Sections 115–121 follow the left field line. Sections 115 and 116 house the best seats in this price category as they are located on the infield corners before the outfield grass begins.

The Upper Boxes consist of the grandstand seating in Sections 200–214 around the infield. Sections 200–208 are in front of press box and offer Rows AA–JJ. In Sections 209–214, the rows continue to Row PP. Fans seated in Rows JJ–PP enjoy the shade cast by the sunroof.

The Bleachers are silver colored metal benches without back supports. They are located on the 200 level in outfield foul territory. Section 215 is in left field and Section 216 is in right. Each bank contains Rows AA–PP.

The view from the outfield Lawn is much better than the view from the Bleachers. The well-manicured berm extends above the entire outfield fence — except for where the Blue Monster rises in straight-away center. The Lawn is graded perfectly, allowing excellent views of the entire field. Behind the concourse at the top of the Lawn, several palm trees line the blue iron fence that separates the Lawn from the parking lot outside. The backside of the scoreboard in left field doubles as a giant billboard, welcoming fans to the complex as they drive up.

THE BALLPARK EXPERIENCE. The pre-game experience at the Peoria Sports Complex is livelier outside the main stadium than it is inside. When the ballpark

A view from the left field berm.

gates open one and a half hours before game-time, the field is already raked, lined and watered. Batting and infield practice for both teams take place on the practice fields outside. The home teams both use the fields numbered one and two on their portion of the complex for batting practice. The practice fields all have covered bleacher sections where fans can sit.

The players for both teams access the field through an opening in the right field fence near the foul pole. Fans sometimes walk from the outfield berm to the edge of the runway behind the right field fence and wait for the players to enter. This is a better place to snap photographs than it is to get autographs as game time approaches, but after the game many players linger in this "Autograph Alley."

The game-day experience at Peoria is much more festive when the Mariners are the home team, than when the Padres play before a half empty stadium. No matter which team is playing host, however, stadium management sees fit to prompt fans during the traditional singing of "Take Me Out to the Ballgame" by displaying the lyrics on the scoreboard while pre-recorded organ music plays through the public address system. As mentioned above, the ushers are friendly folks who represent the Peoria Diamond Club, a nonprofit organization that formed in 1993 to support both teams. Originally the group had about ninety volunteers; today, it has more than 500!

At the Kids Zone on the right field concourse, young visitors take their hacks on a miniature Wiffle ball field. Lefty swingers will be pleased to find a shorter-than-usual right field fence at the already tiny diamond.

A unique piece of art appears on the concourse too—a statue entitled "First Mitt." Sculpted by artist George Lundeen, the piece depicts a child with a baseball glove on his hand, reminding those who walk past that baseball is for the kid in all of us. The Peoria Arts Commission acquired the piece in 1995.

The multitude of concession stands at Peoria Stadium combine to make the facility the best-eating ballpark in spring training. In fact, some regular season ballparks fall short of matching the breadth and quality of concessions in Peoria. Not only does the stadium offer a ridiculous number of treats from which to choose, but all items are prepared fresh and served right off the grill. Randy Jones' Barbecue—operated by former Padres Cy Young Award winner Randy Jones, serves Brush Back Ribs, Room Service Cheeseburgers and the Ruthian Hot Dog, which weighs a half pound.

The Peoria concession menu also makes room for local flavors like Indian Fry Bread—a favorite at the Arizona State Fair for decades. The delicious fried dough is served topped with parmesan cheese, crushed garlic, and melted butter. Another stand sells skewers of chicken, peppers, onions and carrots, dipped in a spicy southwestern barbecue sauce. Another serves Grilled Rib Eye Sandwiches. The sandwich includes an actual whole rib eye that is placed on the grill at the time each customer orders and seared while the customer waits. When cooked to perfection, the steak is placed between bread, and topped with sizzling peppers and onions. Other favorites include Louisiana Sausage, Polish Sausage, Turkey Sausage, Bratwurst,

Jerk Chicken, Frozen Yogurt, Funnel Cake, Espresso, Gyros, huge Philly Cheese-steaks, and Kettle Corn. The beer list includes Red Hook, Fat Tire, and Pyramid Ale.

Visitors from Seattle were delighted to find Rick "The Peanut Man" Kaminski tossing nuts in the Peoria grandstand prior to his passing in 2011. The Peanut Man made the trip from Seattle to Peoria each March to get his arm tuned up for his regular season gig at Safeco Field.

ON THE TOWN. Not long ago Peoria consisted mainly of desert farmland. Today, it is a sprawling urban retail center that contains nearly every type of national chain imaginable. There is a **Hooters** (16550 North 83rd Avenue) restaurant not far from the sports complex, a **Cheesecake Factory** (16134 North 83rd Avenue), a **Chick-Fil-A** (16657 North 83rd Avenue), a **Famous Dave's** (16148 North 83rd Avenue), a **PF Chang's China Bistro** (16170 North 83rd Avenue), and so on. For visiting baseball fans there are also many hotels and bars from which to choose within a short distance of the baseball grounds. The most convenient hotel for road-trippers is **La Quinta** (16321 North 83rd Avenue), which is actually visible from inside the stadium. It rises from the far side of the parking lot beyond the left field fence. There are several other hotels within a mile of the complex as well.

Surprise Stadium

(SURPRISE) Kansas City Royals *and* Texas Rangers

Surprise Stadium
15960 North Bullard Avenue, Surprise
623–222–2000
http://www.surpriseaz.gov/files/springtraining/
http://texas.rangers.mlb.com; http://kansascity.royals.mlb.com
Opened: 2003. Seating Capacity: 10,714
• 9 miles east to Peoria (Mariners/Padres)
• 15 miles east to Glendale (Dodgers/White Sox)
• 17 miles east to Maryvale (Brewers)
• 25 miles east to Phoenix (A's)

Surprise Stadium played an integral role in the expansion of the Cactus League. It lured to Arizona not one but two teams—the Kansas City Royals and Texas Rangers—that had previously spent the entirety of their spring lives in the Grapefruit League. Unlike previous Cactus League construction and renovation projects that provided new facilities for teams already in Arizona (such as the projects in Maryvale, Mesa, Peoria and Scottsdale), the Surprise complex tilted the balance of power between the two spring circuits. And it paved the way for other Grapefruit League stalwarts like the White Sox, Reds, and Dodgers to also migrate to the Grand Canyon State. When the $48.3 million, 132-acre, Surprise Recreation Campus debuted in 2003, it increased Cactus League membership by 20 percent—from 10 teams to 12—bringing the Cactus League that much closer to leveling the playing field between itself and the Grapefruit League. By 2010, of course, when the Reds landed at Goodyear Ballpark via Sarasota, the two leagues would each have 15 teams.

As its sheer acreage might suggest, the Surprise Recreation Campus is more than just a spring training attraction. In addition to baseball facilities for two major league teams and both teams' minor leaguers, the complex also houses the Maricopa County Library, a tennis complex, a community park, an aquatic center, and government offices. Located on the former site of Luke Air Force Base, the complex

As in Peoria, the back of the scoreboard also serves as a greeting sign.

sits 25 miles northwest of downtown Phoenix, anchoring the growing community of Surprise.

Both the Royals and Rangers signed 20-year lease agreements to play in Surprise upon their arrival, so both clubs will be in town through at least 2022. The baseball amenities include six full practice fields for each team, as well as a practice infield apiece, 18 practice pitching mounds, eight batting tunnels, and a 37,000-square-foot building that contains clubhouses, locker rooms, weight rooms, training rooms, administrative offices, and kitchens. The Rangers' fields and facilities appear parallel to the left field line of the main stadium, while the Royals' portion of the complex sits behind the home plate grandstand. Five of each team's six practice fields mimic the field dimensions of Surprise Stadium, while the sixth replicates the dimensions of each team's regular season park. The Royals' field measures 330 feet down the lines, 375 feet to the outfield gaps, and 400 feet to center field, just like Kauffman Stadium. The Rangers' field measures 350 feet down the lines, 379 feet to the gaps, and 400 feet to center, just like Rangers Ballpark. These lighted fields serve the teams' respective entrants in the Arizona Rookie League each summer.

The complex actually opened as the instructional league headquarters for both teams in December of 2002, while the main stadium was still under construction.

Surprise Stadium officially opened in February of 2003. The Royals beat the Rangers 6–3 in the stadium's inaugural game, but only after a prolonged attempt to block its funding by John F. Long. Long, who was a legendary figure in the development of the West Phoenix suburbs had built Maryvale in the 1950s and later donated the land for Maryvale Baseball Park. When the Arizona Sports and Tourism Authority was formed, Long grew resentful and perhaps began to feel obsolete. No longer would a handful of well-moneyed developers spur projects from which they themselves would reap financial benefit, but a public financing mechanism would prevail. When the Sports and Tourism Authority committed $26 million to the Surprise project in 2001, Long filed a lawsuit challenging the constitutionality of the funding that had been approved by Maricopa County voters via a 2000 referendum. According to the act of legislation, the Authority — which has since funded many other Arizona stadium constructions — parlays the proceeds from a 30-year hotel tax and rental car surcharge into funding for stadium construction and tourism promotion. As projects arise, the Authority issues low-interest bonds to cover its contributions, and then retires the debt over time using tax revenue. Despite repeated defeats in lower courts, Long continued to appeal until his case finally reached the Arizona Supreme Court, which refused to hear it in December of 2002.

The irony of Long's suit — which sought to end the Sports and Tourism Authority's funding of stadium projects — was that it ultimately resulted in the Authority spending $6 million more than the $26 million it had originally intended to spend on the Surprise project. During the duration of Long's litigation, the Authority was legally unable to issue the $26 million in bonds necessary to fund its share of the Surprise construction costs. Fearful of losing the Royals and Rangers to other cities if the stadium was not completed in time for the start of the 2003 Cactus League season, the city of Surprise took a considerable gamble. In order that construction could continue, Surprise agreed to fund the entire cost of the project, with the understanding that the Authority would reimburse it in the amount of $32 million pending a victory in court against Long. The Authority's contribution was increased by $6 million to compensate Surprise for its added financial risk and for the consequences that the added financial burden had on the overall development of the city. As a result of having to redirect funds to the Recreation Campus, Surprise had to delay the construction of its new police department, court house and wastewater facilities plant.

For Surprise, the Sports and Tourism Authority and the two baseball teams involved, all was well that ended well. Surprise Stadium opened on time in 2003. That season, the Royals drew an average crowd of 4,534 fans per game, an increase of 53 percent from their final season at their Baseball City complex in Florida, and the Rangers drew an average crowd of 5,095, an increase of 67 percent from their final season in Port Charlotte, Florida.

Today, the Royals average about 5,000 fans per game, while the Rangers draw about 7,500. The Surprise Saguaros of the Arizona Fall League also use Surprise Stadium in November and December.

As for Mr. Long, he passed away in 2008 at the age of 87. He was a giant among Phoenix's early fathers and a generous philanthropist in his later years. But his memory was tarnished as far as many fans of the Cactus League are concerned by his steadfast opposition to Arizona's effort to build new baseball parks in his final years.

Surprise Stadium was designed by the accomplished ballpark specialists at HOK Sport. Groundbreaking for the project took place in May of 2001 with a pair of Hall-of-Famers pitching the first spades into what was at the time barren desert. George Brett did the honors for the Royals, while Nolan Ryan did the same for the Rangers. The field inside the stadium was dedicated "Billy Parker Field" in March of 2003 in honor of the late William David Parker, a second basemen who spent parts of three seasons in the major leagues with the California Angels (1971–1973). After his playing career, Parker settled in Surprise where he worked in construction and coached several youth sports teams. When Parker died in February of 2003 at age 56, the city thought it fitting to name the new field after him since he had loved baseball and had given generously of his time and energy in support of youth athletics.

The first thing fans see upon arriving at Surprise Stadium is a large and colorful

A view from the left field berm.

sign at the far side of the parking lot. The billboard-sized welcome message features the home teams' logos, and the Surprise Recreation Campus logo, which portrays a baseball player swinging at an oversized ball that shimmers like the sun, set amidst the backdrop of a regal blue mountain range. At street level outside, the sign appears to be an ordinary one-story structure. Inside the park, however, the sign — or rather, the scoreboard on its other side — towers over the playing field from its perch atop the left field berm. That is because the field is sunken 19 feet below street level. In fact, the entire seating bowl is below grade, excepting the limited number of club seats that flank the press box and cast shade on the concourse and Lower Dugout Boxes.

White steel gates supported by brick pillars separate the stadium's outfield berm from the massive parking lot. The Royals' team building anchors the left field corner of the stadium while the Rangers' building occupies the same space in right field. These buildings offer attractive brick exteriors at street level and interior decks overlooking the concourse and field. The white steel and large glass windows of these buildings create an image reminiscent of the five-story office building that spans the outfield of the Rangers regular season park in Arlington. The outfield lawn, meanwhile, spans the entire expanse between the foul poles, including a roped off parcel in straight-away center that serves as the lower half of the hitter's backdrop, recalling the center field lawns beyond the fences in Arlington and Kansas City. Atop the roped off portion of the lawn rises a green wall, to further ensure that hitters will be able to see the baseball as it leaves the pitcher's hand.

Unlike at most professional ballparks, fans enter Surprise Stadium through gates located in the outfield. One large gate stands in the left field corner and another in the right field corner. A wide concourse surrounds the entire field, running behind the last row of dark green seats. Fans can walk laps around the stadium, while only losing sight of the field for a brief few steps in straight-away center when the path veers behind the hitter's backdrop.

The cozy field dimensions ensure great views from all seating areas. The field measures 350 feet to the foul poles, 379 feet to the power alleys and 400 feet to center. The bullpens are in home run territory behind the outfield wall (Royals in left, Rangers in right), arranged so that the pitchers throw toward the foul poles. In order that fans can see the pitchers warming up, chain-link is substituted for the green fence and advertising signs that otherwise rise at the back of the warning track. Astroturf, for some reason, takes the place of real grass in the bullpens. As with all other aspects of the stadium, the Royals' dugout is on the third base side, while the Rangers' is on the first base side.

Behind the last row of infield seats, brick pillars rise on the concourse, supporting the beige press box and the three sections of second level seats on either side. The pillars contribute to a retro effect. The red, white and blue bunting that hangs from the second level adds another old-time touch. The face of the press box reads "Billy Parker Field." A silver aluminum roof tops off the structure behind home plate.

The wide concourse surrounds the entire field, leaving room for signs to honor the Rangers and Royals.

Both of the home teams' logos have been replicated generously throughout the park — on the concourses, on the center field fence and on the left field scoreboard. The crystal clear video board in the center of the scoreboard is used mainly to show commercials between innings. The board also hosts nightly hot dog races between one weenie that wears relish, one that wears ketchup, and one that wears mustard. The top of the scoreboard supports a round white face clock, while the lower-middle portion of the board displays the speed of each pitch immediately after it is thrown. Far-off mountain peaks span the entire outfield. The most breathtaking of the peaks rise beyond the left field berm. If only the stadium planners had placed the scoreboard on the right field berm instead of the left, more fans would enjoy this view. But then the scoreboard would not have been able to serve the aforementioned dual purpose that it does, offering a billboard-sized welcome message on its reverse side. For the benefit of those sitting on the spacious outfield berm, the small upper deck includes ribbon scoreboards on both the first and third base lines. These are a rarity in the spring game.

As mentioned above, neither the Rangers nor the Royals had trained in Arizona before 2003. The Rangers, who played as the Washington Senators from 1961 to 1971, trained in Pompano Beach, Florida, from 1961 through 1985 and then in Port Charlotte from 1986 to 2002. Charlotte County Stadium, which today hosts the Tampa Bay Rays during March, had become too small and rundown by the time the Rangers departed. It is only successful today because it underwent a substantial renovation before the Rays arrived. But the Rangers didn't just leave Florida because their Port Charlotte complex was lacking. They also desired to base their minor league headquarters closer to their regular season home in Texas. A move to Arizona solved both problems.

Upon entering the American League as an expansion team in 1969, Kansas City set up camp at Terry Park in Fort Myers, where the team remained through the 1987 spring season. From 1988 through 2002, the Royals trained a few miles west of Orlando at a complex known as Baseball City. The training complex/amusement park attracted neither very many baseball fans to Grapefruit League games nor tourists to its theme park. The facility has since been destroyed. (For more information on the Baseball City complex, refer to the Champion Stadium chapter, which discusses spring baseball's history in the Orlando area.)

The defection of the Rangers and Royals from the Grapefruit League represented a major coup for the Cactus League in its quest to become the premiere spring training site of Major League Baseball. Today's Arizona stadiums are, on the whole, newer and more fan-friendly than most stadiums in Florida. Arizona's spacious camps are more attractive to baseball's teams and players than the cramped quarters that exist in much of Florida too. The highways are less congested in Arizona, the ballparks are clustered closer together, and games are hardly ever rained out. Florida still has its beautiful beaches, but only time will tell how long that saving grace staves off what would appear to be an inevitable shift of spring baseball dominance from the tropical Southeast to the desert Southwest. With the exodus of just one more team from the Grapefruit League to the Cactus League, the spring game's junior circuit will have completed the metamorphosis prompted by the Surprise Campus's opening and will at long last have more teams than the Grapefruit League.

GETTING TO THE PARK. The Surprise Recreation Campus is located a mile and a half west of the intersection of Bell Road and U.S. Route 60 (Grand Avenue). From Phoenix, take Route 60 to Bell Road. Turn left on Bell Road and then right on Bullard Avenue. There is no off-site parking or public transportation, so the only option is to park in the dusty lot operated by the city of Surprise Recreation Department. As game-time approaches, particularly when the Rangers are hosting, the traffic tends to back up. Likewise, getting out of the parking lot can be a bit of an ordeal. On the plus side, Surprise offers one of the few free parking lots to be found in today's spring game. Another option is to stay at the nearby Holiday Inn Express (16540 N. Bullard Ave.) and to walk to the game.

The Surprise Recreation Campus is only a short drive along Bell Road from the Peoria Sports Complex, and because both complexes house two teams, the Cactus League schedule often allows fans the opportunity to attend a day game at one facility followed by a night game at the other.

SEATING. The Surprise Stadium seating bowl contains 7,000 fixed seats and room for more than 3,600 fans on its outfield lawn. There are five different seating categories: Lower Dugout, Upper Dugout, Infield (the seats of which are located mostly in the outfield), Plaza, and Lawn. Section 100 is directly behind home plate, while even numbered sections continue on the right side of the field and odd numbered sections on the left side. All of the fixed seating is provided in the form of green plastic stadium chairs that offer cup-holders and plenty of legroom. Not only is there a welcome absence of bleachers inside the stadium, but there is no mid-level walkway, thus ensuring that lateral pedestrian traffic never interrupts sight lines. The gradual slope of the seating bowl keeps all fans low to the field. The front row is located at field level where only a short green metal fence separates fans from foul territory. The friendly ushers allow for undeterred seat-hopping on the first level, but only Upper Dugout ticket holders are allowed access to the stairway leading to the Upper Dugout sections.

The Lower Dugout seats are the best in the ballpark, appearing in Sections 100–112. Sections 100–106 are behind home plate while Sections 107, 109 and 111 are behind the Royals' third base dugout, and Sections 108, 110 and 112 are behind the Rangers' first base dugout. Sections 100–102 contain Rows E–V, while Sections 103–106 contain Rows B–V, and Sections 107–112 contain Rows D–V. In all sections, Rows M–V are shaded by the upper deck.

The Upper Dugout sections are not "dugout" seats, despite their name. They are second level seats, albeit second level seats on the first base (Sections 202, 204, 206) and third base (201, 203, 205) lines. Rows A–F all provide excellent views and the roof provides relief from the sun.

The so-called infield sections (113–120) present an even greater misnomer than the Upper Dugout sections. Four-fifths of these seats reside in outfield foul territory. Only Sections 113 and 114 are on the infield and even then, they appear on the outfield side of the corner bases. All of these sections contain Rows A–V.

There are two sections of Plaza seats in either outfield corner. Sections 121 and 123 are in foul territory near the left field foul pole and Sections 122 and 124 are in foul territory near the right field pole. Because the Plaza sections angle seat-holders back toward the infield, they provide better sight lines than Infield Sections 117–120, which angle fans toward center field, forcing them to look over their shoulders to see home plate.

The Lawn seating area is among the best in the spring game, providing a perfect slope that allows fans to see over those in front of them. The grass is cut low, and is thick and comfortable. The thin horizontal slats of metal atop the outfield fence allow for a better view of the game than the chain-link fence that appears in the same spot at most other spring parks. The cozy field dimensions also help make the area a top-notch place to watch a game, as fans are not that far from the infield.

THE BALLPARK EXPERIENCE. The game-day atmosphere at Surprise Stadium is festive and friendly, although the stands are usually only about half full when the Royals are playing. Ranger attendance used to be rather lackluster as well, but in the wake of the team's success in 2010 and 2011, it has risen dramatically. Batting practice takes place outside the stadium on the practice fields. The main stadium does not open until an hour and a half before the game. Fans are, however, allowed to walk freely about the complex, with many choosing to wait behind the outfield fences of the practice fields for home run balls. Unfortunately green plastic mesh covers these fences, serving to block the dusty breeze and to prevent fans from interacting with outfielders to the extent that they might otherwise.

Inside the stadium, two shops sell apparel related to the home teams. In addition to housing concession stands and rest rooms, the concourse also allows fans to peer into batting cages in left field (Royals) and right field (Rangers). A carousel and small Wiffle ball field reside on the right field concourse too.

When the Rangers are the home team, the fans sing "Cotton Eyed Joe" during the seventh-inning stretch, just like at Rangers Ballpark in Arlington. This is a good dancing/stomping song that some of the fans really enjoy.

Most of the concession stands are located in the outfield corners of the concourse. The majority of these offer traditional ballpark fare, while private vendors operate stands on the left field concourse. The Surprise Grill offers a foot-long Octoberfest Sausage, topped with grilled peppers and onions. Servers chop the peppers and onions at the stand before placing them on the griddle and then transferring them to the sausage bun. The German sausages are never pre-packed, but rather served right off the grill. The grill-master uses a metal meat thermometer to tell when they are fit for consumption. Other favorites to be found in this part of the park include Homemade Ice Cream, Steak Sandwiches from Uncle Jimmy's

Cheesesteaks, and Barbecue Sandwiches courtesy of the "Battle of the Barbecue" stand. The barbecue counter aspires to let fans decide whether they prefer Texas- or Kansas City–style "Q." However, the only real choice is between which type of sauce — Kansas City or Texas — fans want. The Beer Garden in left field foul territory offers different brews on tap, while large cans of PBR and Sierra Nevada are also available. Frozen Margaritas and glasses of Wine are sold as well. Once upon a time Surprise Stadium offered deep-fried Oreos and Twinkies at its Fry-Bread Stand, but the sale of those artery-clogging indulgences was eventually discontinued.

ON THE TOWN. Surprise's population increased from 7,000 in 1990 to more than 30,000 by 2000, to nearly 120,000 by the time of the 2010 Census. If the east Phoenix suburb of Tempe is a college town, the west Phoenix suburb of Surprise is a retirement and commuting town. Surely many young professionals make the drive to Phoenix to work each day, but it is also not uncommon to see senior citizens riding along the breakdown lanes of the city's streets behind the steering wheels of modified golf carts.

As far as places to stay, eat, and drink in Surprise, fans will find plenty of options just a mile or two from the ballpark on Bell Road. The familiar chains prevail, including **TGI Fridays** (14127 W. Bell Road), **Carrabba's Italian Grill** (14043 W. Bell Road), **Buffalo Wild Wings** (13882 W. Bell Road), **Applebee's** (13756 W. Bell Road) and **Starbucks** (13706 W. Bell Road).

Those looking for a place with a bit more local character and an outdoor patio head to **Fuzzy's Sports Grill** (18795 N. Reems Road). Fuzzy's serves a half pound Angus beef burger and meaty chicken wings, as well as a sampling of other treats. The friendly wait staff makes fans feel right at home during spring training.

Camelback Ranch–Glendale

(GLENDALE/PHOENIX) Los Angeles Dodgers *and* Chicago White Sox

Camelback Ranch
10710 West Camelback Road, Glendale/Phoenix
623–302–5000
http://web.camelbackranchbaseball.com
http://losangeles.dodgers.mlb.com;
http://chicago.whitesox.mlb.com
Opened: 2009. Seating Capacity: 13,000
• 8 miles east to Maryvale (Brewers)
• 11 miles north to Peoria (Mariners/Padres)
• 14 miles north to Surprise (Rangers/Royals)
• 15 miles southwest to Goodyear (Indians/Reds)

THE LARGEST SPRING TRAINING VENUE OF ALL, Camelback Ranch–Glendale is perhaps the most Arizonan of the Cactus League ballparks. More than any other park in the Arizona circuit it incorporates and reflects the desert landscape in its design. To establish a uniquely Southwestern identity, Glendale decided to identify its ballpark as a "ranch," rather than a stadium or ballpark. Similarly working to establish a rustic motif, the press box behind home plate looks more like a hunter's lodge than a stadium façade. Stonewalls along the concourses and outfield berm areas meanwhile, separate the various interior spaces of the park, appearing where fencing or concrete barriers would ordinarily stand. The design also leaves most of the seats exposed to the sun, utilizes desert colors atypical of stadium décor, and offers funky irregular angles. These effects make the park feel as if it couldn't reside anywhere else but in the stark desert landscape of the Grand Canyon State.

The ballpark complex or "campus" as the Dodgers and White Sox like to say, sits on a plot of land nestled between the Glendale Municipal Airport and Glendale's two regular season pro sports venues— Jobing.com Arena, where the NHL Phoenix Coyotes play, and University of Phoenix Stadium, home of the NFL Arizona Cardinals. The campus actually falls within the western city limits of Phoenix, but the

The seats at Camelback Ranch are wider and more comfortable than those found at most parks (John Verive/Flickr).

land is owned by the city of Glendale. Thus, the two municipalities had to work out a tax revenue sharing plan before the complex could be developed to serve as a home to the White Sox, who'd previously been playing in Tucson, and the Dodgers, who'd been anchored for decades prior in Vero Beach, Florida.

Today, the White Sox and Dodgers manage and operate the facility, unlike in most spring cities where the local parks and recreation departments usually steward ballpark operations. Both teams arrived at Camelback amidst some controversy in 2009. In moving from Vero Beach where their much-ballyhooed Dodgertown predated even the club's move from Brooklyn to Los Angeles, the Dodgers were bucking tradition in favor of modern amenities and the practical reality that it made a whole lot more sense for a West Coast team to spend the spring in Arizona than in Florida. Still, the game's old-timers and romantics loved Dodgertown, steeped in lure and tradition such as it was. With its Live Oaks growing in the stands and its uncovered player benches, Holman Stadium was the quaintest and most iconic Grapefruit League ballpark ever built. Thus, there was a fair amount of resistance to the Dodgers' proposed move to the Cactus League as momentum built in 2007 for the planned Camelback campus that the Dodgers would share with another team. Similarly, the White Sox faced some resistance to moving, but for different reasons. The Chicago club's proposed relocation from Tucson to Phoenix foreshadowed the end of Tucson's long run as a Cactus League outpost. The team's move made it clear to close observers of the circuit that the Rockies and Diamondbacks—not wishing to be the only two teams left outside Phoenix Valley — would soon move north too. Thus, the city known as "The Old Pueblo" and Pima County in which Tucson resides stuck to a lease agreement with the White Sox that said the club would remain at Tucson Electric Park through 2012. Eventually the White Sox paid what amounted to a $5 million ransom to get out of the remaining four years of their lease and move. And as suspected, two years later the Rockies and Diamondback followed suit, moving to Salt River Fields at Talking Stick.

It is understandable that both the Dodgers and White Sox wanted to relocate. The current facility they share is one of the finest in all of spring training. Clearly, no expense was spared in the design and development of the Camelback Ranch–Glendale campus. Each team has six full-sized practice fields, a practice infield, batting cages, pitching stations, and an expansive clubhouse. The practice fields lie beyond the outfield of the main stadium, with the Dodgers' portion of the complex oriented past left field and the White Sox's portion past right field. A narrow lake, stocked with fish, and utilized for irrigation, runs through the middle of the complex. This nicely-landscaped water body separates the two teams' workout areas. The Dodgers' tract includes a small orange grove in homage to Walter O'Malley's citrus orchard at Dodgertown. The pathways are named after Dodgers' legends in another tribute to the Vero Beach campus.

Groundbreaking for the complex took place in November of 2007, with Dodgers broadcaster Vin Scully and then-owners Frank and Jamie McCourt among the dignitaries hoisting ceremonial shovels. Over the next year, the 141-acre plot, intended to eventually anchor a yet-to-be-developed entertainment district, became a vibrant green oasis, thanks to the architectural work of Dallas-based HKS and the expenditure of more than $100 million in construction costs. The project was funded by the city of Glendale, which will be making payments of between $13 million and $22 million from 2013 through 2038 to pay off its debt. Supposedly, the Camelback campus will return that much and more to the municipality as new revenue derived from the anticipated ballpark entertainment district materializes in the years ahead.

While the earth-tones of the Sonoran Desert are featured heavily throughout the complex and stadium, no other design element is quite as distinctive as the gabion walls — made from desert stones held in place by metal framing — which appear throughout the stadium. The caramel coloration of the ballpark seats and dugout roofs is also unusual. The not-quite-brown, not-quite-yellow hue helps to give the stadium its desert character. The press box and luxury suite level also looks more like a rustic desert ranch than part of a sports stadium. Part of this is due to its brown color and part to the lack of any real roof overhead. A brim of five wooden slats rings the upper level, providing limited sun-relief to the fans in the upper levels of the grandstand and no escape from the occasional rainstorm.

The field itself is sunken 12 feet below street level and all of the seating appears below a wide but mostly un-shaded concourse that encircles the field. The seating options, too, surround the entire field, with the wider-than-usual caramel seats extending deep into the outfield corners. There are four different Berm seating areas (right field foul territory, right field home run territory, left field home run territory, left field foul territory) and two outfield patios. The Dodgers use the third base dugout and their clubhouse sits at the back of the left field Berm and patio area, while the White Sox use the first base dugout and their clubhouse is behind the right field foul pole. Both clubhouse buildings have roofs that slope toward foul territory.

The symmetrical field measures 345 feet down the lines, 380 feet to the power alleys, and 410 feet to straightaway center. The bullpens are in straightaway left (Dodgers) and right (White Sox) and oriented so the relievers throw parallel to the mesh outfield fence. The rest of the outfield wall takes the form of solid green padding, with the occasional advertising sign appearing on its face. A small green screen and grove of desert trees compose the hitter's backdrop, while further in the distance appears the sort of mountain-view for which the Cactus League is famous. The scoreboard atop the right field Berm is not a solid structure but consists of several interconnected parts (face-clock, video board, line-score, stadium name, home team logos) essentially allowing fans to look "through" it. Usually ballpark designers just put advertising in the spaces of the board not being used to convey information, but not in Glendale where fans find this novel variation.

Camelback has the most unique scoreboard in the Cactus League (John Verive/Flickr).

While the ballpark and campus were still being developed, the project was often referred to as "the Camelback ballpark project," in reference to the longtime name of the barren plot of land just west of Loop 101 on which it was being constructed. Eventually, the city of Glendale impressed upon the two resident teams and the city of Phoenix its desire that the Glendale name be in some way incorporated into the official moniker. Thus, by the time the ballpark opened on March 1, 2009, the campus and ballpark were known collectively as Camelback Ranch–Glendale. The park opened with the White Sox defeating the Dodgers 3–2 in an inaugural game witnessed by more than 11,000 people. Keyed by a Gordon Beckham pinch-hit home run, the White Sox scored three runs in the top of the ninth inning to claim the win. The Dodgers and White Sox went on to attract nearly 230,000 fans to the 30 games they combined to host that first season, which seemed pretty impressive at the time, but later paled in comparison to the 360,000 Salt River Fields at Talking Stick drew when the Rockies and Diamondbacks opened that park two years later.

In any case, both the White Sox and Dodgers have continued to draw well since moving to Glendale, with the Dodgers typically attracting crowds of about 8,000 per game and the White Sox averaging 6,000. Even a respectable crowd leaves Camelback Ranch looking half empty, however, as the ballpark can accommodate 10,000 in its comfortable stadium chairs, and nearly 4,000 more on its lawns. The 2012 spring season was a historic one for Camelback as it set a Cactus League single-game attendance record on March 17th. On a windy Friday night, 13,655 fans turned out to watch the Giants and Dodgers play to a 3–3 tie. After that record-setting game, another 13,648 filled the seats the very next day for a game between the Angels and Dodgers. Entering the 2013 season, those two crowds ranked first and second in Cactus League history. The old record had belonged to Peoria Stadium, which drew 13,629 to a game between the Cubs and Mariners in 2010.

Both the White Sox and Dodgers are committed to play at Camelback through 2028. Both teams also hold options that don't expire until 2018 to develop two parcels abutting the campus's current footprint. The Dodgers' entry in the Arizona Rookie League uses Camelback Ranch during the summer months, while the White Sox's minor leaguers play their developmental league games in the Appalachian League instead.

The Dodgers' history in Vero Beach was as rich as it was long. The Brooklyn Dodgers arrived in the sleepy Atlantic Coast city in 1949. In the years to follow, the Dodgers revolutionized the way major league organizations approached spring training. Prior to Dodgertown, the big league players in each system trained independently from the minor leaguers. But Dodgers general manager Branch Rickey envisioned and created a "baseball college" where all players in the Brooklyn system came together to learn to play "Dodger baseball." From 1949 through 2008, every player who was the property of the Dodgers practiced at Dodgertown. (For more information about Dodgertown, refer to the Tradition Field chapter.)

As for the White Sox, their spring history was a more transitory one, but they

There is very little shade to be found in the Camelback grandstand at gametime (Nick Panico, Wikimedia Commons).

still had deep roots in the Grapefruit League before the layover they'd spend in Tucson prior to their move to Camelback. The Chicagoans set up camp in 17 different cities between 1913 and 2008, spending the largest chunk of time (1960 through 1997) in Sarasota, Florida.

Now both of these historic franchises have staked their spring flags at Camelback Ranch–Glendale. Presumably, as the area around the ballpark becomes further developed and the loyal fans that follow both the White Sox and Dodgers establish traditions of visiting the Cactus League, Camelback will put to good use its plentiful seating and the ample room it allows for fans to roam its grounds.

GETTING TO THE PARK. Camelback Ranch sits not far from Glendale Municipal Airport on the far western outskirts of Phoenix. From Loop 101, the ballpark can be accessed via the Camelback Road exit. Follow Camelback west for two miles and the ballpark appears just after Camelback crosses 107th Avenue. The parking system at the ballpark is a bit chaotic but is the only option for visiting fans. Elderly and disabled fans may be chagrined to note the rather long walk from the parking lots to the stadium gates. On the plus side, parking is free.

SEATING. The Dodgers draw better at Camelback than the White Sox do. Between 2010 and 2012, the Ranch welcomed six of the ten largest crowds ever to view a Cactus League game and the Dodgers hosted five of those games, with the other pitting the White Sox versus the Cubs. The Giants, Angels and Cubs almost always draw well as visitors, especially later in the spring and on weekends. Typically, though, fans are able to purchase walk-up tickets on game-day.

Ticket prices at Camelback are not cheap. Games are divided into regular and premium dates so that prices are higher when better opponents come to town. Thus, when a top-tier opponent visits, the box seats behind home plate sell for $44, and even a Berm ticket costs $13. In a nice design touch, the placards on the seats are designed to look like baseballs with the seat number in the middle.

There are two levels to the seating bowl, separated by a mid-level walkway. The main concourse, meanwhile, runs at the very top of the bowl. Both tiers of seating rise at a very gradual grade. The lower tier includes just ten rows (only six behind the dugouts), while the upper tier contains between 19 and 22 rows. The lower tier includes three different pricing options: Home Plate Box (Sections 14–16), Dugout Field Box (Sections 6–13 on the first base line; Sections 17–24 on the third base line), and Baseline Field Box (Sections 1–5 in right field; Sections 25–29 in left field). All of these seats provide close-to-the-field sight-lines and quality views. Even in the Baseline Field Box sections, the seats are nicely angled back toward the infield so that fans don't have to crane their necks to follow the action.

Behind this ring of Box seats, fans find the Infield Box and Baseline Reserved seats on the second tier. These sections are deep—meaning they include a great many rows—but they're not "nosebleed seats" thanks to the very gradual rise of the stadium. The Infield Boxes extend from Section 106 at first base, to Section 115 behind home plate, to Section 124 at third base. Sections 102–105 in right field and 125 to 128 in left field compose the Baseline Reserved.

The two smaller Berms appear immediately beyond the Baseline Field Box sections in the outfield corners, while the larger Berms are in left and right field home run territory. The outfield spots provide generally superior views than the lawns in deep foul territory, since the outfield lawns face the infield.

THE BALLPARK EXPERIENCE. If snowbirds flock to Arizona to soak up the sun that's been hiding back home, then Camelback Ranch–Glendale delivers … and then some. Due to the orientation of the park, which partially faces the afternoon sun, there is practically no shade to be found behind home plate or on the third base side of the seating bowl when afternoon games begin. The small amount of shade on the first base side of the grandstand increases only slightly as the innings pass. It is no wonder that the ushers—mostly friendly elderly gentlemen in brown shirts—wear wide-brimmed straw hats. Indeed, fans attending Camelback would be wise to pack a nice big hat and a bottle of sunscreen. Fortunately, fans find a shaded stretch of the concourse behind home plate, where standing is allowed.

Before the game, fans are free to wander the campus and to visit the various fields where minor leaguers and sometimes major leaguers are practicing. Fans will notice that one field on either side of the campus takes on the dimensions of the home team's regular season park. The Dodgers' orange grove is beyond the left field fence of the Dodger Stadium replica field.

Roaming the complex offers ample opportunity to collect autographs as the player footpaths are separated from the fans only by rope barriers. There is also a bandstand where musical acts and other entertainers sometimes greet fans as they arrive at the park. This is particularly utilized for weekend and night games.

The ballpark food includes fan favorites like the foot-long Farmer John brand Dodger Dog, and Chicago-style hot dogs with all of the fixings. The freshly-made Burritos and Tacos are also popular, as are the Hawaiian Noodles. To cool off, fans have a choice of "yard-sized" Frozen Drinks, Italian Ice, and freshly-squeezed Lemonade.

A souvenir stand in the right field corner sells the hat of every Cactus League team, so that even visiting fans can add to their wardrobe. Bottles of Coppertone sunscreen can also be purchased at the stands.

It is a tradition for the Dodgers and White Sox to kick off the Cactus League season with a game against each other. Then the two teams play another three games against one another as the spring continues. These matches provide a festive game-day atmosphere. The White Sox fans try to drown out the Dodgers fans when they cheer. Likewise, when the White Sox fans assert their presence at the park, the Dodgers rooters try to outdo them. All of this plays out amidst a jovial and playful backdrop, of course, as no one takes the outcome of spring games too seriously. Like the players, the fans are just warming up for the regular season.

ON THE TOWN. Like many of the other ballparks west of downtown Phoenix, Camelback Ranch–Glendale sits amidst a landscape that is still a work in progress. The ballpark campus is complete and beautiful, but fans are still waiting for a festive

Camelback Ranch seats more fans than any other Spring Training facility (Nick Panico, Wikimedia Commons).

ballpark neighborhood to be built surrounding it. Supposedly, this will happen in time, and bars and restaurants aplenty will abound West of Loop 101. In the meantime, fans may visit nearby **Westgate City Center**, a short drive east of Camelback. There, they'll find an entertainment district full of water fountains, shops, bars, and restaurants. **Jimmy Buffett's Margaritaville** (6751 N. Sunset Boulevard) is a popular spot, as is **Saddle Ranch** (9375 W. Coyotes Boulevard) where they have a mechanical bull. Those seeking a more familiar eating and drinking experience can visit **McFadden's** (9425 W. Coyotes Boulevard). Westgate also offers quality Mexican restaurants, steakhouses and plenty of bars. Westgate also houses the Phoenix Suns' **US Airways Center**, and the Phoenix Coyotes' **Jobing.com Arena**.

Goodyear Ballpark

(GOODYEAR) Cincinnati Reds
and Cleveland Indians

Goodyear Ballpark
1933 South Ballpark Way, Goodyear
623–882–7525
http://www.goodyearaz.gov/index.aspx?NID=1119
http://cincinnati.reds.mlb.com; http://cleveland.indians.mlb.com
Opened: 2009. Seating Capacity: 10,311
• 16 miles northeast to Glendale (Dodgers and White Sox)
• 18 miles north to Surprise (Rangers and Royals)
• 20 miles east to Maryvale (Brewers)
• 20 miles northeast to Peoria (Mariners and Padres)

WHEN THE CITY OF GOODYEAR allocated $123 million derived from municipal bonds to build a two-team training complex, surely its leaders didn't envision the two resident clubs perennially finishing last and next-to-last in the Cactus League attendance ledger. But such has been the case since Goodyear Ballpark's opening. In 2012, the average Cactus League game attracted 7,420 fans. The Cleveland Indians, however, drew just 4,677 per game to Goodyear Ballpark, and the Cincinnati Reds drew only 3,867. The Goodyear teams' woeful totals were actually inflated by a two-for-one ticket promotion available to Goodyear residents all season long and by another program that offered seniors and children half-price tickets. Yet those measures couldn't prevent the home teams from finishing fourteenth and fifteenth in Cactus League attendance for the third year in a row. Thus, the ballpark ran at a multimillion-dollar loss once again.

At first glance, visitors to Goodyear may find themselves asking why the local investment in a baseball future has failed to yield the influx of tourist dollars that Salt River Fields at Talking Stick and Camelback Ranch-Glendale have generated. After all, Goodyear Ballpark's ultra-modern façade is attractive enough, set behind a pretty palm court and adorned by the most ambitious sculpture in all of spring training. The park is different, but inviting, with its dark wood paneling, generous

The "Ziz," by sculptor Donald Lipski, is named after a giant mythic bird (courtesy Jim Tootle).

use of windows, and shiny metal trim. The interior, likewise, is clean and modern, even if it seems designed more for functionality than for the sake of aesthetic charm. The seating bowl is appropriately sunken below the field, with all of the seats set below a wide concourse that encircles the field. The park also delivers the requisite berm seating areas and mountain views that are staples of the Arizona baseball experience. Indeed, it's difficult to figure why the seats are two-thirds empty most days at Goodyear Ballpark.

Upon closer inspection, one may begin to piece together a puzzle that explains why the two Ohio teams that call the Goodyear Ballpark and Recreation Complex "home" have failed, thus far, to attract the gushing crowds other Arizona teams enjoy. To begin, the old adage in real-estate — location, location, location — would seem to apply. Goodyear's baseball complex is the westernmost one in the Cactus League. In fairness, it's only about twenty-five miles from downtown Phoenix, but in an era when East Valley teams (Giants, Cubs, Angels, Diamondbacks, Rockies) reign as the Cactus League's top draws, there doesn't seem to be enough in Goodyear to motivate fans to take even a short "roadie" west.

Currently, Goodyear is growing, though. The ballpark is being touted as the anchor of a ballpark village that will one day offer the sort of dining, retail and convention spaces that make the city a hub of commerce and activity. This formula has worked in the West Valley before. For example, Surprise was little more than a bedroom community for Phoenix before its ballpark catalyzed the sort of development and economic growth the folks in Goodyear are hoping to achieve. For the time being, though, there isn't much for a visiting fan to do in Goodyear, besides watching a game.

The similar profile of Goodyear's two home teams also likely works to minimize crowds. Both the Indians and Reds have brought respectable clubs to Goodyear in the years since the ballpark's opening. The Reds have actually brought some big names in Joey Votto, Jay Bruce and Aroldis Chapman. But neither home team has yet brought a player the general baseball public has deemed a must-see attraction — on the order of Ichiro Suzuki, Barry Bonds, or Albert Pujols, who in their primes drew swarms of marauding fans to Cactus League parks. Part of the problem may be a more general one related to the two home teams. Neither the Reds nor Indians come from a big-market baseball city. Sure, both teams have loyal regular season followings, but their fan bases are neither as large nor as well-moneyed as the ones that follow the Cubs, Giants, Dodgers, Angels, Yankees, Mets, Red Sox, etc. Cleveland and Cincinnati are both more than two-thousand miles from Arizona, as well, which equates to about a thirty-hour drive to reach Greater Phoenix from either city. While once there was a tradition of Reds fans making the fifteen-hour drive to Sarasota or of Indians fans making the road-trip to Winter Haven, now an Ohioan wishing to visit spring training must take a more expensive flying-vacation. Though the Indians had trained in Arizona before, from 1947 to 1992, that generation of Tribe rooters was accustomed to visiting Tucson. Thus, whatever nostalgia might have brought old-time Clevelanders west was minimized by the team's relocation to Greater Phoenix. As for the Reds, they had always trained in the Grapefruit League before arriving in Goodyear in 2010. Thus, the two fan bases don't have traditions of visiting the Cactus League: they don't have favorite hotels, wateringholes, recreational activities, and so on. And most importantly, they don't have cherished memories of visiting the Cactus League in the recent past to draw them back.

Finally, there is the ballpark in Goodyear itself, which surely plays some role in its dreadful performance at the turnstiles. Goodyear Ballpark does have its selling points, which this chapter details, but it has some less-than-perfect aspects too. Aside from the fact that the park is located in the middle of nowhere, the most common complaints from fans are that the park provides too little shade (which could be said of several Arizona ballparks) and that it lacks character. There's certainly nothing offensive or glaringly wrong with the park, but it doesn't present, in its own right, a compelling reason for fans to leave the East Valley cocoon, when they could more easily visit Salt River Fields at Talking Stick or Scottsdale Stadium or Tempe Diablo Stadium.

Hopefully someday soon the streets surrounding this patch of former farmland will come to present the sort of multi-faceted entertainment district that fans find in many of the spring hubs closer to Phoenix. Or perhaps either the Reds or Indians will win a World Series and prompt throngs of rooters to plan a feel-good trip to Goodyear the next spring. In the meantime, the city will continue to pay more than $6 million annually in interest on a ballpark project that has yet to deliver on the promise of baseball riches. The good news is that both resident teams signed 20-year lease agreements with Goodyear, upon their respective arrivals, meaning that the Indians should be training in Goodyear through 2028, while the Reds should be in town through at least 2029. So, there is ample time for Goodyear to rebound.

The Goodyear Ballpark and Recreational Complex was initially designed to house just the Indians, who arrived in Goodyear via Winter Haven in 2009. Then, when the Reds opted to leave Sarasota and join their Ohio brethren in Arizona, the Goodyear City Council approved an additional round of financing to expand the facilities. Thus, the Indians had Goodyear Ballpark all to themselves in 2009, then the Reds arrived in 2010.

Before the games began at Goodyear Ballpark, the city held a grand opening event in February of 2009. The citizens of Goodyear and other West Valley communities like Avondale, Tolleson, Buckeye and Litchfield Park were invited to tour the new baseball digs. That was when the 60-foot, 6-inch Fiberglas statue outside the ballpark's home plate entrance was officially unveiled and dedicated. The statue,

Palms trace the outfield, creating a lovely backdrop for a game (courtesy Jim Tootle).

known as "The Ziz," sits atop a water display, surrounded by palms. Its height measures the same distance between the pitcher's rubber and home plate, of course. With its white finish and red stitching, it looks like a giant flattened baseball. It almost looks like a ball in motion, moving so fast that it's a streak or blur of rawhide. According to its creator Donald Lipski, it was inspired by the Romanian sculptor Constantin Brancusi, who created a series of pieces entitled "Bird in Space."

The grand opening event also introduced fans to the Indians, who were on the field working out for part of the day. Fans toured the facility, sampled the ballpark cuisine, ran the bases, and played Wiffle ball at the Kids Zone on the right side of the concourse. It was a fun day, yet the ticket office in Goodyear sold only 4,181 tickets to the park's inaugural Cactus League game, which took place on February 25, 2009. Thanks to a free ticket promotion with nearby Luke Air Force Base, the actual crowd was a little bit better than the tickets-sold figure, but the park was still half empty on its Opening Day. Nonetheless, the Air Force provided F-16s for a flyover, and Indians legend Bob Feller threw out the ceremonial first pitch. Then the Indians lost 10–7 to the Giants in a game highlighted by Tim Lincecum's first appearance of the spring for the visitors—a scoreless first inning.

By the time the Reds arrived the next spring, the 100-acre practice complex a quarter-mile south of Goodyear Ballpark had been expanded to include a grand total of 12 full diamonds, four practice infields, and two sprawling clubhouse and administration buildings. The Reds and Indians both enjoy year-round access to two practice fields apiece for player development activities. The rest of the fields are used by Goodyear's recreation department when spring games and workouts aren't taking place. While this complex wasn't designed with ease of walking access for fans at the top of the priority list, there are parking lots on Wood Boulevard for fans wishing to watch workouts. The Indians' portion of the complex is closer to the main stadium than the Reds' portion.

As for Goodyear Ballpark, the exterior façade of the Populous-designed facility is certainly distinctive in the world of pro sports. It looks more like the entrance of a shopping mall than a sports venue, with its wood paneling, glass, and metal signage announcing the ticket and clubhouse shop retail spaces. Inside, the structure behind the grandstand climbs to a height of three inauspicious stories, housing the press box and some luxury suites on the lower of the raised two floors and a party deck upstairs. The plain beige structure could use some adornment. Aside from the smart approach to seating that allows for excellent sight-lines from the comfortable plastic chairs of the main bowl and from the outfield lawn areas, the most noteworthy aspects of the park are its right field party deck and the views it allows of the mountain ranges that run behind the first base side of the grandstand and the third base side. The fans seated along the first base line can see the White Tank Mountains rising on the left side of the stadium, while the fans seated along the third base side enjoy the looming Estrellas behind the right side of the stadium. The fans seated behind home plate, meanwhile, enjoy an outfield view that showcases the tall palms growing atop the narrow berm. The seats along the baselines that run from the dugouts nearly all the way to the foul poles are exposed to the sun, and even behind home plate the small grandstand roof provides less than complete sun-relief. There are free-standing shade screens on the baseline concourses, but they are no match for the potent March sun.

The Indians inhabit the right side of the park, taking the first base dugout, while the Reds use the third base dugout. The bullpens are adjacent to one another in left field home run territory, set between the outfield fence and start of the seating berm. The Indians' relievers use the pen closest to the foul line. The field measures 345 feet down the lines and 410 feet to center. The batter's eye in straightaway center takes the form of a green wall. The scoreboard sits atop the berm in left field.

Aside from the Indians and Reds, both teams' rookie league squads use the Goodyear facilities during the Arizona League's summer schedule. The facility is also used for an annual Fourth of July festival and for a variety of community events throughout the year.

Prior to arriving in Goodyear, the Indians had trained in Winter Haven from 1993 through 2008. They arrived at that Central Florida town accidentally enough, after having planned a move from Tucson's Hi Corbett Field to a brand new training complex awaiting them in Homestead, Florida. After Hurricane Andrew laid waste to that facility, though, the Indians moved to Winter Haven's Chain of Lakes Park instead. The Indians' first spring in Winter Haven will be forever remembered for a tragic boat accident on Little Lake Nellie in Clermont, Florida. On March 22, 1993, Cleveland pitchers Steve Olin and Tim Crews lost their lives and fellow pitcher Bobby Ojeda was seriously injured when the speedboat they were using crashed into a dock. That tragic first spring in Winter Haven, was not, in fact, the Indians first foray into the Grapefruit League. The Tribe had ventured to the Sunshine State beginning in 1923 when they made camp at Henley Field in Lakeland. In 1928 they departed for New Orleans, where they trained until moving to Fort Myers for the 1940 and 1941 spring seasons. They trained in Clearwater in 1942, then stayed north during the World War II years of 1943 to 1945, utilizing a camp in Lafayette, Indiana. After spending 1946 in Clearwater, the Cleveland club set up camp at Hi Corbett Field in 1947. Along with the Giants and Cubs, the Indians helped form the backbone of the early Cactus League. (For more information on Hi Corbett Field and the Indians' time in Tucson, please refer to the Salt River Fields chapter.)

As for the Reds, they were a Grapefruit League stalwart dating back to the 1920s, when they trained in Miami and Orlando. They moved from Orlando to Tampa in 1931 and remained there (excepting the war years when they trained in Bloomington, Indiana) until 1987, spending much or their time at Al Lopez Field. Next, they played in Plant City, where the local park featured the same outfield dimensions as Riverfront Stadium and seated 6,700 fans. But the Reds never drew well at Plant City Stadium, so they jumped at the chance to fill the void left by the White Sox when Chicago announced its intention to depart Sarasota's Ed Smith Stadium for a new home in Tucson after the 1997 season. The Reds moved into Ed

Fans sun themselves on the outfield seating berm (courtesy Jim Tootle).

Smith and spent more than a decade there before finally following the path paved by their Sarasota predecessors to the Cactus League.

Hopefully both Ohio teams that have chosen to make their spring camps in Goodyear will eventually lay down strong roots that fortify new traditions that bring many fans to Goodyear Ballpark in the decades ahead. The stadium is certainly an able enough one to accommodate greater masses than it's seen to date, and as more fans seek it out there will be increased impetus for the surrounding community to develop the restaurants, sports bars and retail spaces that are also important elements of the spring experience.

GETTING TO THE PARK. Goodyear is the westernmost outpost in today's Cactus League. Though the ride from Phoenix is something less than scenic, it really doesn't take long to span the 25 miles between the league's unofficial hub and Goodyear. Visitors should take the I-10 (Papago Freeway) to the Estrella Boulevard exit and turn south. The ballpark is on the left. The park can also be accessed from Bullard Avenue. Parking costs $5.

SEATING. The designers of the Goodyear Ballpark seating bowl did several things right, but also committed a few small faux pas. The fact that all of the seats in the grandstand appear below the main concourse is a major plus. It's also nice that they're comfortable plastic seats. There are no bleachers in this facility. This is a relatively small stadium by modern Cactus League standards, as well, with room to house just over 10,000. As a result, all of the seats are close to the field. The berms are narrow but nicely sloped and large enough given the small crowds the park typically attracts. The drawbacks include some outfield sections that angle the seats a bit more toward the outfield than home plate, a more obstructive than usual screen to protect fans sitting between and behind the dugouts, and a tarp in left field foul territory that blocks views for those seated in Section 105. Ordering tickets in advance, of course, is never a necessity; it's rare that crowds in Goodyear approach the 7,000 mark. And the friendly ushers don't seem to mind fans upgrading their seating location once the first couple of innings have passed.

The main seating bowl spans nearly all the way down the outfield lines, ending a short distance from either foul pole. There are three main ticket designations—Infield Box, Outfield Box, and Outfield Reserved—in addition to a small Club Section on the third base side, a partially shaded Pavilion in right field home run territory, and two different Berm seating areas. The seating bowl begins with Section 101 in deep left field foul territory, then makes the turn behind home plate at Section

Games have been sparsely attended since the Indians and Reds arrived in Goodyear (courtesy Jim Tootle).

112, and finishes in deep right with Section 123. The blue stadium chairs are attractive and comfortable, but tend to heat up in the sun, especially when left unoccupied. The concession concourse atop the twenty-four rows of seats offers a nice shaded place from which fans enjoy excellent views of the field.

The appropriately named Infield Boxes occupy sections 106 through 118 on the infield. In most sections, Row A is down at field level, while the section ends with Row Z. The Sections behind the third (107–109) and first (115–117) base dugouts begin with Row E. These are all great seats, with unobstructed views thanks to the absence of a mid-level walkway as is found at many of the minor league and spring training facilities.

The Club Seats occupy the uppermost portions of Section 106 and 107, just beyond the Indians dugout on the third base line. There, fans find wider seats, food and beverage delivery service, and plenty of shade (thanks to a special roof).

The Outfield Boxes are, on the whole, quite good. They begin where the Infield Boxes end on either side of the diamond and continue for three sections along either foul line. Sections 103–105 in shallow left field foul territory offer nice views of the Estrella Mountains across the diamond, while Sections 119–121 in shallow right field foul territory showcase the White Tanks.

The two outermost sections of the seating bowl on either side are tapered to fit into the outfield corners and angled back toward the infield. Indeed, the seats in Outfield Reserved Sections 101 and 102 in deep left are superior to the less artfully angled seats of Section 104 in the leftfield Outfield Boxes. Similarly, Outfield Reserved Sections 122 and 123 in deep right offer better views of the infield than nearby Section 120.

The larger of the two Berms runs from the left field foul pole to the batter's eye in deep center. It is narrow and placed behind the two bullpens. From this left field location the glare of the sun is not as bothersome as it is for those sitting on the smaller Berm on the other side of the batter's eye. The Berm in right-center is also raised higher than the one in left, and is set farther from the infield.

The Pavilion in right offers first-come first-served seating to ticket holders who have opted for this seating option. The uppermost seats of the Pavilion that are closest to the right field line are definitely preferable, since they are shaded by a small roof. The all-you-can-eat Pavilion menu includes hot dogs, hamburgers, pulled chicken, cookies, chips and soft drinks. Beer and wine are also available at regular concession stand prices.

THE BALLPARK EXPERIENCE. Goodyear Ballpark does not go to tremendous lengths to provide sun relief for fans. It's a shame the Indians and Reds play only about two night games apiece each spring. Under the lights, this is a much more enjoyable park than it is beneath a hot sun. And it's a more scenic one too, as the Ziz sculpture and tall palms outside the home plate entrance are beautiful when illuminated.

The typical spring brings furry Indians' mascot Slider to town, as well as the

The press box level behind home plate is utilitarian in appearance (courtesy Jim Tootle).

Reds' Gapper. The two are particularly hilarious when paired together on days when the Indians and Reds play one another. Most springs see five or six such matchups when both home teams square off.

While the winner of the spring training series between the two home teams wins little more than bragging rights, Goodyear Ballpark also houses the Ohio Cup on the concourse behind home plate. This three-foot-high trophy is awarded each year to the winner of the six-game regular season series the Indians and Reds have played since the advent of interleague play. The trophy resides in Goodyear during spring training, and then goes home with whichever team won the regular season series the previous year. In the event that the two teams tie 3–3 during the regular season, each team displays it at its home stadium for a portion of the regular season. The Ohio Cup actually dates back further than the dawning of interleague play, which began in 1997. In earlier times the Reds and Indians played a "Battle of Ohio" exhibition each spring at Cooper Stadium in Columbus, Ohio and the winner of that game won the trophy.

More than just displaying this piece of Buckeye State hardware, Goodyear Stadium treats visiting Ohioans to a couple of their favorite hometown flavors: Cincinnati's famous Skyline Chili is available in Goodyear, as is Cleveland's Bertman's Mustard. Other concession highlights at Goodyear Ballpark include the Hot Dog

Nation stand behind home plate, which offers a great variety of dogs, a Mexican food stand, a Philly Cheesesteak cart, and the frozen Margaritas.

A kids' zone on the right field concourse offers a Wiffle ball field and other activities, while fans find the Outfield Box sections just beyond the dugouts the best places for collecting autographs.

ON THE TOWN. Unlike in the more densely populated East Valley, where fans find the spring ballparks practically piled on top of one another, and hopping club and dining scenes filling the spaces in between, nightlife in the West Valley typically rates somewhere between sleepy and deceased. Eventually, the plan in Goodyear is to build a festive entertainment district near the ballpark. In the meantime, fans must settle for some familiar chain restaurants on North Estrella Parkway, a couple of miles from the park and for one very solid local sports bar. Clearly, **Augie's Sports Grill** (15605 W. Roosevelt Street) is the highlight of the post-game scene in Goodyear. The festive sports bar offers plenty of televisions, an outdoor patio, and some delicious pretzel sticks among other pub foods.

Spring Training Sites
Since 1914, Team by Team

Listings include sites for each team since the founding of the Grapefruit League in 1914. Previous club names of franchises that have moved are in parentheses.

ARIZONA DIAMONDBACKS

1998–2010	Tucson, AZ
2011–Present	Scottsdale, AZ

ATLANTA BRAVES
(BOSTON BRAVES, MILWAUKEE BRAVES)

1914–1915	Macon, GA
1916–1918	Miami, FL
1919–1920	Columbus, GA
1921	Galveston, TX
1922–1937	St. Petersburg, FL
1938–1940	Bradenton, FL
1941	San Antonio, TX
1942	Sanford, FL
1943–1944	Wallingford, CT
1945	Washington, DC
1946–1947	Fort Lauderdale, FL
1948–1962	Bradenton, FL
1963–1997	West Palm Beach, FL
1998–Present	Lake Buena Vista/ Kissimmee, FL

BALTIMORE ORIOLES
(ST. LOUIS BROWNS)

1914	St. Petersburg, FL
1915	Houston, TX
1916–1917	Palestine, TX
1918	Shreveport, LA
1919	San Antonio, TX
1920	Taylor, AL
1921	Bogalusa, AL
1922–1924	Mobile, AL
1925–1927	Tarpon Springs, FL
1928–1936	West Palm Beach, FL
1941	San Antonio, TX
1942	Deland, FL
1943–1945	Cape Girardeau, MO
1946	Anaheim, CA
1947	Miami, FL
1948	San Bernardino, CA
1949–1952	Burbank, CA
1953	San Bernardino, CA
1954	Yuma, AZ

1955	Daytona Beach, FL
1956–1958	Scottsdale, AZ
1959–1990	Miami, FL
1991	Sarasota, FL
1992–1995	St. Petersburg, FL
1996–2009	Fort Lauderdale, FL
2010–Present	Sarasota, FL

BOSTON RED SOX

1912–1918	Hot Springs, AR
1919	Tampa, FL
1920–1923	Hot Springs, AR
1924	San Antonio, TX
1925–1927	New Orleans, LA
1928–1929	Bradenton, FL
1930–1931	Pensacola, FL
1932	Savannah, FL
1933–1942	Sarasota, FL
1943–1944	Medford, MA
1945	Atlantic City, NJ
1946–1958	Sarasota, FL
1959–1965	Scottsdale, AZ
1966–1992	Winter Haven, FL
1993–Present	Fort Myers, FL

CHICAGO CUBS

1913–1916	Tampa, FL
1917–1921	Pasadena, FL
1922–1942	Catalina Island, CA
1943–1945	French Lick, IN
1946–1947	Catalina Island, CA
1948–1949	Los Angeles, CA
1950–1951	Catalina Island, CA
1952–1965	Mesa, AZ
1966	Long Beach, CA
1967–1978	Scottsdale, AZ
1979–Present	Mesa, AZ

CHICAGO WHITE SOX

1913–1915	Paso Robles, CA
1916–1919	Mineral Wells, TX
1920	Waco, TX
1921	Waxahachie, TX
1922–1923	Seguin, TX
1924	Winter Haven, FL
1925–1928	Shreveport, LA
1929	Dallas, TX
1930–1932	San Antonio, TX
1933–1942	Pasadena, CA
1943–1944	French Lick, IN
1945	Terre Haute, IN
1946–1952	Pasadena, CA
1953	El Centro, CA
1954–1959	Tampa, FL
1960–1997	Sarasota, FL
1998–2008	Tucson, AZ
2009–Present	Glendale/Phoenix, AZ

CINCINNATI REDS

1914–1915	Alexandria, LA
1916–1917	Shreveport, LA
1918	Montgomery, AL
1919	Waxahachie, TX
1920	Miami, FL
1921	Cisco, TX
1922	Mineral Wells, TX
1923–1930	Orlando, FL
1931–1942	Tampa, FL
1943–1945	Bloomington, IN
1946–1987	Tampa, FL
1988–1997	Plant City, FL
1998–2009	Sarasota, FL
2010–Present	Goodyear, AZ

CLEVELAND INDIANS

1914	Athens, GA
1915	San Antonio, TX
1916–1920	New Orleans, LA
1921–1922	Dallas, TX
1923–1927	Lakeland, FL
1928–1939	New Orleans, LA
1940–1941	Fort Myers, FL
1942	Clearwater, FL
1943–1945	Lafayette, IN
1946	Clearwater, FL
1947–1992	Tucson, AZ
1993–2008	Winter Haven, FL
2009–Present	Goodyear, AZ

COLORADO ROCKIES

| 1993–2010 | Tucson, AZ |
| 2011–Present | Scottsdale, AZ |

DETROIT TIGERS

1913–1915	Gulfport, MS
1916–1918	Waxahachie, TX
1919–1920	Macon, GA
1921	San Antonio, TX
1922–1926	Augusta, GA
1927–1928	San Antonio, TX
1929	Phoenix, AZ
1930	Tampa, FL
1931	Sacramento, CA
1932	Palo Alto, CA
1933	San Antonio, TX
1934–1942	Lakeland, FL
1943–1945	Evansville, IN
1946–Present	Lakeland, FL

HOUSTON ASTROS (COLT .45'S)

1962–1963	Apache Junction, AZ
1964–1984	Cocoa Beach, FL
1985–Present	Kissimmee, FL

KANSAS CITY ROYALS

1969–1987	Fort Myers, FL
1988–2002	Davenport, FL
2003–Present	Surprise, AZ

LOS ANGELES ANGELS OF ANAHEIM (ANAHEIM ANGELS, CALIFORNIA ANGELS)

1961–1965	Palm Springs, CA
1966–1979	Holtville, CA/ Palm Springs, CA
1980–1981	Palm Springs, CA
1982–1983	Casa Grande, AZ/ Palm Springs, CA
1984–1992	Mesa, AZ/Palm Springs, CA
1993–Present	Tempe, AZ

LOS ANGELES DODGERS (BROOKLYN DODGERS)

1913–1914	Augusta, GA
1915–1916	Daytona Beach, FL
1917–1918	Hot Springs, AR
1919–1920	Jacksonville, FL
1921	New Orleans, LA
1922	Jacksonville, FL
1923–1932	Clearwater, FL
1933	Miami, FL
1934–1935	Orlando, FL
1936–1940	Clearwater, FL
1941–1942	Havana, Cuba
1943–1945	Bear Mountain, NY
1946	Daytona Beach, FL

1947	Havana, Cuba
1948	Santo Domingo, Dominican Republic
1949–2008	Vero Beach, FL
2009–Present	Glendale/Phoenix, AZ

MIAMI MARLINS (FLORIDA)

1993	Cocoa Beach, FL
1994–2002	Viera/Melbourne, FL
2003–Present	Jupiter, FL

MILWAUKEE BREWERS (SEATTLE PILOTS)

1969–1972	Tempe, AZ
1973–1985	Sun City, AZ
1986–1997	Chandler, AZ
1998–Present	Maryvale/Phoenix, AZ

MINNESOTA TWINS (WASHINGTON SENATORS)

1912–1916	Charlottesville, VA
1917	Atlanta, GA
1918–1919	Augusta, GA
1920–1929	Tampa, FL
1930–1935	Biloxi, MS
1936–1942	Orlando, FL
1943–1945	College Park, MD
1946–1990	Orlando, FL
1991–Present	Fort Myers, FL

NEW YORK METS

1962–1987	St. Petersburg, FL
1988–Present	Port St. Lucie, FL

NEW YORK YANKEES

1914	Houston, TX
1915	Savannah, GA
1916–1918	Macon, GA
1919–1920	Jacksonville, FL
1921	Shreveport, LA
1922–1924	New Orleans, LA
1925–1942	St. Petersburg, FL
1943	Asbury Park, NJ
1944–1945	Atlantic City, NJ
1946–1950	St. Petersburg, FL
1951	Phoenix, AZ
1952–1961	St. Petersburg, FL
1962–1995	Fort Lauderdale, FL
1996–Present	Tampa, FL

OAKLAND ATHLETICS (PHILADELPHIA ATHLETICS, KANSAS CITY ATHLETICS)

1914–1918	Jacksonville, FL
1919	Philadelphia, PA
1920–1921	Lake Charles, LA
1922	Eagle Pass, TX
1923–1924	Montgomery, AL
1925–1936	Fort Myers, FL
1937	Mexico City, Mexico
1938–1939	Lake Charles, LA
1940–1942	Anaheim, CA
1943	Wilmington, DE
1944–1945	Frederick, MD
1946–1962	West Palm Beach, FL
1963–1968	Bradenton, FL
1969–1978	Mesa, AZ
1979–1983	Scottsdale, AZ
1984–Present	Phoenix, AZ

PHILADELPHIA PHILLIES

1914	Wilmington, NC
1915–1918	St. Petersburg, FL
1919	Charlotte, NC
1920	Birmingham, AL
1921	Gainesville, FL
1922–1924	Leesburg, FL
1925–1927	Bradenton, FL
1928–1937	Winter Haven, FL
1938	Biloxi, MS
1939	New Braunfels, TX
1940–1942	Miami, FL
1943	Hershey, PA
1944–1945	Wilmington, DE
1946	Miami, FL
1947–Present	Clearwater, FL

PITTSBURGH PIRATES

1901–1916	Hot Springs, AR
1917	Columbus, GA
1918	Jacksonville, FL
1919	Birmingham, AL
1920–1923	Hot Springs, AR
1924–1934	Paso Robles, CA
1935	San Bernardino, CA
1936	San Antonio, TX
1937–1942	San Bernardino, CA
1943–1945	Muncie, IN
1946	San Bernardino, CA
1947	Miami, FL
1948	Hollywood, CA
1949–1952	San Bernardino, CA
1953	Havana, Cuba
1954	Fort Pierce, FL
1955–1968	Fort Myers, FL
1969–Present	Bradenton, FL

ST. LOUIS CARDINALS

1914	Augustine, FL
1915–1917	Hot Wells, TX
1918	San Antonio, TX
1919	St. Louis, MO
1920	Brownsville, TX
1921–1922	Orange, TX
1923–1924	Bradenton, FL
1925	Stockton, CA
1926	San Antonio, TX
1927–1929	Avon Park, TX
1930–1936	Bradenton, FL
1937	Daytona Beach, FL
1938–1942	St. Petersburg, FL
1943–1945	Cairo, IL
1946–1997	St. Petersburg, FL
1998–Present	Jupiter, FL

SAN DIEGO PADRES

1969–1993	Yuma, AZ
1994–Present	Peoria, AZ

SAN FRANCISCO GIANTS (NEW YORK GIANTS)

1908–1918	Marlin Springs, TX
1919	Gainesville, FL
1920–1923	San Antonio, TX
1924–1927	Sarasota, FL
1928	Augusta, GA
1929–1931	San Antonio, TX
1932–1933	Los Angeles, CA
1934–1935	Miami, FL
1936	Pensacola, FL
1937	Havana, Cuba
1938–1939	Baton Rouge, LA
1940	Winter Haven, FL

1941–1942	Miami, FL
1943–1945	Lakeland, NJ
1946	Miami, FL
1947–1950	Phoenix, AZ
1951	St. Petersburg, FL
1952–1983	Phoenix, AZ
1984–Present	Scottsdale, AZ

SEATTLE MARINERS

1977–1992	Tempe, AZ
1993–Present	Peoria, AZ

TAMPA BAY RAYS

1998–2008	St. Petersburg, FL
2009–Present	Port Charlotte, FL

TEXAS RANGERS (WASHINGTON SENATORS)

1961–1986	Pompano Beach, FL
1987–2002	Port Charlotte, FL
2003–Present	Surprise, AZ

TORONTO BLUE JAYS

1977–Present	Dunedin, FL

WASHINGTON NATIONALS (MONTREAL EXPOS)

1969–1972	West Palm Beach, FL
1973–1980	Daytona Beach, FL
1981–1997	West Palm Beach, FL
1998–2002	Jupiter, FL
2003–Present	Viera/Melbourne, FL

Bibliography

PERIODICALS

Angel Magazine, 2004

Arizona Daily Star, 2004

The Arizona Republic, 2002–2004

The Baltimore Sun, 2003–2012

Baseball Weekly/Sports Weekly, 1993–2004

The Boston Globe, 2000–2012

The Bradenton Herald, 2004

Dodgers Dugout, 2004

Florida Spring Training Guide, 2004

Florida Today, 2002–2004

The Houston Chronicle, 2000–2012

The Lakeland Ledger, 2004

The Maine Sunday Telegram, 2003

The Miami Herald, 2004–2012

On Deck: The Official Magazine of the Pittsburgh Pirates, 2004

The Palm Beach Post, 2002–2004

The Philadelphia Inquirer, 2003–2004

The Phoenix Business Journal, 2002–2012

The Phoenix Guide, 1995

The Seattle Times, 2004

Sports Illustrated, 1988–2012

The Sporting News, 2000–2004

The Sun-Sentinel of South Florida, 2002–2004

The Tampa Bay Times, 2002–2012

The Tampa Tribune, 2003–2012

TSA Monthly, 2003–2004

Tucson Weekly, 2001–2002

USA Today, 1992–2012

BOOKS

Bouton, Jim. *Ball Four*. New York: Macmillan, 1990.

Coleman, Ken, with Dan Valenti. *Grapefruit League Road Trip*. New York: Pelham, 1988.

Cramer, Richard Ben. *Joe DiMaggio: The Hero's Life*. New York: Simon and Schuster, 2000.

Dobbins, Dick. *The Grand Minor League: An Oral History of the Old Pacific Coast League*. San Francisco: Woodford, 1999.

Garrity, John. *The Traveler's Guide to Baseball Spring Training*. New York: Andrews McMeel, 1989.

Kahn, Roger. *The Era: 1947–1957, When the Yankees, the Giants, and the Dodgers Ruled the World*. Lincoln: University of Nebraska Press, 2002.

Knight, Graham. *Arizona Spring Training Ballpark Guide*, Baseball Enterprises, 2012.

Mining Towns to Major Leagues: A History of Arizona Baseball. Society for American Baseball Research, 1999.

Pahigian, Joshua, and Kevin O'Connell. *The Ultimate Baseball Road Trip*. Guilford, CT: Lyons, 2012.

Ritter, Lawrence. *Lost Ballparks: A Celebration of Baseball's Legendary Fields*. New York: Penguin, 1994.

Shatzin, Mike, and Jim Charlton. *The Baseball Fan's Guide to Spring Training.* Reading MA: Addison-Wesley, 1988.

Shaughnessy, Dan, and Stan Grossfeld. *Spring Training: Baseball's Early Season.* Boston: Houghton Mifflin, 2003.

Sullivan, George. *Big League Spring Training.* New York: Henry Holt, 1989.

Sullivan, Neil J. *The Dodgers Move West.* New York: Oxford University Press, 1987.

Total Baseball. Sixth Edition. New York: Total Sports, 1999.

Veeck, Bill, with Ed Linn. *Veeck, as in Wreck.* New York: Putnam, 1962.

Zinsser, William. *Spring Training: The Unique Story of Baseball's Annual Season of Renewal.* New York: Harper and Row, 1989.

WEB SITES

www.all-baseball.com
www.arizona-liesure.com
www.arizonensis.org
www.azcentral.com
www.ballparkdigest.com
www.ballparkreviews.com
www.ballparks.com
www.ballparkwatch.com
www.baseball-almanac.com
www.baseballlibrary.com
www.baseballparks.com
www.baseballpilgrimages.com
www.baseballtour.com
www.cactusleague.com
www.cubspringtraining.com
www.espn.com
www.floridagrapefruitleague.com

www.heraldtribune.com
www.lee-county.com
www.mlb.com
www.modernerabaseball.com
www.naplesnews.com
www.nationalpastime.com
www.ouraaa.com
www.playballexperience.com
www.redsoxconnection.com
www.sfgate.com
www.springtrainingmagazine.com
www.springtrainingonline.com
www.sportsbusinessdaily.com
www.sun-sentinel.com
www.tampabaylive.com
www.tampabayonline.net
www.tcpalm.com
www.thegrandstand.homestead.com
www.wesh.com

Index